Questions of Competence

Culture, Classification and Intellectual Disability

Intellectual disability – more commonly described as 'mental retardation' or 'learning difficulties' – is a socially constructed phenomenon that varies in important respects cross-culturally. This collection of original essays examines the classification of people as competent and incompetent in the United States, England, Wales, Greece, Greenland, Uganda and Belize. The contributors, anthropologists and sociologists, argue that it is time for a new understanding of intellectual disability. In contrast to medical and psychological models, a social model of intellectual disability emphasises the cultural and individual variability of incompetence, the intimate relationship between cultural categories of competence and incompetence, and the role of social interaction and networks in its social construction. This book is a timely and original contribution to ongoing theoretical and policy debates about disability.

RICHARD JENKINS is Professor of Sociological Studies at the University of Sheffield. He is the author of *Lads, Citizens and Ordinary Kids* (1983), *Racism and Recruitment* (1986), *Pierre Bourdieu* (1992), *Social Identity* (1996), and *Rethinking Ethnicity* (1997). He has done anthropological fieldwork in Northern Ireland, England, Wales and Denmark.

Questions of Competence

Culture, Classification and Intellectual Disability

edited by

Richard Jenkins

CAMBRIDGE
UNIVERSITY PRESS

PUBLISHED BY THE PRESS SYNDICATE OF THE UNIVERSITY OF CAMBRIDGE
The Pitt Building, Trumpington Street, Cambridge CB2 1RU, United Kingdom

CAMBRIDGE UNIVERSITY PRESS
The Edinburgh Building, Cambridge CB2 2RU, United Kingdom
http://www.cup.cam.ac.uk
40 West 20th Street, New York, NY 10011–4211, USA
http://www.cup.org
10 Stamford Road, Oakleigh, Melbourne 3166, Australia

© Richard Jenkins 1998

First published 1998

Printed in the United Kingdom at the University Press, Cambridge

Typeset in Plantin 10/12 pt   [SE]

A catalogue record for this book is available from the British Library

Library of Congress cataloguing in publication data
Questions of competence: culture, classification and intellectual
disability / edited by Richard Jenkins; [contributors, Michael
Angrosino . . . et al.].
    p.   cm.
Includes bibliographical references and index.
ISBN 0 521 62303 0 (hb)
    1. Mentally handicapped – Cross-cultural studies. 2. Learning
disabled – Cross-cultural studies. I. Jenkins, Richard, 1952– .
II. Angrosino, Michael V.
HV3004.Q47 1998
362.3 – dc21 98-3022 CIP

ISBN 0 521 62303 0 hardback
ISBN 0 521 62662 5 paperback

Contents

Contributors

MICHAEL ANGROSINO is Professor of Anthropology at the University of South Florida, where he also holds affiliate appointments in the Department of Special Education and the Department of Community and Family Health. He is the author of *Documents of Interaction: Autobiography, Biography, and Life History in Social Science Perspective* (University of Florida Press), *A Health Practitioner's Guide to the Social and Behavioral Sciences* (Greenwood Press), the forthcoming *Opportunity House: Ethnographic Stories of Adult Mental Retardation* (AltaMira Press) and numerous articles on mental health/mental retardation policy and service delivery in the United States. He has also conducted fieldwork in the British and Dutch Caribbean. He served two terms as Editor of *Human Organisation*, the journal of the Society for Applied Anthropology.

TIM BOOTH is Professor of Social Policy in the Department of Sociological Studies at the University of Sheffield. His research interests include learning difficulties, supported parenting and narrative research. He has recently completed a study of now-adult children raised by parents with learning difficulties and is currently working on an action research project aimed at developing an advocacy support network for parents with learning difficulties. His most recent publications include *Outward Bound* (Open University Press, 1990, with W. Booth and K. Simons), *Parenting Under Pressure* (Open University Press, 1994, with W. Booth), *Exceptional Childhoods, Unexceptional Children* (Family Policy Studies Centre, 1997, with W. Booth) and *Growing Up With Parents Who Have Learning Difficulties* (Routledge, 1998, with W. Booth).

WENDY BOOTH is a Research Fellow in the Department of Sociological Studies, University of Sheffield. Her research interests include self-advocacy and parents with learning difficulties. She has recently completed a study of now-adult children raised by parents with learning difficulties. She is a member of the Maternity Alliance Disability Working Group and adviser to Huddersfield People First. Her most recent publications include *Outward Bound* (Open University Press, 1990, with T. Booth and K. Simons), *Parenting Under Pressure* (Open University Press, 1994, with T. Booth) and *Growing Up With Parents Who Have Learning Difficulties* (Routledge, 1998, with T. Booth).

CHARLOTTE AULL DAVIES is Lecturer in the Department of Sociology and Anthropology, University of Wales, Swansea. In addition to research on people with learning disabilities and the transition to adulthood, her research interests lie in the areas of ethnicity, language and nationalism. She is the author of *Welsh Nationalism in the Twentieth Century: The Ethnic Option and the Modern State* (Praeger, 1989).

PATRICK DEVLIEGER is an Assistant Professor of Human Development in the University of Illinois at Chicago's Institute on Disability and Human Development. His fieldwork sites have included Zaïre, Zimbabwe and the United States. His current research interests include disability and spirituality, disability derived from gunshot trauma in Chicago, and the history of disability in Zimbabwe.

RICHARD JENKINS is Professor of Sociology at the University of Sheffield. Trained as a social anthropologist, he has undertaken field research in Northern Ireland, the West Midlands region of England, south Wales, and western Denmark. In addition to intellectual disability and competence, his research interests include ethnicity, social identity in general, the transition to adulthood and the social construction of deviance. His most recent books are *Pierre Bourdieu* (Routledge, 1992), *Social Identity* (Routledge, 1996) and *Rethinking Ethnicity: Arguments and Explorations* (Sage, 1997).

NANCY LUNDGREN is Associate Professor of Anthropology and Women's Studies at Antioch College, Yellow Springs, Ohio, USA. She received her BA degree in sociology at the University of Hawaii, and MA and PhD degrees at the University of Massachusetts, Amherst. She specialises in political economy, socialisation, 'race' and gender; her culture area is the African Diaspora. She was a Fulbright Scholar to Belize, where she has done the major part of her research on the reproduction of systems of inequality. Recently she has expanded her research to Africa, where she taught during 1995–6 and is continuing a collaborative research project with a local resident in Ghana.

SYLVIA VAN MAASTRICHT was born in The Hague, Holland. She took an undergraduate degree in Pedagogics and a Master's degree in Orthopedagogics, both at the University of Leiden. She has worked with children and adults with learning difficulties in Holland, England, Wales, Greece and Ireland. She is currently working for the North-Western Health Board, Ireland, as Counsellor for the Handicapped, and doing her PhD as a part-time student in sociology and anthropology at the University of Wales, Swansea.

MARK NUTTALL is a Lecturer in the Department of Sociology at the University of Aberdeen. He has carried out social anthropological fieldwork in Greenland, Scotland and Alaska. His publications include *Arctic Homeland: Kinship, Community and Development in Northwest Greenland* (University of Toronto Press, 1992), *White Settlers: The Impact of Rural Repopulation in Scotland* (Harwood Academic Publishers, 1996, with Charles Jedrej), and *Protecting the Arctic: Indigenous Peoples and Cultural Survival* (Harwood Academic Publishers, 1998).

SUSAN REYNOLDS WHYTE has been engaged in field research on misfortune and health in eastern Uganda at intervals since 1969. She is co-editor, with B. Ingstad, of *Disability and Culture* (University of California Press) and author of *Questioning Misfortune: The Pragmatics of Uncertainty in Eastern Uganda*, (Cambridge University Press), a study of Bunyole. As Professor at the Institute of Anthropology, University of Copenhagen, she is also involved in applied health research and research training in Uganda through a programme supported by the Danish International Development Agency.

1 Culture, classification and (in)competence

Richard Jenkins

This collection of essays is about the social categorisation of individuals as 'incompetent'. Juxtaposing discussions of 'incompetence' and 'competence' in different cultural settings, the contributors hope to encourage readers to question the nature and status of these notions. Although, for stylistic reasons, I will not retain the inverted commas around these and similar words throughout this chapter, they are meant to indicate their contested and problematic character. Nor is it our intention to render them less contested or problematic: quite the reverse, our aim is to provoke questions and raise creative doubts.

This enterprise builds on the small amount of work that has adopted a comparative perspective on 'mental retardation' (Dybwad 1970; Edgerton 1970; Kidd 1970; Manion and Bersani 1987; Zevenbergen 1986) and follows on the heels of a session discussing these issues at the 1994 meeting of the American Anthropological Association. It is also part of the trend that has produced a recent collection of papers offering a cross-cultural perspective on disability, in its widest sense (Ingstad and Whyte 1995). Thinking about these topics in the widest of contexts is increasingly being recognised as vital, if we are to understand them better (cf. Barnes 1996).

(In)competence

'Competence' is the capacity or potential for adequate functioning-in-context as a socialised human. It is generally taken for granted and axiomatic. In this definition, *capacities, potentials* and *adequacies* are to be understood as socially constructed and ascribed – and hence locally variable – rather than 'objective' attributes of persons. *Axiomatic* suggests that the competence of most individuals is not in doubt until it *is* in doubt: in the absence of evidence to the contrary, competence can be presumed, by self and others. In all local settings there are, however, those to whom the presumption of competence is not extended or from whom it has been withdrawn. That they must strive to be competent – more accurately, to be *seen* to be competent – is among the most telling indicators of their exclusion from the fellowship of competence. As Tim and Wendy Booth argue in Chapter 3, the presumption of *in*competence may also be axiomatic: in Britain this presumption is a powerful constraint upon people who are categorised as 'having learning difficulties'.

Categorisations of incompetence may have historical affinities with other categorisations of persons. In any local cultural context, what it means to be 'properly' human in the abstract, and the particular meaning(s) of individual human-ness, are typically the taken-for-granted bedrock upon which mutual sociality is constructed. But human-ness is socially defined and culturally variable. Doubt – or more than doubt – about the full humanity of some individuals or collectivities appears to be common. Historically, cross-culturally, and in our own backyards today, there are many instances in which individuals and collectivities have been, or are, denied their full humanity by others.

A familiar case is racism. Here members of entire social categories are defined as inhuman or as inferior humans and treated accordingly. The categorisation of persons as fundamentally incompetent has, indeed, some things in common with racism. Like 'racial' inferiority, incompetence is typically attributed or ascribed to others; it is unlikely to be self-ordained. Like 'race', it is often bound up with socio-cultural models of the body. Physical impairments, for example, have considerable impact upon socially defined 'human-ness' in some local contexts (Whyte and Ingstad 1995: 10–11; Murphy 1987). Categorisations of incompetence and 'racial' categorisations are often dimensions of hierarchical schema of human adequacy and acceptability: as sexual partners, mates, affines, colleagues, neighbours and so on.

Historically, ever more precise definitions and measurements of both incompetence and 'racial' difference were central to the burgeoning science and statistics of 'normality'. 'Racial' Otherness was equated or associated with incompetence or inadequacy, as in the typification of Down's Syndrome as 'mongolism', and in nineteenth-century ethnic classifications of mental degeneracy and idiocy (Miller 1995: 217). In the twentieth century there has been an even more consequential history of the racialisation of intelligence and competence (Fraser 1995; Herrnstein and Murray 1994; Jensen 1969). Inspired scientifically by Galton and the eugenic vision, the pursuit of 'racial' fitness was taken to the point of mass extermination (Burleigh 1991; Burleigh and Wippermann 1991). 'Racial' fitness, entangled with notions about individual incompetence, produced Nazi euthanasia programmes (Burleigh 1994). Less dramatically, in the contemporary world local political economies of (in)competence are, as Nancy Lundgren discusses in Chapter 9 with respect to Belize, located within wider racialised hierarchies of dependency and underdevelopment that have their roots in colonialism and empire. This may result in axiomatic presumptions of 'racial' incompetence.

Attributions of incompetence do not, of course, necessarily equate with dehumanisation. Local and cultural variability is manifold. In the area of Uganda where Susan Reynolds Whyte has done fieldwork (see Chapter 7) or in north-western Greenland (see Mark Nuttall's account in Chapter 8) it appears that 'mental' incompetence does not in any straightforward sense equate with diminished or problematic personhood. Nor, as these authors suggest, should we expect to find *one* over-arching understanding of competence in any local context: (in)competence is likely to be entangled with other domains of classifying persons.

One of these domains is age and the life course. Human infants are – by definition – unable to look after themselves and, in the first instance, they lack language. Children are typically considered as at least less competent than adults, in the sense that they are imperfectly socialised and psycho-socially immature. Infants and children, however, are presumed to be on their way to competence. Older people may also be defined as less competent: they may become more physically dependent and, perhaps, communicatively and intellectually impaired. In their case, however, this is a departure from previously existing states of competence. Childhood and senility are thus states-of-being that are understood as 'normal': either a transitory pre-condition of competence, or a loss of adult competence that is a regrettable part of the scheme of things. In any local setting there may be a link between these kinds of incompetence and models of adequate human-ness, but it is not inevitable. In the United Kingdom, for example, there are some connections: in everyday understandings of the child-like innocence of people with learning difficulties, in the almost axiomatic presumption that they cannot become 'proper' adults (Jenkins 1990), and in the attribution to them by psychologists, on the basis of authoritative formal disgnostic testing, of putative 'mental ages'. In the United States the category of 'mental *retardation*' is itself suggestive of the same kind of developmental model of incompetence.

'Race'-as-incompetence and age-related incompetence are attributes of social categories rather than conditions that are specific to individuals (although they are *also* conditions of individuals, and individuals may be exempted from the presumed incompetence attaching to their categorical identification). This collection of essays, however, is primarily concerned with something else: individual incompetence that is locally understood as something other than inherently categorical, transitory or chronologically appropriate. The incompetences in which we are interested are locally understood as *definitive* characteristics of *individuals* (although they may also generate collective categorisations). Even in the Belizean case described by Lundgren in Chapter 9, where (in)competence is axiomatically hierarchised as a collective ethnic attribute, it still boils down to an individual matter. Not all Garinagus are incompetent, not all Creoles are competent, hence the importance in Belizean schools of testing.

The incompetences in question are also different from physical disabilities or emotional and personality disturbances. To use categories with which we as Western social scientists are comfortable, this book is about how *intellectual* or *cognitive* incompetences are understood in different local cultural settings. However, since distinctions such as intellectual-emotional or intelligence-personality do not necessarily travel well, drawing this particular heuristic boundary gets us immediately into difficulties. This issue provides our collection with one of its themes.

The first thing that a comparative perspective tells us is that intellectual incompetence does not *only* mean 'learning difficulties' or 'mental retardation'. Nor does it necessarily mean *all* of the conditions or states-of-being that these labels conventionally identify. These are classificatory categories of Western medicine and psychology, defined according to locally specific criteria. They are not 'natural' or 'real' in any sense, other than in their social construction as such. They are cultural constructs or folk models – albeit very powerful ones – and they presuppose too many important things to be analytical categories of comparative anthropological usefulness. For example, conditions such as deafness, cerebral palsy or schizophrenia – which are not defined as 'mental retardation' – might in any given cultural context be included in the category which is, locally, the closest cognate classification to 'mental retardation'. Further, whether or not there exist in any local setting categories which approximate to the North American 'retardation' or the British 'learning difficulties' is always in principle a moot point, to be resolved by investigation. The ethnography presented in subsequent chapters by Whyte (from Uganda) and Nuttall (from Greenland) makes all of these points. Thus one key question is: can we produce an analytical category of 'intellectual incompetence' – or incompetence more generally – which possesses comparative utility?

The first answer to this question is that, in order to transcend the limitations of Western diagnostic categories, it is necessary to document *local* models. There may be no better approach to this than the anthropological, specialising as it does in understanding local points of view (which is not to underestimate the difficulties involved in doing so: Geertz 1983: 55–70; Holy and Stuchlik 1983). The second answer, if we are to approach those local models with an open mind, is that we need a comparative approach that does not presume an 'objective', quantitative model of deficit (although the realities of impairment cannot be ignored either). Finally, our starting point should be 'competence' – culturally defined and context-dependent – no less than 'incompetence'. A foundational assumption of any inquiry must be that notions of competence and incompetence presuppose and reciprocally entail each other. Hence the notion of (in)competence, to denote classificatory fields which necessarily encompass both competence and incompetence.

Local models

How are we to interpret and analyse the ways in which (in)competence can be understood locally? There are many different threads here, and no self-evident best way to weave them into a coherent pattern. The following are among the places from which one would have to start.

- Is (in)competence acknowledged at all in the cultural context in question?
- What are the criteria of classification and/or processes of diagnosis?
- What aetiological models are deployed to understand (in)competence?
- Is intellectual (in)competence differentiated from physical (in)competence?
- Does the general distinction between the physical and the intellectual-mental make sense in the particular local cultural context?
- Is a distinction made between emotional incompetence and intellectual deficit? This involves asking whether, and how, the former is recognised.
- Is a distinction drawn between permanent and temporary incompetence?
- Is there an explicit or implicit hierarchy of (in)competences?
- How, if at all, are physical and intellectual (in)competences integrated into an understanding of general practical (in)competence?

In fact, we must ask whether a model of (in)competence that is open-ended and sensitive to local meanings, yet capable of delineating a sufficiently distinct domain of social phenomena to permit a comparative perspective, is possible at all. This raises issues of ontology and metaphysics that are as difficult as they are ancient and ethically disturbing (e.g. Cockburn 1991; Chapman and Jones 1980; Hirst and Woolley 1982; Singer 1979).

One approach to competence which may allow us to make a start on some of these questions, is to think in terms of that which is *predictable*, *usual* or '*normal*' (to introduce another troublesome word). The point of departure here is the non-deviant rather than its opposite (Jenkins 1998):

- Is 'normality' – or something approximating to it – a meaningful local category?
- If so, how do locals understand and talk about 'normality'? How does this help to constitute deviance, etc.?
- Is there a local differentiation, for example, between moral normality or deviance, and other kinds of conformity and difference?
- What is the place of sexuality and understandings of reproduction in these categorisations?
- How are incompetence or abnormality explained locally? How are they related to ideas such as 'normality'?
- Are there specific aetiological schema for explaining specific kinds of abnormality or incompetence?

Questions about 'normality' inexorably lead one to think about *social control*. Considering social control as an aspect of the interactional practices and institutional constitution of everyday life prompts further questions:

- Are the incompetent recognised interactionally at all?
- If not, what happens to them?
- What difference does it make in an individual's day-to-day life to be classified as intellectually incompetent?
- Is incompetence locally seen to be a social problem?
- Have specific institutions and practices been developed to 'deal' with the 'problem'?
- What social possibilities are open to those who are classified as incompetent?
- What *must* they do or not do?
- Who classifies (in)competence or (ab)normality locally, and in what institutional settings and contexts?
- How do these issues relate to local public–private distinctions?
- What implications does (in)competence have for one's rights and duties as a member of society?

Questions such as these lead, in turn, to a consideration of *social identity*: the ways in which collectivities and individuals are distinguished in their relations with other collectivities and individuals; the establishment, signification and organisation of relationships of similarity and difference between collectivities and individuals:

- How does (in)competence relate to concepts of social adulthood?
- To gender?
- To other dimensions of social identity, such as ethnicity or, if locally appropriate, 'race'?
- How is ageing related to conceptions of (in)competence?
- How does intellectual incompetence affect membership of the category 'human'?

- What does it mean to be 'human' in the local cultural context?
- What are the implications of different *kinds* of incompetence for 'being human'?
- Does being categorised as incompetent prevent or disrupt the achievement of full person- or selfhood (however these are understood) in the local context?
- How do people who are categorised as intellectually incompetent see themselves?
- And how do they see others?

These are infinitely more complex questions than is suggested by posing them so baldly. The last two, in particular, raise epistemological questions about communication with people who may, for example, possess few communicative skills and have cognitive impairments. These questions are thorny enough if the researcher is working in a culture where s/he has a native linguistic competence (e.g. Atkinson 1988; Atkinson and Williams 1990; Booth 1996; Booth and Booth 1996; Flynn 1986). For anthropologists, working as they often are on cultural and linguistic *terra infirma* (if not utterly *incognito*), they are posed even more sharply.

Thinking about social identity entails asking *who* identifies individuals as competent or incompetent? Localities are – in ways which are complex and often contradictory – components of wider arenas of communication, decision-making, resource/penalty allocation, and identification. In the modern world, the attribution of (in)competence is unlikely be a purely local matter. Indigenous or local models may be at odds with external or metropolitan models, over response and treatment as well as classification and diagnosis. As Nuttall's discussion of Greenland in Chapter 8 illustrates, metropolitan models – particularly in-so-far as they are Western scientific bio-medical models, bound up with the organisational practices of the state – are likely to be consequential in different ways, and to different degrees, than local models or indigenous knowledge. Taking a different tack, Lundgren, in Chapter 9, discusses the damaging internalisation of metropolitan models in the ex-colonial periphery. She also suggests, however, that in a place like Belize, where the majority of the population can be said to fall short of metropolitan ideals of competence, some of the *extremes* of incompetence may be less visible. But in all respects, power is an issue that is never far away.

'Mental retardation' and 'learning difficulties'?

To talk about Western bio-medicine, and the state, in the context of (in)competence, is to talk about classificatory categories such as *mental retardation* in North America, and *learning difficulties* or *learning disabilities* in the United Kingdom. Although these might appear to be straightforward diagnostic categories, they are, in fact, difficult notions to grasp with clarity or precision. There is not even consensus about appropriate terminology; for example, 'learning disabilities' means something quite different in the United States than it does in the United Kingdom (Murphy 1992).

A consistent feature of campaigns in Western societies on behalf of people who are classified in this way has been successive changes in terminology. In the United Kingdom this has involved progressive shifts of nomenclature: from 'idiocy', to 'feeble-mindedness', to 'mental subnormality', to 'mental handicap', to 'learning difficulties', and finally, on the part of the Department of Health, to 'learning disabilities'. In the United States, by the same process:

> *defectives* became *mental defectives*, *imbeciles* became *high-grade* and *low-grade imbeciles*, *moron* became the *higher-functioning mentally-retarded*. More recently *the mentally retarded* have become *mentally retarded persons* and now *persons with mental retardation* and, in some circles, *persons with developmental disabilities* or *persons specially challenged*. (Trent 1994: 5, italics in the original)

The politics of correctness here are integral to strategies aimed at enhancing the individual worth and social value of the people concerned, in their own eyes and in the eyes of others, and improving their care. However, categorical ambiguity of this kind might also indicate unease about the nature – the social and ontological status – of the people concerned. It is difficult not to agree with Trent's further observation:

> In this process, essence has been apparently liberated from existence, being from descriptions of it. Behind these awkward new phrases, however, the gaze we turn on those we label mentally retarded continues to be informed by the long history of condescension, suspicion and exclusion. That history is unavoidably manifest in the words we now find offensive. . . . While our contemporary phrases appear more benign, too often we use them to hide from the offense in ways that the old terms did not permit. (*ibid.*)

The more recent labels are not more accurately descriptive: everyone, for example, has *some* learning difficulties, however trivial. They are not necessarily less stigmatising either – the polarity of *any* category can be subverted. Nor is the fact that 'learning difficulties', for example, appears to command most assent at the moment among those working in the field in the United Kingdom sufficient to dictate its use. Other categories have their advocates, and the strength of support for particular labels among the labelled is a matter of assertion rather than evidence. For the purposes of thinking comparatively, these categories that are so locally specific are unlikely to prove helpful.

So, throughout the rest of this discussion I will avoid categories such as 'mental retardation' or 'learning difficulties', other than to place them in inverted commas as categories of everyday local use. However, terminology is sometimes necessary. I have reluctantly chosen to accept the argument of Hattersley *et al.* that the best term, for the conditions and states-of-being that are called 'mental retardation' or 'learning difficulties', is 'intellectual disability':

'Intellectual' is a more accurate description than 'mental', which is a term associated with psychiatry rather than learning; 'disability' directs attention to the need *to enable* the person by whatever means are possible, recognising that impaired movement, vision, hearing and speech commonly compound the learning difficulties further. (Hattersley *et al.* 1987: 3–4)

Since it has not passed into widespread use, this expression has the virtue in this context of not yet being particularly locally or culturally specific. So, where necessary, I shall talk about *intellectual disability*. Other contributors, however, talk about 'learning difficulties' and 'mental retardation' and I have not intervened in this respect.

A general definition of intellectual disability might stress social and cognitive incompetence: difficulties experienced by an individual in doing things as well as most other people in the appropriate cultural context. In use, however, the concept clearly means more than this. In contemporary Western industrial societies, a clinical diagnosis of 'mental retardation' or 'learning difficulties' will typically draw upon three criteria:

• a measured IQ below a particular (arbitrary) score;
• the identification of the condition during early childhood;
• 'behavioural' problems.

The latter criterion is increasingly being questioned by professional opinion (although where there is no organic pathology it is the most likely reason for *referral*). The first two criteria, however, are professionally consensual and, in increasingly elaborated versions with respect to tested intelligence, relatively well-established over time (Miller 1995: 213).

There is less consensus with respect to *aetiology*. Clinical conventional wisdom suggests that in only 25–30 per cent of cases so diagnosed is intellectual disability associated with an identifiable organic pathology; Zigler and Hodapp (1986: 51–4), arguing at the same time for a slightly lower overall prevalence rate than is generally accepted, suggest that the figure is closer to 50 per cent. The rest – between a half and three-quarters of the category in question – attract a variety of labels, of which the United States has, perhaps, been most productive:

retardation due to sociocultural factors, familial retardation, retardation due to environmental deprivation, nonorganic retardation, and cultural-familial deprivation. (Zigler and Hodapp 1986: 8)

In other words, the bulk of the category consists of people who have been categorised as significantly less bright than the general population average, without there being any clear diagnosis or understanding of the reasons for their incompetence.

Talking about aetiology raises issues that are fundamental to the comparative enterprise. The identifiable organic pathologies – Down's Syndrome, iodine deficiency, lead poisoning, Fragile X syndrome, and so on – have in common the fact that they are, albeit in differing degrees, definitively embodied. They are more or less visible. In the archaeological record individuals with hydrocephalus or Down's Syndrome are as pathologically identifiable as modern individuals with the same conditions (Brothwell 1960; Cronk 1993; Murphy and McNeill 1993: 126–7, 129; see also the case referred to by Nuttall in Chapter 8). An individual with a condition of this sort in one cultural context is, in some senses – *although in some senses only* – 'the same' as a person with the same condition in any other cultural context. In any and every cultural setting it is possible to identify a population presenting the symptoms of the organic pathologies or impairments that are intellectually disabling. However, how those symptoms are understood locally, and how the individuals concerned are treated, is culturally and contextually variable. The pathologies are not in themselves determinate; but they do exist and they can be discovered.

But, what about the up to 75 per cent – in Britain or the USA – who are less visible? How are people such as these cross-culturally visible? Do such people exist at all in other cultural settings? One comparative approach to these issues is historical.[1] We encounter an immediate problem, however. As Berrios argues (1995: 225, 233), most historical accounts of the topic treat the modern point of view as by definition superior to that of past generations, and the past as 'a preparation for the present'. This may simply be a general problem in the writing of history, but it highlights a serious difficulty with respect to our particular area of inquiry. The question of appropriate categories is the tip of an epistemological iceberg: it is not merely that talking about 'learning difficulties' or 'mental retardation' with respect to earlier periods is anachronistic – it certainly is – but that the *categories* of people that these words denote did not exist in, say, the nineteenth century.

To put this another way, the last two centuries or so in Western industrialised states have witnessed two connected trends. In the first, the criteria for identifying – or, if you prefer, socially constructing – intellectual disability, have become more broadly based and inclusive as they have become ever more sophisticated. One interpretation links this to the expansion of the notion of citizenship following the American and French revolutions, and its subsequent definition by exclusion, by defining who was *fit* to exercise the responsibilities of citizenship (Goodey 1995). Another argument sees it as a consequence of 'urbanisation, literacy and a cash economy' (Thom 1995: 251). Writing about the nineteenth century, the same author goes on to argue that:

The concept of idiocy became a stigma when it was used as technical term to isolate, to identify the non-productive or those who disturbed the peace of a working day. . . . When both handicap and criminality were lumped together under the notion of degeneracy, as they were in the very different systems of mensuration of Lombroso, Broca and Galton, the problem of being labelled an idiot became more than merely technical for those so-called defectives. (Thom 1995: 252)

These interpretations do not conflict. Theoretically one can generalise them further, by invoking Foucauldian visions of classification, confinement and control, on the one hand, and understandings of the social construction of deviance deriving from symbolic interactionism and the labelling perspective, on the other (see Cohen 1985, for a suggestive combination of this kind). They can be summarised in the evocative notion of the 'invention of the feeble mind' (Trent 1994).

The second trend is that *within* this period it appears that the size of the category of intellectually disabled persons has been variable over time:

A majority of the individuals shut away as 'feeble minded' at the height of the first wave of mass segregation, as recently as the turn of this last century, would today be ordinary citizens. (Goodey 1995: 239–40)

This variation is not trivial, and must be understood in terms of classificatory practices rather than in 'real' terms (Zigler and Hodapp 1986: 59–63, 90–111). At different times, more or less people, and different kinds of people, have fallen under the purview – the gaze – of the institutional and bureaucratic systems that have been developed to address the problem of incompetence. This is partly a consequence of differing levels of concern about the threat that their incompetence was believed to pose, and partly due to changing methods for identifying incompetence and variations in their use.

In the absence of proper statistical series it is impossible to be precise, but the long-term trend over this period has probably been for an expanding proportion of the population of the industrialised democracies to be classified as intellectually incompetent in various ways and to varying degrees. Some small part of this is doubtless a reflection of the increasing capacity of medicine to preserve fragile life. However, this trend also reflects something else: the gradual expansion, responding to general labour market changes, of the general category of people classified as 'disabled' (Oliver 1990; Stone 1985).[2]

A different point, and more significant for the numbers, is that many people who are today in receipt of services for the 'mentally retarded' or 'people with learning difficulties', had they lived a century or two ago would have been earning their living, albeit in precarious unskilled poverty, as relatively unremarkable members of the community. These belong to the 'up to 75 per cent': the modern population of 'people with learning difficulties' or 'the mentally retarded', who are so defined at least as much by their inclusion in a bureaucratised system of health and social services as by their putative disability. Their 'equivalents' in former times cannot in any straightforward sense be identified as 'mentally retarded' or as 'having learning difficulties'.

There is, therefore, neither necessity nor even likelihood that all – or indeed any – of the 'up to 75 per cent' will be visible in every cultural setting. This is further support for my earlier argument: categories such as 'learning difficulties', 'mental retardation' and 'intellectual disability' are unstable, context-dependent, and likely to be unhelpful as analytical tools for comparative analysis, whether historical or cross-cultural. Even more dramatically, this implies that there may not even be a stable phenomenon that can be compared in these terms. All models may thus be local models.

Can it really be this problematic? This answer is yes, probably. In societies such as the UK or the USA, most people who are classified as 'having learning difficulties' or 'being mentally retarded' are people who have been assessed in childhood as less intelligent than the average – the implication being that the cognitive deficit, even if not congenital, is disruptive of 'normal' development – to a degree that is considered by expert opinion to be severe enough, or sufficiently troublesome to others, to require identification and intervention. This, of course, need not be a bad thing. Without diagnosis and identification, after all, how can 'special needs' be assessed, much less met? Fine, but we are obliged to ask whether, and to what extent, those 'special needs' are endogenous or are the product of categorisation and exclusion from mainstream society. The chapters which follow by Angrosino, Devlieger, Davies, and Booth and Booth deserve particular attention in this respect.

From a comparative perspective, further questions about the local specificity of (in)competence are implied by the 'retardation as a product of urbanisation and industrialisation' school of thought. These highlight the notions of adequate *function* that are central to classifications of (in)competence. One of them is whether small-scale societies, with simple subsistence technologies, have different thresholds of competence – or different thresholds of tolerance of incompetence – than industrialised, urban societies.

Society, technology and environment

A cross-cultural perspective upon intellectual (in)competence is elusive. Observations on the topic are scattered throughout the ethnographic literature, but there are few specialist studies. It is, therefore, impossible to generalise with any confidence about variation in the *definition* of (in)competence between cultures. We can say, however, that there is no uniformity between local cultural contexts in the *treatment* of people who are defined as incompetent. This can be seen in the chapters which follow. Neither incompetence nor intellectual disability – nor indeed disability more generally (Ingstad and Whyte 1995; Marshall 1994, 1996) – are consistent, 'natural' or self-evident categories. This is not to ignore the fact that, for a range of reasons, individuals differ in their intellectual and physical capacities. Nor is it to overlook the likelihood that some distinction between competence and incompetence is drawn in all societies. However, *where* the line is drawn, and what it *means*, varies enormously.

To make this point with a recent European example, it is only within the last twenty to thirty years or so that people with cerebral palsy have been removed from the 'retarded' or 'learning difficulties' categories (and, even so, their experiences of everyday interaction may not have been much improved thereby). To take another example, Islam appears to encourage a relatively high degree of tolerance of the less competent. There is an extensive and long-standing body of Islamic law which deals with their rights. This too varies, however. Thus it is incompetent men rather than women – and usually only men with property at that – who are legally protected. Nor is there a cultural consensus within Islam about nature or causation: diagnoses and treatments range from the opinions of modern scientific medicine, to attributions of *djinn* possession which entail exorcism at a shrine. There is also regional variation: while the threshold of tolerance for the incompetent may – by dint perhaps of the necessities of the desert nomad's existence – be low among the Bedouin, this does not seem to be true, for example, in Pakistan (Miles 1992).

Might there be a relationship, therefore, between the treatment of incompetence and either technological complexity or subsistence pressure? In 1970 Robert Edgerton, whose ethnography of 'mentally retarded' people in California in the early 1960s (Edgerton 1967) remains a rare example of a study of a non-institutional setting, examined the available cross-cultural evidence (Edgerton 1970). His aim was to question the then-conventional wisdom which suggested that the 'simpler' the society – if only in terms of technology – the more tolerance there was likely to be for 'simple' people. He asked whether intellectual disabilities have become more visible and more problematic as societies have become functionally more complex and cognitively more demanding.

Within the limits set by the small amount of evidence he could muster, Edgerton found no one pattern of tolerance or rejection of incompetence, nor any way of consistently relating either to socio-technological complexity. With respect to environmental stress and subsistence pressure, much the same was true. In some societies the incompetent are (or were) perceived as a problem, in others less so, and in yet others not at all. Take, for example, hunter-gatherers. Edgerton's summary of ethnographic accounts of the Inuit – which is supported by Nuttall's discussion later in this volume – suggests a range of responses to intellectual incompetence, from abandonment to sanctification. The Phi Tong Luang of northern Thailand, even though living on the extreme margins of subsistence, none-the-less appeared to attempt to rear all of their children. By contrast, however, the more securely affluent Chippewa and Algonkin peoples of north-eastern North America have a well-documented history of fatal intolerance towards the disabled and the incompetent.

Edgerton's was a very limited exercise, but it allowed him to reject technological or environmental *determinism* as a framework for explaining cultural variation in the understanding or treatment of those people who can be described as having intellectual disabilities. This does not, however, mean that the environment is unimportant. At least three significant environmental factors affect the *incidence* of intellectual disabilities.

First, the harsher the environment, the less likely it is that incompetent or physically disabled members of the group will survive. If mortality rates for 'normal' infants are routinely high, how much more vulnerable will a child be who is slower or more sickly than the rest? In such circumstances the issue of tolerance may simply not arise. Second, subsistence pressure can be a significant *cause* of intellectual deficits. In particular, certain kinds of malnutrition in children – for example, kwashiorkor – may produce, if allowed to persist in the medium to long term, irreversible brain damage and cognitive deficits. Malnutrition is, of course, not randomly distributed among the world's populations, so we can expect to discover variable and cumulative concentrations of pathologies of this kind.

Third, there are other environmental causes of intellectual disabilities. For example, one organic pathology which results in severe intellectual disability is congenital hypothyroidism ('cretinism') caused by an underactive maternal thyroid gland. This may be caused by iodine deficiencies in the mother during pregnancy, and is common to the point of being endemic in many areas of Asia, South and Central America and Africa

(Hetzel 1989). It has, for example, become an acute problem in Bangladesh due to the leaching of iodine from the soil by recurrent major flooding, and, hence, its disappearance from the local food chain and diet. The condition is preventable by fairly simple interventions – the adequate supply of iodated salt, for example – but, at the moment, it remains a problem of significant dimensions.

Industrial and other pollution may also cause relevant organic pathologies. One notorious example was the concentrated discharge, by the Chisso Corporation, of heavy-metal effluent into Japanese coastal waters at Minamata Bay between the early years of this century and the 1970s. This resulted in a major increase in serious impairments and brain damage, particularly in children, in the local fishing community (Michiko 1988; Smith and Smith 1975). This Japanese case suggests that among the things about which we are still ill-informed are the responses of people in small-scale communities to abrupt increases in the incidence of serious physical or intellectual impairments and their concomitant disabilities, how these responses are culturally variable, and the implications of such situations for local institutions and practices.

Cosmology: culture and nature

If, with respect to cultural variation in models of (in)competence, there are no straightforward relationships between environmental factors and socio-technological complexity, what about the relationships between local models of humanity or personhood and definitions of (in)competence? Although they are present throughout this collection, these issues are explored in particular depth in the chapters by Charlotte Davies, on Wales, Susan Whyte, talking about eastern Uganda, and Mark Nuttall, in the context of north-western Greenland.

Different peoples live, to some extent, in different worlds. Ideas about the self, the nature of humanity, and the place of humans in the world, are culturally variable (Carrithers, Collins and Lukes, 1985; Jackson and Karp 1990; Morris 1994), and this has implications for our discussion. If, for example, being a 'complete' person is believed to be related to a metaphysical quality of individuals – what European cultures might call the soul – then much will depend upon whether people who are categorised as less-than-competent are believed to possess that quality. On the other hand, if the criteria of full humanity are more material – bodily integrity, for example – then the outlook for some incompetent or disabled people will be worse than for others. Looking at the expanses imagined by cosmologies, the conventional scientific model of a 'mechanical universe' has different implications for understanding incompetence than a world-view in which the forces of motion and causality are thought of in spiritual terms. And so on.

These issues underline the usefulness, and relative shortage, of systematic evidence from a range of cultures and local contexts. Marshall's discussions of evidence from Micronesia (1994, 1996), for example, explore the local relationship between models of personhood and attributions of disability, and the inappropriateness of World Health Organisation-style Western models. In another context, Miles (1992) suggests that since Pakistani children are expected to be obedient to the will of their parents, anything other than this is regarded as a disruption of the normal *moral* order, as embodied in Allah's creation. Behavioural problems which in the UK or the USA might offer a basis for a diagnosis of intellectual disability, are thus likely to be interpreted morally, as *djinn* possession, to be dealt with by exorcism rather than educational or medical intervention.

In the absence of cross-cultural evidence we may learn from history. In the European past, even the very recent past, popular cosmology envisaged a moral universe teeming with a host of spirits, some of whom were not even clothed in the thinnest of Christian camouflage. A child of 'normal' parents who would today be diagnosed as having intellectual disabilities, might then have been identified as a 'changeling', not human at all, a poor substitute for the healthy child which had been stolen by envious fairies or trolls (Schoon Eberley 1991). The consequences of such a diagnosis could be fatal: one recommended treatment for a changeling was to drive the impostor out using fire, another was exposure to the elements. There is evidence that these harsh remedies were actually resorted to (e.g. Jenkins 1977): the abandonment of the incompetent to their fate can be attested in the nineteenth-century British Isles as well as the twentieth-century Arctic.

In other contexts, however, some incompetent persons were tolerated by Christians, even protected by the Church, as 'holy innocents' or 'sacred fools' (Billington 1984: 16–31; Scheerenberger 1983: 25ff.): intellectual deficits were interpreted as signs of spiritual grace, 'simple' states of nature that were closer to God than the immorality and corruption of culture. 'Holy innocence', as is clear from contemporary accounts, could also be understood as a state of perpetual childhood. In both cases an analogy was drawn with humanity before the Fall and the expulsion from Eden. Less benignly, of course, the historical record is also clear that the incompetent might be branded another kind of fool, and exploited for purposes of public and private entertainment.

Notions about perpetual childhood and the innocence of people with intellectual disabilities remain current. Most people, however, no longer live in a world of magical possibilities, peopled and moved by invisible spirits. Secular and scientific rationalities coexist with and are at least as important as a multiplicity of religious world-views (in many of which the deity or deities seem to have withdrawn from the daily management of the world). The enchanted, moral universe is challenged by a model of the world derived from 'objective' statistical probability and the mechanical laws of physics and the other natural sciences.

The philosopher Ian Hacking has argued (1990) that one of the most powerful ideas in this modern cosmology, originally developed by nineteenth-century statisticians such as Galton, is 'normality'. The concept of normality does two things simultaneously: it *describes* as normal that which is most *typical* or the usual state of affairs; it then *asserts* that this is also the way things *ought* to be. The propagation of the average (and the above average) thus becomes a moral imperative. People with intellectual disabilities, from this point of view, are neither average nor normal. To revisit earlier points about the limited significance of organic pathologies in the aetiology and classification of intellectual disabilities, the statistical plotting of a normal curve of distribution for measured intelligence has probably been the single most influential factor in the definition and creation of a category of persons known as the 'mildly mentally retarded'. Before the advent of the bell-shaped curve, the category simply did not exist.

Ideas about normality were developed in nineteenth-century Europe in the context of two related ideologies. The first was a racism which asserted – on the basis of 'proof' – the inferiority of the colonised and disadvantaged peoples of the world. The second, the Eugenics movement, similarly grounded in 'evidence', aimed to improve the 'fitness' of the European population (which was often understood in terms of 'race') by discouraging the breeding of the 'unfit' and the 'inferior'. Both assumed that Europeans, particularly *Northern* Europeans, were the apex of human evolution, the normal yardstick against which the other races of humanity could be measured and found wanting.

There is little point in pouring anachronistic scorn on the ideas of an earlier time. But, as discussed earlier, those ideas were and still are consequential in the classification and treatment of intellectual incompetence. At the relatively trivial end of the spectrum, in 1866 Down characterised the syndrome which now bears his name as 'Mongolism', a reference to the eye shape which characterises the condition and a direct analogy with the 'Mongoloid race'. More significant is a well-documented and continuing predisposition in Europe and North America to label as incompetent or intellectually disabled disproportionately more black or Asian people than white Europeans (Mercer 1973; Tomlinson 1981).

Most important of all, however, was and is the dominance of a model of 'normal' humanity, legitimated by the authority of science, which claims that its criteria of adequacy and competence are 'objective' and, therefore, beyond doubt or reproach. Among the consequences for those who were labelled as 'mental retarded', 'subnormal' or 'feeble minded' were institutionalisation and seclusion. Compulsory sterilisation and abortion were routine, as was the forced breaking-up of families whose parents were deemed 'unfit'. These individual assaults and indignities may be less common, but they have not yet vanished.

At its worst, this model of human normality led to the activities of the notorious 'euthanasia' units of the German state between 1939 and 1945 (Burleigh 1991, 1994). Thousands of intellectually and physically impaired children and adults were killed. The processing of the victims – the decision whether to kill or not – was left to committees of scientific specialists: physicians, psychologists and physical anthropologists. Their professorial and scientific authority legitimated the mass murder which they directed, and many held senior academic posts in Germany until relatively recently (Müller-Hill 1988). Nor were such visions of a better world confined to Nazi Germany. As witnessed by research (e.g. Koch 1996), and by recent controversy in the press (see *The Observer*, 24 August 1997), disturbingly similar perspectives on incompetence and fitness have informed Social Democrat policy and practice with respect to compulsory sterilisation in Scandinavia until relatively recently.

Science, despite its claims to the privileged possession of universal objective knowledge, is but one cultural framework among many, albeit a powerful one. The scientific notion of 'normality' does not exist in isolation. Other cultural themes and threads are also important. Although the absence of proper comparative material makes it impossible to be certain, recent international scandals about the treatment of people with intellectual and other disabilities in Greece, Ceauşescu's Romania, China, Hong Kong, Macao and Bulgaria, indicate the interaction of modern notions of 'objective normality' with other – more 'traditional'? – cultural models of the natural and the unnatural, the human and the less-than-human.

These scandals also suggest another angle on these issues. To judge from the content and presentation of the stories which have emerged in the British press over the past few years, the harsh treatment of people with intellectual and other disabilities may be becoming a marker of difference in popular discourse, a visible index of 'Otherness', 'underdevelopment' and cultural distance. It is something that 'they' do (conveniently forgetting, of course, a long and relatively recent history of scandals in Britain and elsewhere: cf. Ryan and Thomas 1987).

The relationship between ideas about culture and nature offers one key to a better understanding of cross-cultural variation in the treatment of the incompetent. Two variations on this theme may, in different ways and with differing degrees of significance, be relevant. Deeply rooted in human experience, the first concerns the difference between humans (cultural) and animals (natural). Classification, however, is never that simple. There are always anomalies. Domesticated animals, or children prior to socialisation, may each be anomalous, depending upon the culture concerned. So may children with obvious birth defects, or children who fail to thrive or become competent adults. What matters is how the anomaly is resolved: classifying or re-classifying the child as animal or human, part of nature or culture, is one option. The 'changeling', for example, is a representative of the natural world. Anomaly can also be handled differently, however, by sanctification, as in the case of the 'holy innocent'. However it is achieved, upon the resolution of the classificatory problem depends the subsequent treatment of the individual concerned.

The second theme is more recent and returns us to ideas about normality. Here the distinction is between the natural (normal) and the unnatural (abnormal or deviant). Here, by the classificatory logic of statistical frequency – and, indeed, by the classificatory logics of transformation and inversion which are so familiar from structuralism – *culture*, being typical for humans, becomes part of human *nature*. Thus incompetence in things cultural – the inability to learn language, etc. – may be interpreted as an indication of an unnatural and inferior humanity. Although not an animal, the person with intellectual disabilities may be classified as sub-human, an unnatural monstrosity.

The two classificatory themes are not the same. Nor do they deal necessarily with similar issues (although each has a bearing on the boundary between humanity and the rest of the cosmos). However, each allows the classification of individuals who are categorised as incompetent as something less/other than human. In conjunction they are a powerful means of social exclusion, even to the point of extermination.

Contesting classifications

The classificatory boundary between culture and nature occurs in one form or another in *all* cultures. While it may permit the derogation of incompetent individuals as less than human, it does not demand it. Other cultural themes may be of considerable significance in protecting or positively valorising the incompetent. The most obvious, perhaps, is *religion*, the discourse about the sacred (exemplified in the earlier reference to 'holy innocence'). Religion may or may not be relevant, but it is important to consider questions such as:

- Does local religion categorise the incompetent as equal to or inferior to their competent brethren?
- Does local religion privilege incompetent people, theologically or otherwise?
- How does this relate to notions of human essence, such as 'the soul' (a question which refers back to the discussion of humanity and personhood)?
- Is a distinction drawn locally between spiritual essence and intellect?
- Where appropriate, what is the relationship between local religion(s) and more universalistic religions such as Christianity or Islam?

Religion – even different versions of the same religion – may either negate or support dehumanising classifications; religions differ widely in this respect. Hindu and Buddhist theologies of reincarnation understand the human–animal distinction as one point on a continuum of ascent towards the eventual dissolution of individuality. This does not, however, *dictate* the benign treatment of the incompetent. Incompetence or intellectual disability may, for example, be interpreted as a penal aspect of the soul's *karma*. Nonetheless, such evidence as there is (Sen 1992) suggests that there are relatively high levels of public tolerance for people with intellectual disabilities in, for example, India.

Of necessity, religions interpret the relationship between culture and nature. It is somewhat artificial therefore to distinguish religion too sharply from other discourses on the culture–nature theme. However, religions – particularly universalistic religions – may also draw another boundary: between the believer and the unbeliever, the saved and the damned. In respect of both of these boundaries, religion is an important influence upon the classification and treatment of 'proper' human beings.

Universalistic religions such as Christianity and Islam, which view all souls as, in theory, prospective candidates for conversion and salvation, might be thought to be benign by definition. Unfortunately this is not so. To take fundamentalist Protestantism as an example, much depends upon whether people with intellectual disabilities are deemed by a particular sect to be capable of being 'born again'. One may also encounter the belief, inspired by the Second Commandment of the Old Testament, that the birth of a child with intellectual disabilities is a punishment for the sins of the parents or grandparents.

Religious salvation is generally a matter for the hereafter. Secular movements and ideologies may, however, seek salvation in the here-and-now. One characteristic variation upon this cultural theme is, in varying ways, concerned with the achievement of greater *equality*, however that may be defined. A relatively modern ideology, developing alongside the idea of normality, the pursuit of equality can be understood as an expres-

sion of the celebration of the *average* which is one – and only one – of normality's central themes. Two obvious possibilities here are socialism, on
the one hand, and variants on the liberal advocacy of universal human
rights, on the other. There may be others. There is certainly a range of
questions to be asked:

- How do universalistic notions of human equality articulate with individual variability with respect to (in)competence?
- Are there specific political discourses in the local context about, for
  example, disability rights?
- What are the consequences, for people who are categorised as intellectually incompetent, of various formal national or international
  specifications of civil and human rights?
- How do such matters reflect local–national relationships, or
  insider–outsider themes?
- What have been the local effects of wider changes such as political and
  administrative 'modernisation', and developments in the delivery of
  medical and other services?

And so on. Although equality is conceptually linked to the idea of the
average or the norm, it is necessarily concerned with more than the
middle reaches of the social spectrum. One of the most influential models
of social and economic equality implies that as many people as possible
should at least be included economically within the bottom reaches of the
'average' lifestyle; that there is a minimum 'normal' level of access to
social provision and goods to which everyone is entitled. A different but
no less important understanding of equality is political or constitutional,
the extension of the rights of citizenship to all. This has implications for
participation and inclusion in the political process, and full equality
before the law.

As with religion, however, doctrines of equality do not – as the flour-
ishing of slavery in post-Independence America demonstrated – necessi-
tate that all men and women will be treated as equals. The deciding factor
is eligibility: *who* qualifies for inclusion in equality. But notions of equality, however they are framed, necessarily encourage struggles to extend
the criteria of inclusion. This can be seen most clearly in recent years in
the campaigns of the Disability Rights movements in the United States
and Europe (Oliver 1990), and in the various attempts by legislatures to
put some of those rights, at least, on to a more secure legal footing (Doyle
1995). Political discourses of equality also offer an image of a normal way
of life, which could – should – be accessible to all, and imply some redistribution, thus legitimating the participation of the excluded in the wider
prosperity of society.

In all of these respects, the politics of equality have inspired the modern philosophy of care known as 'normalisation' (Wolfensberger 1972). This promotes independent living for people with intellectual or other disabilities, in ordinary community settings wherever possible, and their participation – once again as far as possible – in culturally normative behaviours and activities. Ideologies of earthly equality do not, however, necessarily solve the problems faced by people with intellectual disabilities. They may, in fact, be re-shaped into a new kind of benign oppression: the tyranny of normalisation may be as powerful as the opportunities offered by egalitarianism (Brown and Smith 1989; Chappell 1992). As Wolfensberger himself made clear, normalisation is, at least in part, explicitly ideological; what is moot is whether or not one accepts his notion of the 'good ideology' (1972: 9). The important questions in this respect are:

- Who defines what is 'normal'?
- In whose interests?
- Where does the promotion of normalisation become the persecution (behaviour modification) of non-conformity?
- What happens if people with intellectual disabilities do not want to live independent lives in the community?
- What happens if they do not want to conform to locally normatively-valued patterns of behaviour?

These questions suggest the possibility of a sting in equality's tail: relatively equal access to valued goods and conditions of life may be implicitly conditional upon fitting in to a 'normal' lifestyle or way of life. With respect to the USA and the UK, the chapters by Devlieger and Davies suggest that, according to the dictates of normalising ideologies in local practice, the price of acceptance for people whose being-in-the-world challenges our classificatory boundaries may be the surrender of the independence – to be non-criminally deviant, eccentric, heterodox, non-conformist, or whatever – that is actually definitive of 'normal' adulthood in Western democracies.

And there is yet a further twist to these complexities. Angrosino argues in Chapter 2 that in a liberal capitalist democracy such as the United States the dominant normative themes of independence and self-sufficiency are still, despite decades of high unemployment, powerfully expressed in the notion of 'earning your own living'. Accepting the label of 'disability' is one of the few ways in which an individual can achieve an honourable exemption from the responsibility to 'pay your own way' (cf. Wadel 1973). As Deborah Stone has put it: 'Disability accounts for a substantial proportion of income redistribution and, in much smaller measure, for the distribution of some fundamental privileges and duties of citizenship' (1985: 4).

A similar theme can also be traced in van Maastricht's account of a day centre for 'people with learning difficulties' in Wales in Chapter 6. Despite the public importance of a progressive rhetoric rooted in normalisation, 'created dependency' was the – doubtless unintended – consequence of their insulation from the harsh realities of a world governed by the market, via their categorisation as 'disabled', as vulnerable individuals.

Finally, another aspect of contested classification is worth considering: the relationship in any cultural context between local folk models of (in)competence and the Western medico-psychological model(s) which have achieved a degree of global hegemony. This suggests a final short list of questions:

- How is the conflict between the different models and understandings, where it exists, expressed?
- What are its consequences for people who are categorised as incompetent?
- How does this relate to relationships between local administration and government and external sources of policy and funding or resources?

These questions are not only relevant with respect to marked cultural diversity or Otherness (from a Western perspective). Even within the settings that are their source, Europe and North America, Western scientific medico-psychological models are likely to have local folk competitors and vernacular variants. This has become more marked with the recent proliferation of alternative therapies.

Nor should the competitive global variety in scientific models be underestimated. The role of the psychological and medical establishments in the mass extermination of intellectually disabled people in Nazi Germany has already been alluded to and is relevant in this context. Between 1920 and 1989, Soviet and Western medical and psychological orthodoxies diverged in many ways, intellectual disability among them (Thom 1995: 257). Today, much work remains to be done before we understand better Chinese medical science and psychology, in this field no less than in others. To return to an earlier point, all models are local models.

In this introductory chapter I have explored some of the matters which arise when one tries to think about (in)competence from a comparative perspective. Doing so has entailed asking questions which permit us to move away from the axiomatic dominance of the Western medico-psychological model, towards a framework within which the socio-cultural construction of the phenomenon can be appreciated alongside the presence of intellectually impairing pathologies. And it is, in the strongest possible sense, the social *construction* of (in)competence, not just cultural variation in *responses* to impairment, that I am talking about. This is the most robust thread which unites all of the contributions. It is as central to Nancy Lundgren's discussion of the routine incompetence of 'normal' schoolchildren in Belize, as it is to the discussions of the experiences and situation of people who are categorised as being 'mentally retarded' or as having 'learning difficulties'.

The chapters which follow were not in any simple fashion commissioned to exemplify the issues, or operationalise the questions, that I have set out above. Each chapter will touch on some of them, as appropriate, but the authors were encouraged to pursue their own intellectual agendas. This is still a relatively new field of inquiry, with nothing to be gained from channelling our endeavours too tightly. In that spirit, this collection is presented as an encouragement to the further research and debate that will help us to move beyond present ethnocentric, and somewhat unimaginative, conventional understandings of (in)competence.

Notes

1 In addition to the texts cited, Scheerenberger (1983), Ryan and Thomas (1987: 11–29, 85–116), and Atkinson, Jackson and Walmsley (1997) offer further perspectives on the history of intellectual incompetence and disability. Rosen, Clark and Kivitz (1976) is a useful selection of late nineteenth- and twentieth-century documentary sources.
2 This brief reference glosses over Oliver's important argument about the role of capitalism in the medicalisation and individualisation of disability as a socially constructed category.

2 Mental disability in the United States: an interactionist perspective

Michael V. Angrosino

This essay deals with 'mentally disabled'[1] persons in the United States. To the average citizen, 'mental disability' equals 'mental incompetence'; mental health professionals and laypeople agree that, because ours is a society oriented to complex technology, anything that impairs cognitive functioning disqualifies someone from full participation in the life of the society. The subtext of this remark is that anything that detracts from individual economic productivity is socially undesirable. Given this negative assessment, some advocates prefer to avoid labels that emphasise a lack of ability. My position, however, is that the label 'mental disability' serves a real – and not always negative – purpose; moreover, accepting the label 'mental disability' need not obscure the fact that the majority of people so designated have the capacity to learn and practise fairly sophisticated coping strategies that enable them to assert a personal identity based on self-perceived competencies.

My emphasis in this paper will be on adults defined as 'mentally retarded'. As explained below, it is often not in the interest of these people to master cognitive skills that have exchange value in the marketplace. It is, however, both desirable and possible for them to attempt to demonstrate competence in those kinds of adaptive behaviour that affect their ability to develop and sustain social interactions. They often fail in such attempts, but so do many people considered 'normal'. Mentally disabled people are incompetent not because of what they don't know (since everyone in our complex society has areas of genuine ignorance), but because, in the course of social interactions, they tend to choose less than fully effective ways to communicate the things they think they do know.

The societal context

Most Americans are, sooner or later, caught up in bureaucracies that categorise, measure and standardise normality, and provide treatment for any deviation from the norm. The public education system may be thought of as the master bureaucracy; it serves as monitor and gatekeeper for the rest. Schoolchildren are relentlessly tested for intellectual competence and behavioural acceptability; deviance – measured by standardised intelligence and 'adaptive behaviour' tests – will almost certainly be discovered and labelled at a fairly early age.

This school-based tracking functions best when it can rely on supposedly objective, discrete categories, with rigid, if arbitrary, boundaries. The American Association on Mental Deficiency defines 'mental retardation', in part, in terms of 'deficits in adaptive behavior' (Edgerton 1979: 2), but psychometricians have been busy converting this impressionistic and culture-specific variable into a quantifiable, scalable – and presumably transcultural – entity (Leland 1973). The bureaucratic mind is not inclined to recognise that children may be competent in different tasks at different times in their lives, or that a person with 'mental retardation' may have other conditions, such as mental illness of either a chronic or episodic nature, that confound the expression of retardation. Children with impairments such as epilepsy or cerebral palsy, who show marked deficits in 'adaptive behaviour' but not necessarily 'sub-normal' scores on the IQ tests, are generally grouped with those with 'mental retardation' since it is easier for schools to maintain categorical programming than individualised training.

As a result, children who are tracked into special education programmes tend to live out a self-fulfilling prophecy: denied the kinds of intellectual stimulation routinely available to their 'normal' colleagues, they are readily socialised into intellectual incompetence and patterns of behaviour that indelibly mark them as deviants. 'Clinical retardation' – traceable to an organic dysfunction – accounts for only 25 per cent of all cases of 'mental retardation'; the rest are cases of 'sociocultural retardation' (Edgerton 1979: 49), among whom behaviours recognised as 'retarded' (patterns of speech, habits of holding the body, ways of walking, styles of dress) are *learned*. Only 5 per cent of 'mentally retarded' persons fall into the 'severely' or 'profoundly' retarded categories (Friedman 1976: 16). All the rest – including, presumably, some of the 'clinically retarded' – are capable of learning to modify their behaviour.

Schools cannot cope with those who are 'dually diagnosed', so only those 'retarded' persons with no symptoms of emotional or behavioural disorder, or manifestations of psychosis, survive in the special education system. The rest are relegated to the mental health system, which in most states is a separate bureaucracy with its own funding, personnel and channels of service provision.

Labels such as 'mental retardation', 'mental illness', 'emotional disturbance', or 'behavioural disorder' impose an arbitrary segregation of conditions that are experientially interconnected. They are grouped together – but not truly re-integrated – under the generic label 'mental disability', which is in turn treated as a sub-set of the broad category of 'disability'. The social reality of such a class can be challenged on socio-cultural and philosophical grounds (Krefting and Groce 1992: 3): it is unfair and irrational to define people on the basis of what they are supposed not to be able to do. A clear statement of this 'labeling model' was provided by the civil rights attorney Paul Friedman (1976: 14):

A person is 'mentally retarded' when 'we' say he is. Mental retardation is not a fact, but a label or classification applied to a very diverse group of people – often for purposes of segregating or restricting them, although sometimes for purposes of providing services not available to all in the community.

We tend to think first of the negative consequences of labelling, but the label can be positively functional. Since the United States lacks universal health insurance, virtually the only way many people – particularly the indigent, but also the 'working poor' – can receive medical and associated services is by accepting a designation of disability. One major component of the vast social security system is devoted to providing benefits for those who pass the test of being too disabled to work. Moreover, the 1990 *Americans with Disabilities Act* secures a range of major civil rights protections for those who can persuade the powers that be that they are disabled. Hahn (1987), for one, argues that people with 'mental retardation' and their advocates should see themselves as a 'minority group' on a par with those oppressed because of race, ethnicity, gender, or sexual preference. This would allow them to maintain their solidarity – and the benefits of the 'disabled' label – even as they argue for political empowerment.

So, while we may decry the irrationality of the arbitrary standardisation and bureaucratisation of a diversity of symptoms, both behavioural and organic, and complain about the constitution of an entire social class defined by its disabilities – its incompetence, as it were – the institutions of government make it virtually impossible to act in accordance with any other standard of reality. It is simply not in the economic, legal or political interest of most persons defined as disabled to contest their designation. At the time of writing, no fewer than 116 separate acts or amendments at the federal level – most of which have analogues at state level – have been enacted to provide support for people defined as 'mentally retarded' (Gudorf 1995: 16). The person so diagnosed is inescapably involved in a complex of categorical definitions that have the force of law.

The history of mental disability as a formal designation in the United States has been traced by Appelbaum (1994). The currently dominant philosophy of deinstitutionalisation and community care is surveyed by Bruininks *et al.* (1981), Halpern *et al.* (1980) and Miller (1982). The fallacy of the community care movement was that 'the community' as an abstract concept makes little sense in late twentieth-century America, with its moribund urban cores, geographically dispersed suburban agglomerations, and high degree of mobility. It might have made sense to release formerly institutionalised persons to a traditional folk community, where they could count on ties of kinship and the active ministrations of churches, craft guilds or traditions of patronage.[2] But to release them to 'the community' as it exists in the United States today is to condemn them to alienation. Given that such people start out with some deficits in cognition, and have spent time in institutional environments that exacerbated their intellectual and behavioural deficits, they are sadly ill-equipped for life in the diffuse and scarcely nurturing 'communities' into which they have been released.

An industry has quickly sprung up, providing 'community-based' services to deinstitutionalised clients; private 'vendors' receive some state monies to care for deinstitutionalised clients of the states. The reality of the situation, however, is that their clients need multiple services: health care, psychotherapy, education, housing, transportation and so forth. It is difficult enough for 'normal' people to negotiate the maze of available services; persons with mental deficits clearly need help to do so. The services are usually available, but in bewildering profusion, with access limited by criteria described in confusing legal terms. There are no fewer than 135 different federal agencies, functioning in 1,100 different state and local welfare jurisdictions, each bringing its own eligibility criteria, funding schedules and procedures to bear on the ability of persons with 'mental retardation' to find assistance (Scheerenberger 1983: 250). How can someone with cognitive deficits and marginal ties to existing community networks make sense of this system? One answer has been 'case management', a kind of super-service provided by an agency whose main function is to link clients to all the services they need and to co-ordinate their interactions with other agencies (Gelman 1980). Case management is extraordinarily complex and time-demanding; it has, however, generally been assigned to the lowest paid entry-level social workers or mental health counsellors, who, burdened with enormous case loads, quickly burn out and leave the system, creating more dislocation and lack of continuity. The political climate now favours budget-cutting over human service. Case management, as an abstract function with no easily quantifiable 'end-product', has been an easy target.

The result of these trends is a very large population of deinstitutionalised persons with a variety of problems lumped together as 'mental disability'. They are ill-served by the agencies set up to help them, and generally fail to integrate themselves into 'the community', not only because of their own deficits but because 'the community' itself is not well integrated. Reflecting on her experiences as a health care professional and as a parent of a child with 'mental retardation', Gudorf (1995: 16) describes the array of special programmes as a 'psychedelic labyrinth' that is constantly 'squirming and changing with the convolutions of Congress and the regulation writers'. Her lament echoes that of a private service provider quoted by Scheerenberger (1983: 111): 'I feel real sorry for new providers trying to figure it all out. They probably won't.'

A heterogeneous group of people is drawn together by an arbitrary social label that emphasises their marginal social position. Victims of a self-fulfilling prophecy, they are not supposed to be productive, so they are not given the opportunity to be productive, and thus are stigmatised (or patronised) as helpless, fit mainly to be the objects of public charity. An enormous bureaucracy sees to the labelling and sorting process, and the economic, legal and political institutions of society conspire to secure the acquiescence of those who are labelled and sorted. The situation bears some superficial resemblance to an *apartheid* state. The job of the anthropologist in such a situation must therefore be to look beneath the surface and account for the ways in which people survive in the face of such obstacles. Doing so might be seen as a back-door way of rationalising those obstacles. I prefer to see it as an affirmation of the human resources of even those who seem to be crushed by 'the system' – resources that can be drawn on by those committed to reform.

The research background

I have been working since 1980 with persons defined as 'mentally retarded' and/or chronically 'mentally ill'. I have been particularly active in two agencies in Tampa, Florida. One, which I will call Opportunity House (OH), is an authorised state vendor, one of the few agencies in Florida that accepts those who are defined as both 'mentally retarded' and 'mentally ill'. Moreover, most of its clients have been in trouble with the law and were remanded to the programme in lieu of prison. The second, which I will call the McBride Foundation (MF), is a private group founded by parents of persons with 'mental retardation' and supported by their contributions and a bequest from a local philanthropist. It establishes financially self-sufficient group residences that provide continuing care for 'retarded' adults once their parents can no longer care for them at home. I have conducted my research while serving as a classroom volunteer at OH and as a member of the Board of Trustees of both OH and MF.

The people I will describe are simply those with whom I have had the most intensive and extended contact over the past fifteen years; they do not form a statistically valid cross-section of the range of persons with 'mental retardation'. The clients of OH are atypical in that they are psychiatrically disordered in addition to being 'mentally retarded'; they have also been involved with the criminal justice system as well as the special education and mental health systems. Although they are often baffled by the circumstances of their lives, they are probably more sophisticated about the ins-and-outs of the health and human service bureaucracies than most adults whose experience has been exclusively in one or other of the sub-systems of the bureaucracy. The clients of MF are atypical in that they have lived most of their lives under the care of unusually informed, committed parents/caretakers. They tend to be more dependent and behaviourally immature than the streetwise clients of OH. The latter, most of them from dysfunctional or absent families, are considered to be potentially dangerous 'delinquents'; those at MF are 'nice kids from good homes'. The two groups demonstrate an interesting range of variation, and their patterns of behaviour are certainly suggestive, but no generalisations emanating from this study are definitive in the quantitative sense.

All the residents of the MF homes are white or Hispanic; OH serves a higher percentage of African Americans.[3] The residents of both agencies fall into the 18–45 age range. OH is exclusively male, while MF operates (separate) homes for men and women. The numbers are too small to allow for statistically meaningful correlations related to ethnicity or gender, although I will discuss their *perceptions* of both factors in so far as they figure in the interaction strategies clients have developed to cope with their environments.

Because of the small population size and its non-randomised selection, I have opted for interpretive, rather than quantitative, methods for data collection and presentation (Ferguson *et al.* 1992), in the hope of revealing the experiential meaning of disability. Nevertheless, this qualitative view of the lives of people characterised as 'mentally disabled' developed from more formalised policy-analytical and ethnographic studies of vendor agencies in Tennessee (Angrosino 1981a), and from quantitative surveys of programmes in the fifty states (Angrosino 1981b). The illustrative material that follows should be taken as a stimulus to further research, rather than a definitive statement of the issues.

Conceptual issues

Societal factors predispose people, once labelled 'disabled' by the health and human service bureaucracies, to accept that designation. But anthropological research suggests that the real experiences of such people are more diverse and more complex than the simple label implies. When I began observing community-based programmes, I encountered clients (and their advocates) who were willing to accept all that the label entailed because of the presumed benefits discussed above. But they did not exhibit the uniformity of behaviour that might have been expected had they been thoroughly enculturated into the bureaucratic system. Their diversity might have been no more than random variation among people whose limited faculties made them impervious to regimentation – but the more I observed, the more I was struck by the volitional nature of their responses. These people were under inescapable economic, legal and political pressures that led them to agree that they belonged to the generic category of 'the disabled'. They were confused by the huge, arbitrary, impersonal bureaucracy and continued to feel marginalised, even though they were part of a 'community' agency. None the less, they were manifestly trying to present themselves to significant others in what they thought was their best light.

Robert Edgerton and his group at the University of California–Los Angeles pioneered the 'socioecological' study of persons with 'mental retardation'. Edgerton's classic longitudinal study of deinstitutionalised clients from a large state hospital (1967), offers ample ethnographic evidence of the ways in which even those with limited faculties could cope with the new demands of life outside the 'total institution'. Not all of their coping strategies have been positive, but a picture of ongoing adaptation has emerged from the UCLA research. 'Labelling theory' suggests that a uniform label results in a homogeneous (stigmatised) response. However, my own field studies (Angrosino 1981a, 1981b, 1992a, 1992b, 1994; Angrosino and Zagnoli, 1992) echo the UCLA research (e.g. Langness and Levine 1986) in suggesting that 'disability' is best understood as an umbrella term covering a range of coping strategies, some successful in the eyes of both 'the disabled' and the public at large, others considered successful only by the former, still others unsatisfactory to both.

My view is strongly influenced by symbolic interactionism, most particularly by the proposition that 'culture' is not a fixed entity, but an ongoing set of responses to specific interactional challenges. Social interaction is like a game of football: it has official rules, but players are encouraged to rethink their strategies in different situations. No two football matches are exactly alike even though all follow the same rules and are covered by the same label. Some people clearly play the game more skilfully than others, but even the 'losers' in a particular contest are operating within the general norms and expectations of the game. The upshot of my own research is that even people with mental impairments – as measured by standardised tests – are capable of strategising within the social rules, so as to create situations that seem most comfortable to them. It is arguable that they fail in that attempt more than do people of 'normal' intelligence; but for me the important fact is that, despite all odds, they continue to try to play the game.[4]

Although medical anthropology/sociology has de-coupled the concepts of 'disease' (a syndrome recognised by the biomedical establishment) and 'illness' (a person's self-perception of feeling incapable of carrying out desirable functions), it remains common to equate 'disability' with 'illness'. That is, if one is *labelled* 'disabled', one will necessarily *feel* and *act* 'disabled'. The influential notion of 'stigma' as associated with disability – referring to a permanent, externally imposed attribution, internalised by those who bear it – reflects this position (e.g. Ainlay *et al.* 1986). This assumption has been challenged by researchers from a variety of disciplines (e.g. Batavia *et al.* 1991; Frank 1986), who point out that persons defined as 'disabled' can create a sense of 'normality' in their day-to-day lives, do not necessarily think of themselves as 'ill' in an ongoing way, and only choose to play the 'sick role' when it suits them to do so. Although the bulk of such research has been conducted among those with 'physical disabilities', my own research suggests that these same attitudes are not at all uncommon among those with 'mental disabilities'.

If 'disease' is a defined biomedical malfunction and 'illness' a recognised social role, then 'disability' may best be understood as a statement of personal identity. But, following the logic of symbolic interactionism, we might say that identity itself is a social, rather than psychological, product. One's sense of identity is continually constructed from ongoing interactions and is responsive to the effects of one's immediate situation on behaviour. Interactionists eschew such terms as 'personality' or 'character', which imply continuities of intrapsychic structures, in favour of such concepts as 'the social self' or 'personal identity' (Carson 1969).

Following Harrington and Whiting (1972: 488), we may divide identity into three principal components: *attributed status* (that which is assigned by society), *subjective status* (that which one thinks one fulfils) and *optative status* (that which one wishes to fulfil). A healthy identity has these three factors in balance. But what of persons who, for one reason or another, experience a discrepancy between their self-image and the image that society holds of them? The common assumption has been that persons with 'mental retardation', who are labelled in a stigmatising way, have weak identities because they uncritically accept their attributed status and assume that their subjective status is deficient or defective; they are rarely encouraged to have an optative status at all. The UCLA research and my research (which both use life histories extensively) argue against this assumption. To be successfully 'disabled' is to play a variety of roles, some acquiescing to 'illness' when it seems beneficial to do so, others clearly – even aggressively – stressing presumed competencies and personal choice. The identities of 'mentally disabled' persons, like those of their 'normal' peers, are not single entities that last forever. Identity is constantly re-negotiated; people play various roles as demanded by changing circumstances. 'Normal' people, however, do so with seeming fluency; the 'mentally disabled' are often caught shifting gears, or making inappropriate choices from their repertoires.

With slight modification to Zetlin and Turner's scheme (1984), we may characterise four basic styles in the personal adjustment of persons with 'mental retardation'. *Blame attributors* openly acknowledge their disability, but avoid responsibility for its consequences by accusing others of having victimised them, or for having 'made me this way'. They expect others to help them because, after all, it's those others' fault that they can't help themselves. *Tactical dependers* also acknowledge their disability, but survive mainly by finding helpful, co-operative 'benefactors' who compensate for their incompetence. They like to think that they have 'conned' or manipulated those benefactors into helping them. *Acceptors* don't think of their condition as anyone else's fault (although some of them see it as *their* fault); they take whatever help is offered to them because they don't see any alternatives. *Deniers* refuse to accept the attribution of disability and tend to refuse as well all offers of assistance – 'Why should you help me? I don't need any help!'

These coping styles might seem like another level of arbitrary, even stereotypical, labelling. But, from an interactionist perspective, we can see that they are complexes of more variety than at first appears. I shall illustrate them by looking at some aspects of the lives of four of the people in my study population.[5] In each case, I will look at how the basic style is modified to suit four distinct interactive contexts – within the self; with other retarded persons; with professional staff; with 'normal' outsiders – thereby demonstrating the shifting relationships among attributive, subjective and optative statuses as identity is redefined in interaction.

Chad Clemmons

Chad, a thirty-two-year-old white man, has been a client at OH for the past eight years. He recently graduated to 'independent living' status and shares an apartment with two other graduates. They all meet bi-weekly with a staff member of the agency, but are no longer under direct supervision. Chad works at a local branch of Wendy's, a national fast-food chain that has made a significant effort to employ disabled people. Chad has always had a problem controlling his temper; he encountered the juvenile justice system because of persistent assaults on authority figures (teachers, counsellors, a police officer) who 'got in my face'. After several years of behaviour modification therapy, he has learned some positive ways of dealing with his anger. He is, however, subject to periodic bouts of depression. Even when he is feeling better, he adopts a reserved, almost aloof demeanour and often seems lost in his own thoughts. He has a minor speech impediment that none the less looms very large in his own thinking, and he avoids speaking to strangers if at all possible. He does not know who his father is, and he maintains only very infrequent contact with his mother, an alcoholic who lives in another part of the state.

Chad may be characterised by his tactical dependence. He is not put off by the label 'mental retardation' since it seems to him to explain much of what he has trouble controlling in his life. 'Normal' people who exhibit uncontrollable anger are 'degenerates' and those who are depressed are 'wackos', he says; at least his behaviour has a root cause that absolves him of any blame. But even though he declines to take responsibility for the way he behaves, he is none the less disgusted with himself for acting that way. He describes an assault on a teacher in high school:

It was that dumb Mr Cooley. He was like the gym coach or something stupid like that. He was this big, fat ole son-bitch. Yelling, yelling all the time. He says to me, 'You climb up this rope, sonny,' and I just seen red. It wasn't so much the stupid rope. It was the way he called me 'Sonny'. I wasn't no son of his! I just tucked my head down and rammed him right in his stupid gut. Like an ole billy-goat. And then I kept whamming him. But, you know, it didn't even feel good. I heard myself saying to myself, 'Why? Why? This stupid ole Mr Cooley ain't worth it. Why?' But I couldn't stop it. I felt like such a goddam retard jerk when they finally pulled me off him.

Chad is also depressed over his depression:

I hate it when I can't do nothing but just sit there in the stupid room and stare at the stupid wall. It's like I'm floating up on the ceiling and I see myself sitting there like a stupid retard and I want to kick the shit out of me. But I can't.

On the other hand, Chad has a sense that things are getting better. He has learned some techniques for controlling his anger and the anti-depressants seem to be working. He doesn't care for being a 'pill-head', but thinks it's 'better than being a jerk'. He is pleased to have been commended by his supervisor at work, who recommended that he train to work the cash register. He is reluctant to do so, because 'working the front' would mean having to deal directly with the customers, and he feels safer in the back just making sandwiches. Nevertheless, he says, 'I could do it if I really wanted. Maybe some day I will. Maybe after my birthday.'

Within himself, then, Chad's identity configuration consists of a positive attributed and optative status coupled with a negative subjective status. How does this configuration translate into social interactions?

Chad assumes that all other people with 'mental retardation' are just like him. His acceptance of the label leads him to believe that there is a uniformity among his peers, despite ample evidence to the contrary. For example, he assumes that Harry and Scott, his apartment-mates, have had extensive therapy to allow them to control their anger 'and now they're really cool'. In fact, explosive anger was a problem for neither of them and they often tease Chad when he goes off to pound his pillow, a strategy recommended by his therapist. But nothing will convince Chad that the 'coolness' of Harry and Scott is the result of anything but the same therapeutic process that is changing his own life. Chad sees other retarded people as extensions of himself, and hence as people who are not to be relied on. In his own withdrawn way, he can have a good time bantering with Harry and Scott, but he often says that he doesn't trust them – 'they're nice guys, you know, but they're just retards'. He will never ask a favour of either of them, because 'they'd just screw it up – they're just retards'. This attitude reinforces Chad's air of 'being in a world of his own' because he seems so disengaged from the people with whom he spends most of his time; to reverse the usual cliché, he is *of* them, but not truly *with* them.

His behaviour and attitude shift dramatically in the presence of staff members. He realises that he is considered a 'graduate' of the programme, and his vision of a more pleasant future – symbolised by his willingness even to consider the possibility of 'working the front' – does not include being returned to the 'secure' facility because the staff think he has 'screwed up' in the apartment. He therefore becomes a marvel of efficiency when the counsellor is due to drop in. Even at his moodiest, he will rouse himself to clean his room and those parts of the common rooms for which he is responsible. He has a pot of coffee waiting, and he showers, and puts on fresh clothes, even if he has just dashed in from work. He scoffs at the suggestion that Harry or Scott might help him straighten up the apartment, just as it would never occur to him to help them when their own counsellors come to visit – after all, 'retards' can't be expected to do anything for each other.

Chad sees himself as dependent on the staff, but this does not mean that he makes himself helpless in their sight. Quite the contrary: he feels he can manipulate them into giving him a positive report by acting as if he can really manage his affairs. The irony is that Chad does not think of himself as competent to do so just yet – he still needs to overcome his emotional problems. So he sees his cheerful competence at the time of the counsellor's visit as a ruse designed to convince the professional that the depressed, anger-filled, moody man has been subsumed into the efficient job-holder and homemaker. He has not yet convinced himself that he can – or should – extend his demonstration of competence beyond these Potemkin villages designed to con visiting authority figures. In fact, he consciously or otherwise keeps himself from going *too* far in his act; he will always manage to miss one spot on his cheek while shaving, or to make the coffee much too strong to drink, or to put on mismatching socks – cues small enough to indicate that he still really needs the protective umbrella of OH, but not large enough to cause the authorities to revoke his privileges of independence.

By contrast, he stands to gain nothing by impressing his supervisors at work with competencies beyond what he can manage at the present time. He knows that his job is secure, because he does exactly what he has to. But he cannot afford, he thinks, to exhibit too much ambition. He believes that he was only recommended to 'work the front' because the managers needed to make positions for 'some other retards' to begin employment 'in the back', not because they thought he was especially worthy. In fact, he quite definitely plays up his retardation in his dealings with supervisors because he assumes that the only reason he was hired in the first place was because the management has a policy of hiring the handicapped. So at the beginning of every shift, he has a manager come to his station to run through the list of steps for the making of the various kinds of sandwiches. He knows the routine perfectly well, but needs to give the manager the impression that he would forget, and fall to pieces, if he were not constantly reminded.

The restaurant has many 'normal' people as well as OH clients in its employ. With these people Chad's trademark aloofness becomes most marked. One older lady has taken Chad under her wing. She sees his dazed demeanour as a sign of his helplessness and thinks that Chad's speech impediment is far worse than it really is. She sees it as her special mission to act as his interpreter, and Chad is content to let her do it. For example, when the movie *The Lion King* opened in town, she fancied that Chad (whom she prefers to think of as child-like) desperately wanted to see it. She took it upon herself to speak to the manager; she persuaded him that Chad was feeling under the weather and needed the afternoon off. The request was granted, and the lady gave Chad money to buy movie tickets and snacks. He didn't really want to see *The Lion King*, but he took the time and the money on the grounds that 'it makes her feel good to do something nice – I don't want to disappoint her'. He further rationalises the scam by pointing out that it wasn't his idea to begin with and anyway, what can you expect from a 'retard'?

Chad's other co-workers are recruited to pick him up and drive him to and from work. He lives a short bus-ride away and is quite capable of using the bus by himself; mastering this skill is, in fact, a prerequisite to graduation to the independent apartment programme. But he does not like to ride the bus, since it forces him to be in contact with a lot of strangers. He does not explain this to his co-workers, who just assume that his reluctance to take the bus is a result of his inability to remember the schedules, keep the right change and so on. So they take turns chauffeuring him. Again, Chad excuses his taking unfair advantage by saying that he never *told* anyone that he needed their help – it was their idea – and anyway, 'if someone got in my face on the bus and I couldn't help myself, then where would I be?'

Many of Chad's peers are very vocal about sex. They weave an elaborate mythology about their prowess in their pre-OH days, and have definite ideas about what they're going to do the minute they have the chance. Chad, however, rarely discourses on this topic. In fact, part of the negativism in his overall subjective status is a result of his believing himself to have failed the test of masculinity. Chad admits to being a virgin; he is almost certainly not alone in this condition, but he is the only one who will own up to it. (The MF men, by contrast, seem to assume that a lack of sexual experience is the norm, and they see nothing untoward in the fact.) The standard gender identification of the OH men is one of exaggerated, aggressive 'machismo' (Angrosino and Zagnoli 1992) and Chad just doesn't live up to the expectation. He rejects suggestions that there are other ways of being a man; the media all show that anything short of the 'tough guy' is a 'miserable wuss' – which is the category to which he consigns himself. Chad is so convinced of his own sexual inadequacy that he believes that 'only another retard would want to be with me', a prospect he views with horror. 'I hate these dumb retard girls. I'd rather be dead than be with them. I'd rather be a queer. . .' His voice trails off: according to the OH code, even an offhanded admission to a homosexual preference is tantamount to a certificate of permanent 'wussiness'. When I asked him whether he'd ever talked to one of the non-retarded women at Wendy's, he looked at me as if I were out of my mind. 'Isn't there someone you'd like to ask to a movie?', I went on. He blushed so furiously that I decided against pursuing the issue.

Chad later confided to me that the only reason he was even tentatively considering the offer to 'work the front' was because doing so might convince one of the 'real girls' that he wasn't a total loser after all. But there is a serious, nearly debilitating, conflict in his attitude. On the one hand, the thought of striking up a friendship with a 'real girl' compromises the elaborate edifice of presumed incompetence that allows him to function within the 'normal' world. He could not act his bashful, helpless self –

which a woman might actually find charming – with a 'real girl', whom he assumes would only be satisfied with a macho brute. But to continue to play the out-of-it dreamer when away from his retarded peers or the staff condemns him to a life either with a 'retarded' girl, an outcome he would consider a terrible defeat, or to a life alone.

No objective observer would say that Chad's is a functionally balanced identity. Indeed, his awkwardness in compartmentalising his behaviours as suitable for different constituencies probably strikes those who know him as more disordered than the making of honest mistakes. But the conflicts in his life – even those of his own creation – reveal someone of greater depth and ability than simple labels suggest.

Beth Logan

Beth, a twenty-eight-year-old white woman, lives at an MF home. She is the youngest child of a well-to-do couple – he a local television personality, she an attorney – who have made sizeable financial contributions to the Foundation. Mrs Logan suffers from Alzheimer's disease and her worsening condition led her husband to settle Beth with MF two years ago, a step he had hoped to delay for at least ten years. Their other children live out of the state, and it was decided that it would be easier for Beth to stay in the area where she grew up than to pack her off to another part of the country. Beth adjusted well to the transition; she already knew most of the other women who lived at the home, and she gets on well with the 'house-parents' who supervise her home. Beth has a placid temperament and seems perfectly happy with her job – assembling small toys at a sheltered workshop not far from her new home. She enjoys the social activities provided by the MF, but does not care to express her opinions – she gamely goes along with whatever others have planned.

Beth is predominantly an acceptor. She is comfortable with being 'mentally retarded', mainly because it represents security and stability to her. She knows that her 'normal' sisters have had difficult lives – nicely settled now, but only after years of experiments with drugs, unhappy marriages, and dead-end careers. She sees her own life as one of undisturbed placidity. 'I'm mentally retarded', she says matter-of-factly, 'so there are lots of things I can't do. But that's all right. Everybody's always been so kind to me.' 'Normal' people may lead exciting lives, but at great cost – they always seem to be in turmoil. Her own life is dull, but safe, and she's happy about it:

I have a really pretty room. Mrs Wright [the house-parent] picked out really pretty colours for me. We all have breakfast together, and then Mr Wright drives me down to the workshop. I make toys for little children. [She goes into minute detail describing the process of putting the toys together.] Then I come home. My chore is to vacuum the carpets. I like to do it. I like it when everything is clean. Then we have supper. Then I'll call Daddy, and on the weekends he'll come pick me up so I can visit Mommy. She's sick. We watch TV together. [She lists all her favourite shows.] On Sundays after church we usually barbecue. If it's raining we go to a movie. [She summarises the plots of several of her recent favourites.] It's really nice. All the other girls are really nice.

Beth's pleasure in the quiet, unexciting details of everyday life extends into the future. She knows that her mother is dying, and worries that she seems to be the only one her mother consistently recognises; she feels sad for her father. But, for the most part, she sees no reason for apprehension. The rest of her life stretches out in the same serene pattern that has unfolded until now. Change of any kind – a job at a different workshop, the impending retirement of the Wrights, switching 'spaghetti night' from Tuesday to Wednesday – is unthinkable. Beth is a true heir of Candide: for her, everything truly is for the best in the best of all possible worlds.

Beth, like Chad, has generally positive attributed and optative statuses; unlike him she has a positive subjective status as well. Her interaction configuration is quite different from his, although she shares his assumption that all retarded people are alike. In her case, though, this means that they are all quiet, happy, well-adjusted people, not 'screwed-up jerks' as in Chad's view. Beth is impervious to the sulks and peeves of her housemates and the others at her workshop. Outbursts are viewed as whims of the moment, never as expressions of genuine, ongoing anger or frustration. All the retarded people she knows live in nice homes with kind people looking after them; they have loving families nearby; they work in quiet, safe places where they earn a little money by doing things that they feel comfortable doing. What, therefore, could there be to make anyone angry?

As a result, Beth is willing to help any of the others, and to accept their offers of help in return. She likes the fact that at the house everyone is assigned a specific chore so that they never have to fuss or argue over who does what. Beth is pleased to share her clothes, her cosmetics, her music tapes, with her friends and is puzzled when one of the others seems to interpret this as part of a pattern of reciprocity. One of her new housemates, Eliza, is an expert hairdresser. Eliza, who is very chic, was appalled at Beth's dowdy hair-do, and decided to give her a complete make-over. Beth seemed pleased with the results, although it never would have occurred to her that she needed it. Shortly thereafter, Eliza asked to borrow some money from Beth, saying 'Well, I helped you out, so now you owe me a favour.' Beth couldn't fathom why Eliza thought she wouldn't just give her the money when she asked; to her, there was no connection between one favour and another. Needless to say, Beth is frequently taken advantage of, but she never interprets it as such, even when the Wrights or her father point it out to her. As far as she's concerned, everyone is her friend, and she's happy to do what she can to help them.

Beth's acceptance translates into deference in the presence of professionals. She sincerely likes the Wrights, often speaking of them as 'almost like my real Mommy and Daddy, not just like my house-parents', but she never presumes to real intimacy. Several of the other women adopt a little-girl demeanour in the presence of 'Mom and Pop' Wright, but not Beth. For her, their role is to provide the safe haven that her own parents can no longer give; they organise the details of her daily life so that she can function without having to worry too much. As a result, she is careful not to overplay her hand:

I don't think it's real smart to cuddle up to Mom and Pop. They're wonderful and all and I love them but it would be terrible if they thought I was a phony or something. They've got their own real kids – they might get mad if they think we're trying to take their place.

So she does everything in her power to demonstrate gratitude to the Wrights, but always stops short of getting 'familiar' with them. The casual observer might expect Beth, the eternal sunny optimist, to be the resident most apt to give herself over to gushing fondness towards her surrogate parents. But precisely because she thinks of herself as totally dependent on them she fears they will withdraw their attentions if they think she is overstepping her bounds. So she is dutiful, cheerful, co-operative, deferential – but never truly affectionate. She does everything they ask of her in as competent a manner as she can muster, because 'if you're really helpless, they'll help you because they're paid to, not because they really like you'. She is less personally attached to her workshop supervisors, but applies the same logic to that relationship as she does at the group home. The workshop staff think of her as a top-notch worker who always does her job and never complains. She thinks of herself as a person of limited qualifications and therefore places great emphasis on being liked 'for what I am'. It would shame her greatly to think that professionals only helped her because it was their duty to do so. She wants the help – and is sure she needs it – but adopts her idea of a 'professional' demeanour to make sure that it is forthcoming on terms that reaffirm her own self-esteem.

With non-professional others, however, she becomes the coy, helpless child-woman she otherwise disdains. She reverts to baby-talk whenever her father is present, although she can carry on a reasonably adult conversation when he is not there. She used to do so with her mother;

now that her mother is more helpless than she is, Beth strives bravely to be a 'big girl' for her mother's sake. When she meets new people, Beth seems almost to dissolve into a blur of giggles, blushes and lisping baby-talk. She can be quite adorable in small doses. Whenever reporters or potential donors visit the facilities, it is always Beth who is introduced first because she is so 'sweet and irresistible'. The sight of this 'dear, childlike innocent', gamely going about her vacuuming while singing a little song drove at least one benefactor to tears – and to his chequebook – in my presence. Beth seems to slip into this pose naturally; there is nothing of the manipulative cynic in her behaviour, as there is in Chad's. It is simply something she has learned as a survival strategy, and she is stunningly good at it.

Like many of the 'retarded' women we have studied over the past several years (Angrosino and Zagnoli 1992), Beth adopts a traditional gender role. It is as traditionally 'feminine' as Chad's is stereotypically 'masculine'. The critical difference is that she seems willing and able to live up to her ideal. In Beth's view, the only suitable role for a woman is to be a wife and mother. The parents of most of the other MF women actively discouraged their daughters' sexuality; the Logans, more liberal perhaps, were tolerantly bemused at their 'little girl's' eagerness to date. Her father now says, admittedly much to his own surprise, that perhaps marriage might be a real solution for her. 'Beth has the morals of my Baptist grandmother,' says Mrs Wright and so at this point in her life casual dating is no longer on the agenda; only a serious, committed relationship will do. Everyone agrees that she has the stable temperament to be a good wife, and is responsible enough to be a good mother, provided she has lots of help.

The trouble is that all of Beth's protectors think of her in a relationship with a 'normal' man, preferably some sensitive type who will be an extension of their protective selves. Beth, however, dismisses out of hand the notion that she could attract – let alone continue to satisfy – such a swain. She is cheerfully resigned to the prospect of marrying and raising a family with a 'retarded' man. She knows that they would have problems and need extra help – but then she's always needed help, and she's always found it readily, so there is no reason to worry.

Her only concern at the moment is that she has two likely suitors. She has known Barry from her workshop for several years; he is, admittedly, not very exciting, but he is 'steady and reliable'. She knew Mark many years ago from a special education class at her grade school; he was expelled from the programme for some unspecified misconduct. He reappeared in her life as the assistant to the lawn care man hired by MF. He has been quite attentive to her, although he still has a slightly disreputable air. ('He *smokes!*' Beth gasps). Eliza was brutally frank in expressing her preference: 'Barry drools,' she grimaced. Beth reluctantly agreed that Mark certainly cut the more dashing figure, but she admitted that he probably wouldn't make a very good husband or father, and her top priority now is not romantic adventure but a solid, secure future. Moreover, she is realistic enough to know that selling her father on marriage to any 'retarded' man will be difficult – with Mark it would be impossible. But she does not doubt that she will succeed, even if it takes a while. Barry, she guesses, isn't going anywhere. She smiles and shrugs when Eliza snorts, 'I'd rather be a dead virgin than married to Barry.'

John Briggs

John is a twenty-one-year-old black man. Abandoned by his unwed mother as an infant, he was raised in foster care. He was diagnosed as 'mildly mentally retarded' in school but the conditions of foster care meant that he changed homes, and hence schools, with alarming frequency. Whatever benefits might be had from a consistent special education programme were denied him, and he reached adolescence totally deficient in even the most basic academic skills. He ran away from his last foster home and lived on the streets for a few years until he was arrested for attempted rape and sent to OH three years ago. He is, for the most part, a charming young man, an interesting conversationalist with a lively sense of humour. But he seems to have concentrated all his anger, frustration and bitterness on women, and he continues to harbour such a violent sexual fixation that he cannot yet be allowed into the community to work or participate in recreational activities. He agrees that he needs intensive help in overcoming his problems (although he and the staff do not yet agree on what his problems really are) but resents the fact that he has to be incarcerated to achieve those goals.

John may fairly be characterised as a blame attributor. He knows that he has problems doing many of the things other people seem to take for granted but, unlike Chad or Beth, he finds no solace in the label of 'mental retardation'. For him it is a 'death sentence': it means 'I never was nothing and I ain't never gonna be nothing'. Worse, 'mental retardation' for him is not some cruel, but impersonal caprice – it has clear and direct antecedents. 'My so-called mother', he sneers, adding a few choice uncomplimentary epithets, 'she was worse than worthless trash. Throwed me in a dumpster and all but knocked my brains out before I even had a chance.' (In fact, his unwed mother deposited him as an infant with neighbours before leaving town; he was not literally thrown into a dumpster, although the occasional news reports of babies so treated probably gave rise to this aspect of his autobiography.) 'Them foster bitches – they was even worse! Never feed me, do for me no how.' (The record indicates that John suffered various forms of abuse, including sexual, in his foster homes; much of it was perpetrated by the men of the households, although he directs his ire solely at the women.) 'I tell you, a man can't make an honest living on the street – nothing but them bitch whores out there and they'll take every last cent you got.' Although his invective seems full of despair, John is surprisingly hopeful about the future:

I'm gonna learn to drive one day soon – just you wait to see. I don't give a shit about any of that other stuff, just as long as I can drive. Then you watch – I'll be outta here. There's this place somewhere out west where only men live – just bring in women to do stuff, you know, but then they're outta there. It's true. Somebody told me about it. Saw it on TV so it must be true.

Unlike Chad or Beth, whose positive optative statuses correspond to positive evaluations of their attributed statuses, John's positive optative status grows out of an extremely negative attributed status. From a psychological standpoint, it is probable that the highly unrealistic nature of his future ideal – which contrasts sharply with the mundane but attainable ideals of Chad and Beth – is a function of the extreme negativity from which he begins, almost as if no realistic good could come from so dreadful a beginning; only fantasy will clear away the horror.

In many ways John seems to have a positive subjective status. He has an air of self-confidence and is realistic in his assessment of the many skills he does possess. Although academically deficient, he survived by his wits in a very rough environment for many years, and is justifiably proud of his 'street smarts'. But the better one gets to know him, the more one realises that he is consumed by profound self-loathing. So powerful is his personal myth of victimisation that he is convinced that he is 'damaged goods'. Unlike many victims of abuse who come to feel that they must have deserved their ill-treatment, John sees no motive save malice for his plight. He was the innocent in a world of unmotivated wickedness: 'Nobody could go through what I gone through and come out smelling like a rose. No, they made me just what they are – a piece of shit.' Even the street smarts that are a source of pride are also a source of shame: 'If every one of them, from my so-called mother on down, had done the right by me, I wouldn't never have needed to know all that stuff. I'd be just a happy guy, living large.'

Perhaps because of this self-abasement, John is extraordinarily solicitous of other 'retarded' men ('retarded' women he regards as a mutant sub-species of already-tainted womanhood, beneath consideration). He assumes that his victimisation, while not unique, was far more horrendous than anyone else's. Therefore, everyone else is that much less damaged than he is. Rather than provoking his jealousy, the relative state of grace in which he assumes that his peers live is a source of wonder and amazement to him. He is willing to use his street smarts to help his friends, whom he assumes are less adept at dealing with the trickery of the world. Indeed, he insists on taking the lead, lest his friends sully what's left of their innocence by descending to the sorts of stratagems that he has mastered. In some ways, he sees his ability to help his less-tainted friends as a means to his own redemption. 'You know why I'm gonna get over? Because I kept these other guys from the devil, that's why. My escape, that's the reward for my saving them.'

On the other hand, he disdains the professionals with whom he must deal. He initially refused to have anything to do with me, assuming that I was a psychologist or a social worker. When he found out I was a college professor, he concluded that I was probably too weird to be a threat. The staff are simply continuing the work of all those who have kept him down in the past. That so many health and human service professionals are women is further proof of how degraded the whole enterprise must be. Even the men on the staff are nothing but 'pussy in drag'. He does not consider that they have anything worthwhile to teach him; he has lived all his life without knowing how to read, and sees no reason to apply himself to the task now. His only vocational goal, to learn to drive a car, is not on his treatment plan; everything on the plan is 'bullshit' to him. It is important for him to maintain his self-assured pose, and this entails adopting a 'cool' attitude towards staff. The other, more innocent, guys can be child-like and playful with the staff, but he cannot allow himself such cosy feelings, lest he compromise the only worthwhile shred of his self-image.

John is careful, however, not to go too far in his lack of respect for the staff. They provide him with 'three hots and a cot' and he doesn't want to go to jail. His compromise is a kind of joking relationship with the staff, that allows him to make 'nasty cracks' about them under the guise of 'just goofing around'. He does not, however, admit much reciprocity in the relationship; he is barely able to stomach return banter, and the staff quickly learn not to 'push his buttons'.

At the moment, John has limited contact with non-professional 'normal' people, but my experience with him may be an example of his approach. John sees people as representatives of a world of violent deceit; even though individuals may be pleasant one at a time, they are all corrupted by 'the system'. His world-view leads him to believe that everyone tries to victimise everyone else; but he recognises that a special hell is reserved for black people and that the judgements of an evil society fall most harshly on young men like himself. He is certain that most people the world considers 'normal' are potential threats. They can lock you up, destroy your dreams, do whatever they please with you – and always get away with it. On the other hand, he is shrewd enough to recognise 'liberal guilt' – enough white people are sufficiently ashamed of the way society has treated blacks that they can be induced to bend over backward to do him a favour every now and then. His attitude on meeting a new person is wariness verging on hostility. If he senses that he is in the presence of a guilty liberal, he reveals his relaxed, charming side. He has already identi- fied a potential benefactor, the owner of a garage whom he met during his days on the street. He is sure this man will be the one to buy him his getaway car when he is ready for it.

John is proud that 'normal' women – black and white – have found him physically attractive. The woman he attempted to rape was someone he had 'hung around with' for several months; he turned violently aggressive when she told him she wanted to break off the relationship because she had found a rich boyfriend. He sees his sexual prowess as another element in his street-smart persona. It is, however, not one that he cares to acti- vate. Ever since the attempted rape, he has to all intents and purposes dis- avowed sex (except in the fantasy of once-in-a-while 'stuff' in the men-only village out west). It is sufficient for him to have the *image* of a desirable stud. Actually living up to the image takes more emotional energy than he has at the moment. He loves to give advice on sexual matters to his house-mates, who look on him as an unimpeachable authority. But his sense of masculinity has to do with the ability to take off and be independent, and not with entering into relationships, even dysfunctional ones.

Eliza Mercante
Eliza is thirty years old. Her large extended family is part of the long- established Cuban community in Tampa. Her parents were killed in an auto accident when she was a teenager, and she was taken in by her grandparents. Eliza affects a sophisticated demeanour, but she is pain- fully naive, especially when it comes to men. She has 'gotten herself into trouble' on several occasions and has experienced two miscarriages in addition to one completed pregnancy. The baby is being raised by an aunt. Now that the grandparents are in frail health, other relatives have discussed the possibility of taking Eliza in. They believe that she will con- tinue to 'get herself into trouble' on her own, but they cannot bear the thought of putting her in anything that looks like an institution. So when they learned about MF through their church, they decided that it might be the best solution. She took up residence in 1995 and is not, as the house-parents say, a 'happy camper'. She continues to work at a 'real job' – as a hairdresser in a cousin's beauty shop – and is openly scornful of her house-mates who are employed at sheltered workshops or in fast-food

restaurants. She worries that the 'real people' she associates with at work will discover that she now lives in the 'retarded house'. She has never associated with 'retarded' people, and resents now having to share a house with them. She is furious that the social activities arranged by the house-parents usually involve other 'retarded' people, so that she can no longer meet 'normal' people.

Eliza is a denier. She recognises 'mental retardation' as a wholly negative condition suffered by 'helpless geeks' who drool a lot and have to be locked up. Since she doesn't see anything of herself in that description, she believes that she cannot possibly be 'retarded'. She is at a loss to explain why others think of her as such, although she could push the question to the back of her mind while she was living at home. Now that she has been relegated to living with unmistakably 'retarded' people, she is more than ever amazed that anyone would put her in the same category. Her conclusion is that her relatives were distressed by her having had a baby – indeed, since she considers herself a 'good Catholic', she is also appalled – and their decision to send her to the home for 'retarded girls' was their bizarre punishment.

Eliza's denial is not entirely whimsical. As soon as her problem was diagnosed at public school, her parents placed her in a special school run by their church, serving children with a variety of learning disabilities in a setting of small classes and individualised instruction. Since she is not behaviourally disordered, Eliza was not in the school group with the obviously 'retarded' children, and, since everyone at the school was in one special group or another, she never felt stigmatised. She knew that her family was very protective of her, but she also knew that most of the girls of her community complained that they were over-protected – 'It's the Cuban way!' she laughs – so that she never drew the connection between her limitations and her family's behaviour.

In her view she is not 'retarded' – simply forced to live among them until her family cools off – and looks forward to a brighter future: she will reclaim her baby, move to another city where nobody knows her, and start life anew. She thinks she can do it since she has a marketable skill. It will be difficult, she knows, to separate from the community to which she has so many ties, but she is confident that everyone will be happier if she and her baby go away. She thinks that after she works for a while she will earn enough money to start her own beauty shop. When asked about her confidence in managing all the financial aspects of a business, she shrugs and says that she will meet a 'nice guy' who will take care of such things for her. A husband? 'No, no, no. No husband. I want to be an independent woman now. I mean a – what do you call him? – a business partner.' Why does she assume the partner would have to be a guy – wouldn't another independent woman do? 'Oh, I guess so. But guys seem to be good at business. It's like one of the girls at the shop said: Men! They're only good for three things – hit a baseball, screw, open their wallet.'

Since the only negative element on her horizon is the ridiculous notion that people have of her being 'retarded', Eliza is overflowing with self-esteem. She realises that she has in the past been susceptible to the blandishments of men, but feels she has learned her lesson. Anyway, her misadventures left her with a beautiful little girl, so 'all's well that ends well, right?'

Eliza was raised to be polite and accommodating and tries her best to be nice to the other women at the home. But she cannot always disguise her lack of sympathy for them. 'I mean, they're all just so stupid!' she says in exasperation. She is not referring to academic skills – in which she is only modestly proficient – but to social skills. She despises their lack of fashion sense, the way they talk, their gracelessness when dancing or participating in sports, their ignorance of 'the birds and the bees'. She is scornful of their employment in sheltered workshops and fast-food restaurants, as opposed to her own skill at a 'real job', providing a meaningful service to 'normal people'. Her salary as a beautician has not made her wealthy, but, compared with the others, who are dependent on allowances from their families, she could support herself if need be. She has, however, decided that since Beth's father is a 'big TV star' it would be worth her while to let Beth think that she is poor – perhaps Mr Logan might be moved to help her out. Hence her requests – actually demands – that Beth lend her money.

Although forced to live with 'retarded' women, Eliza sees no point in associating with 'retarded' men. She pantomimed barfing when asked if she'd like to attend a dance with the men of another MF home, although she went rather than be left by herself. She grandly condescended to dance with those who asked her, although few dared do so, so dazzled were they by her glamour. Like John – albeit for different reasons – she is a fountainhead of sexual advice, even though she is, for the moment, 'on the shelf'.

Since she considers her residence at the MF home a temporary sojourn based on an error, she treats the staff as equals. She often volunteers herself to the Wrights to 'help keep the retards in line'. She does Mrs Wright's hair and discusses the day's sports news with Mr Wright (she is an avid follower of all the local teams) while the others are watching TV or 'wasting time'. She has frustrated the several social workers who have taken on her case because she assumes that they only want her assessment of the other women.

Eliza has had more – and more positive – encounters with 'normal' others than just about any other person in the study population. In addition to her job at the beauty shop, she has been able to rely on her extended family in the close-knit ethnic community in which she was born and raised. John is as conscious of his racial group as Eliza is of her ethnic community, but he sees his race in negative terms, as a source of his problems; he has never experienced African-American *community*.

At present, Eliza is angry at her family for being angry with her, but she is sure they'll patch things up sooner or later – 'that's the way families are' – even though she thinks she needs to start over again in another place. It is comfortable for her to have these people on whom she can rely, but they assume that they know best, and she thinks she has grown beyond the point where she needs them meddling in her business. She is sure that when it comes time for her to relocate, she will be able to find another city with a nice Cuban community – just not one full of her nosy relatives.

Being Cuban is an important part of Eliza's identity. She is not particularly knowledgeable about the history and politics of the Cubans in Florida, but she knows that they are a hard-working people who have been successful in the United States. She is openly scornful of people of other races or immigrant ethnic groups whose communities have not fared so well. She is proud that she is bilingual – 'You see? These retards can't even speak one language, but I can speak two!' – and has a particular love of the Cuban traditions that survive in her community. 'Ethnicity' is perhaps too abstract a concept to be important to most people with 'mental retardation', but it is central to Eliza's sense of self. Her view of 'ethnicity', centring around a few specific customs, might not be sophisticated, but it provides a larger context for her experiences than is available to the others in the study population. For them the various service bureaucracies have become a substitute for community.

Culture, classification and intellectual (in)competence in America

Cross-cultural comparisons of intellectual (in)competence usually concern the confrontation between folk systems of classification and extrinsic biomedical standards. This paper reflects a different perspective: the people I have studied belong to the same culture as the health and social service professionals whose classifications dominate their lives. They accept the classification, both as a label and as a bureaucratic process. Yet they allow neither label nor process to go uncontested. As functioning social actors they are involved in complex interactions that allow them to develop varied and evolving identities that belie the superficially homogenising label 'mental disability'.

US society is more tolerant of persons with 'mental retardation' than it is of those who are chronically 'mentally ill'; their 'disability' is not commonly seen as their own fault. In the present political climate, they are even less negatively stigmatised than 'normal' people suffering the effects of economic dislocation, who are forced into the increasingly unwilling embrace of public assistance. But that relative tolerance is, at best, expressed as stifling paternalism. 'Retarded' persons are not to blame for their incompetence, and thus deserve assistance; but, under the guise of protectiveness, that supposed incompetence is also a rationale for excluding retarded people from everyday life.

The people discussed above, however, assert their competence in the face of interlocking paternalistic bureaucracies that conspire to tell them that they cannot achieve anything beyond the most meagre of goals. They deal with their intellectual 'incompetence', either by scaling down their own goals or denying that intellectual capacity has anything to do with whatever is really important to them. They then define areas in which they can function: jobs with just enough supervision to make them feel safe, but not so regulated as to be overtly humiliating; social relations with other retarded people as well as selected 'normal' significant others.

The basic issue is, to what extent can 'mentally disabled' people define personally satisfying identities? To the extent that they can do so, then they may be thought of as competent from an interactionist perspective. This is perhaps the only competence that is cross-culturally relevant. The compilation of a satisfying identity is a varied and evolving process, no less so for persons with 'mental retardation' than for 'normal' people. What resources are necessary to put together social identities that allow their bearers to interact in an orderly way with others?

One way in which all people build satisfactory identities is by accentuating the things they think they do well while de-emphasising areas of presumed incompetence. People with 'mental retardation' have to deal with their intellectual deficits, which are unavoidable given their socialisation into the bureaucratic norms. It therefore becomes increasingly important for them to find other aspects of their behaviour that can compensate. Many of them assume that because they are 'retarded' intellectually they must also be physically awkward, even ugly.[6] As a result, they tend to pay particular attention to their physical skills: fixing a perfect sandwich, making the bed carefully, combing one's hair just so, all loom larger in their self-perceptions than might be the case for 'normal' people. But many 'retarded' people have physical competencies that even 'mainstream' people can admire: athletic or musical talents, or readily marketable job skills (like Eliza the beautician).

'Retarded' people are often startlingly conscious of their emotional

lives. Many live in dread lest they 'act out' in ways that others will interpret unfavourably. They are sometimes so preoccupied with ordering
their emotional lives that they seem more disordered (almost robotic)
than they would if they let their emotions flow. They have learned that
those with emotional or mental illness are not accorded the same tolerance as those who are 'merely' 'retarded'. Even those, like the OH clients,
who are officially 'dually diagnosed', try to erase all manifestations of
their psychiatric disorder, even as they embrace for strategic reasons the
qualities presumed to be 'retarded'. My informants seem to accept
'mental retardation' as a permanent condition, for which they can compensate but never really overcome; they view mental or emotional disorder as a wholly negative, albeit transient, phenomenon that can and
should be overcome, through therapy or sheer willpower.

Sexuality is a most significant area of the configuration of identity. It is
very important for my informants to see themselves as functional adults,
which, to them, means sexually competent. There is a tendency among
the men to interpret sexual competence as aggressive – even predatory –
activity; the women are more interested in stable relationships, although
this often implies passivity when dealing with men. This distinction is not
atypical of 'mainstream' society. This area is one of the most problematic
in our society's treatment of adults with 'mental retardation'. While we
are lavish in providing services, we tend to balk at sexuality education.
'Retarded' adults, like 'normal' adults, need to know the basic biology of
sex and how relationships are initiated and sustained. Attitudes are
slowly changing, but there remains an unwillingness to acknowledge the
sexuality of 'retarded' people, or that they can direct their sexuality con-
structively once the subject is open to them. If my observations are
correct – if 'retarded' people can integrate acceptable skills in the workplace, in conversation, in athletics, and so forth – then they need the
resources to integrate sexuality into their identity configurations. Failure
to do so condemns them to perpetual social immaturity (Angrosino and
Zagnoli 1992). As Booth and Booth demonstrate, elsewhere in this
volume, people with mental retardation can even become successful
parents.

Ethnicity and race play an ambiguous role in the formation of
'retarded' persons' identities. On the one hand, mainstream society is
ready to ascribe abnormality – whether criminal, psychiatric or emotional
– to the behaviours of African-Americans, such that black 'retarded'
people suffer additional stigmatisation. On the other hand, ethnicity or
race is not well-integrated into their own calculations of what their problems are or how they might be overcome. Some, like John, have learned to
use racial language to get their way with the white liberals who dominate

social service systems. Others, like Eliza, find solace in the customs of a familiar ethnic community. But these identities are only part of the repertoire of self-image, and rarely the dominant ones. It may be significant that these concepts are important to people like John or Eliza who are in conscious flight from their 'retardation'. Those who accept the designation generally treat 'retardation' as (for good or ill) a primary attribute that subsumes all others.

What will become of people as they age? At the moment, my informants are still of working age; they can shore up their sense of self-worth by dint of the fact that they can, in one way or another, be productive members of society. Self-reliance, as Devlieger points out elsewhere in this collection, remains the critical feature of American culture. But what will become of them in their retirement years? The MF people will, at least, be well cared for. But will they be able to sustain their self-images as 'real people' when they are nothing but objects of care?

I do not mean to imply that the 'retarded' people with whom I have worked have a *conscious* concept of self, personhood or identity. But I have argued elsewhere (Angrosino 1992b, 1994) that they are consistent in their attempts at self-thematisation in their accounts of their lives. They are, after all, products of the larger American culture which has made this sort of introspection a kind of national obsession. My informants may not be as glib about it as their 'normal' confrères, but they are, in good American fashion, very much concerned with their identities – their personal images – although it is possible, as Davies suggests in Chapter 5, that their concepts of personhood are constructed on bases other than those that characterise the mainstream population.

The MF works in conjunction with local (Christian) churches; all of its group homes are built on church property that has been donated or leased at nominal cost. The churches see the affiliation as an expression of their belief in the value of all human beings. Jesus' words, 'Whatever you do to the least of my brothers, you do to me', are often cited by church leaders promoting the affiliation to their congregations. But religion *per se* does not mitigate the circumstances of 'retarded' people – even the clients of MF. The impulse to subsidise the group homes, while undeniably admirable given the shaky financial situations of most churches these days, is a reflection of the paternalism offered to 'retarded' people. There are individual exceptions, but for the most part, the churches feel that they have done their Christian duty once they have signed over the plot of land. Integrating the residents into the congregation's life is rarely attempted, let alone realised. Residents generally attend services at the churches adjacent to their homes, but it does not seem to be an activity that defines their lives. OH, as a state agency, cannot encourage religious activity among its clients; although it does not discourage those who choose to participate, they must find outside benefactors to take them to services elsewhere. There is, however, a lingering tendency on the part of the OH staff to interpret clients' expressions of spirituality as a hangover of the 'religious obsession' that characterises certain forms of psychosis. In any event, most of my informants would not recognise the notion of finding solace in a religious context.

Political ideology is a more potent weapon against stigmatisation than religion. Again, it would be inaccurate to characterise my informants as possessing an articulated 'ideology'. But they recognise the political sources of their situation. They know that the Constitution guarantees them certain rights and that, in democratic principle at least, 'no one is better than anyone else' in America. They can be quite sophisticated about the array of programmes, services and legal protections to which their disabled status entitles them. They have learned to integrate the professional skills of their case managers into their own resource base, to negotiate the complexities of the bureaucracies with which they must interface. And while they may not make the connection, their advocates do not hesitate to link the aspirations of the 'disabled' to the struggles of other minorities suffering discrimination.

Conclusions

Interactionism allows us to perceive lived experience beneath arbitrary labels. The people discussed in this essay illustrate the diversity of interactive strategies that characterise the 'mentally disabled' in the United States. 'Mental disability' is a meaningful designation in so far as it is supported by the force of economic, legal and political exigencies in society; the label influences where people live, the kinds of services that are available to them, the contexts in which they encounter other people. Labels can obscure – and, in their essential unfairness, oppress – but they do not necessarily destroy. 'Mentally disabled' people, like members of other marginalised groups, learn how to survive. They do so by developing competencies different from (and perhaps disvalued by) the 'mainstream'; but they do survive.

I have discussed four coping strategies, four styles of interaction that allow persons with 'mental disabilities' to resolve the tensions within their own senses of identity. But each of these types is a complex configuration of attitudes and behaviours. Far from being helpless automata, 'mentally disabled' people are constantly strategising about how to present themselves to significant others in their environments. Perhaps their greatest failure is that they are so often transparent in their attempts to present themselves to advantage. But they are certainly not lacking in resources for such attempts.

The four illustrative cases suggest that in spite of the pressures to acquiesce, to conform to the negative attributions made by society, 'mentally disabled' people can construct positive ideals of what they would like to be, how they would like to be seen. They are not always realistic in this process – but then again, neither are many 'normal' people. Between the pigeon-hole to which society consigns them and their idealised visions lies the vast ground of their everyday survival.

Notes

1 This term encompasses 'mental retardation', chronic mental illness, emotional disturbance, learning deficits, and a broad range of organic disorders such as hearing or sight impairment, cerebral palsy, certain forms of seizure disorder, etc., all of which compromise one's cognitive abilities. The main descriptive passages in this paper, however, refer specifically to adults diagnosed with 'mental retardation'.

2 'Therapeutic communities' have been created specifically to receive and deal with deinstitutionalised persons with mental illness or 'mental retardation' (Leighton et al. 1963; Roosens 1979; Vanier 1979). Such carefully crafted and self-contained communities do not represent the experience of 'community' in the lives of the majority of those deinstitutionalised (and increasingly, for younger people, never institutionalised) in the United States.

3 Young black men may be more likely to be considered 'criminal' when exhibiting the same maladaptive behaviours as whites. White 'mentally disabled' people can be more 'deviant' in their behaviour when interacting with those outside their immediate social networks than black people in general, and black men in particular. The 'mainstream' is all too willing to consider *any* young black man a 'danger to self and others' (a primary criterion for involuntary commitment).

4 They do not yet have the political clout of other marginalised groups, who can argue for what amounts to rewriting the rules of the game.

5 The four people will be identified by pseudonyms. Certain demographic details have been altered slightly to further disguise their identities. A female colleague, L. J. Zagnoli, has taken the lead in the interviews with the women in the study population. For more detail about the methodology of this study, see Angrosino (1989, 1992b) and Angrosino and Zagnoli (1992).

6 Some do have trouble mastering skills requiring physical co-ordination, but this is not universal; it is unclear how much of this physical clumsiness is learned behaviour, not an inevitable consequence of 'mental retardation' at all. And standards of beauty have little or nothing to do with intellectual competence, as any number of beautiful celebrities demonstrate.

3   (In)competence in America in comparative perspective

Patrick J. Devlieger

> As soon as you set foot in America, you feel the presence of an entire
> continent – space there is the very form of thought.
>
> Jean Baudrillard (1989: 16)

> It hardly needs saying that the disabled, individually and as a group,
> contravene all the values of youth, virility, activity and physical beauty
> that Americans cherish, however little most individuals may embody
> them.   Robert Murphy (1987: 100)

People with disabilities in the United States, in the very way they lead
their lives, reveal American culture. Their lives are especially revealing
because mental retardation is a highly changeable concept, both historically and cross-culturally, and much of its content is continuously drawn
from the dominant culture. This is reflected in language and in its historical change. Since the late nineteenth century, shifts of usage from 'idiot',
to 'feebleminded', to 'mentally defective', to 'mentally subnormal', to
'mentally deficient', to 'mentally retarded', to 'person with mental retardation', have reflected unease with the connotations of earlier terms, and
a never-ending search for the right designation. Michael Angrosino (this
volume) points to both the acceptance and the contestation of contemporary classifications, both as labels and bureaucratic processes, and to self-
thematisation and concern with personal images, suggesting that no label
may ever fit.

My concern here is not to trace the historical development of labels,
but to read into contemporary American culture and to understand
people with mental retardation *as Americans*. It is a reading from the
inside, using American culture as my starting point, working out towards
a cultural understanding of (in)competence. To reach this goal, I will first
make a detour, looking at aspects of the particular life histories of people
with mild mental retardation, drawn from Devlieger (1995a), and
drawing some cross-cultural comparisons with material from African
societies. My reading into American culture will benefit from the relativ-

ity derived from appreciating the predicaments that are inherent in *any* life.

My approach departs from a classical life-course approach, in which 'culture' is not the focus of attention. Nor am I as interested in reading culture via the phenomenon of disability, as in the opposite process: reading into disability, more precisely into incompetence, using culture as my starting point. This approach also differs from what Moffat (1992: 214) labels a constructionist approach. Such an approach looks at the 'processes which explain how common frames of references and sets of shared cultural codes are established and reproduced as the common property of all Americans (or at least most)' (Löfgren 1989: 371). In trying to connect an overall culture with individual lives, I begin with a simple proposition: to understand the people in this study, we need first to understand Americans and their culture. I will also confront this issue by introducing alternative cultural understandings, those of the Songye of Zaïre and the Shona of Zimbabwe.

Life histories and local models of (in)competence

I worked from 1992 to 1995 intensively with twelve young adults in their early twenties, their families, and people associated with them in agencies and schools. This fieldwork took place mostly in Illinois and Indiana. About half of the people had spent most of their lives in small towns before they had moved to live in one of the group homes or apartments offered by their agency. One person had lived continuously in a metropolitan area; the rest had moved several times in their lives, living in different towns and cities across Illinois, and one person also across the country and overseas. The invitation of people to work with me included various sources, such as two professionals in adult agencies, one vocational coordinator in a rural high school, a professional in a speech and hearing clinic, and a colleague graduate student who offered that I work with his sister. This variation of sources also resulted in people labelled with mental retardation from various backgrounds, optimally contributing to the complexity of the study.

Life histories are instructive about life transitions, such as the transition from school to adult life, as well as about American culture. Some brief life histories of people with mild mental retardation may illustrate this point. It is important to recognise that life histories are only in limited ways instructive. What can be learned from life histories about the substance of life transitions is very different in every person. Rather than giving an overview of lives, I wish to point out what I could learn from them.

Brian, for example, became trapped in his transition from school to adulthood because the only alternative for him after school was home. Caught in a situation of restricted mobility, he represented for people in his social environment the antithesis of the expansionist image portrayed in advertising by, for example, the Marlboro Man. In his words, the disability 'is messing me up'.

Sharon's life transition, on the other hand, exemplified the importance of supportive relationships in a life transition. She reported being continuously overwhelmed by dominant relationships in her life, thus confronting the independence, and the manipulation of association, that Americans cherish. In one conversation, just after her adoptive mother had set the record straight about some of the things she had said in an earlier conversation, Sharon collapsed in expressing herself: she felt that she could not answer or speak about anything. I later learned that the development and collapse of our relationship was not unique in Sharon's experience of social relationships. In fact, it happened every time her disability was uncovered.

Steve's life, again by contrast, revealed the total incorporation of his life into a culture of mental retardation, consisting of sheltered work, group home life, and agency-initiated recreational and personal relationships. This subsequently redirected much of his adult script, since the sequence of decisions made by or about him, and the further development of his life, were congruent with the normative expectations of his agency. That as an adult he needed to make money was used to support his moving into a group home; but working in a sheltered workshop diminished in significance the more he became incorporated into the everyday structures of his adult agency.

Tina's life history reveals many of the disturbing themes of American society: child abuse, cancer, divorce. But it also illustrates the impact of the construction of relative notions of success, depending on the person's development of a self-reliant, independent lifestyle. Tina did not portray herself as a success story, because she knew too well that distorted family relationships had led her into her current situation. The information was of little relevance to agency workers, however, who emphasised a view of her as a success, on account of her independent life. Tina could never have been a success in, for example, an African context, since she had been expelled from living with her family. Self-reliance and quick adaptation, however, qualified her as a success in America.

Life histories can bring out elements of a model of American competence that goes beyond the label of 'mental retardation.' Brian and Steve, for example, are both hampered by missing opportunities to exploit the expanding space and mobility which are so much part of the American

heritage. The country's development became inscribed into the development of American personhood. The good immigrant, for example, is the
one who comes from abroad, ignores his heritage and becomes an
American. The good American travels in life without looking back, in
search of a better future, summarised in the phrase 'going west'. In that
sense, Steve's parents know that Steve's leaving home, even if his future
life was unsure, would have been the right thing to happen. In the daily
life of most people at transition age, the personification of expanded space
and mobility is, of course, the automobile, an extension of the house and
of the body. Individual incompetence is hardest to accept at this level.

Sharon's life history demands that we look at the freedom of association and the ability to engage in social relations that are at the heart of the
local American concept of competence. This engagement is goal-oriented; it is the goals that give meaning to the association. In its most ideal
form, contradictions are inherent in competent engagement in social relationships such as these: any assumed subordination or dependence leads
to greater independence, or at least, to an improved mastery of independence. In other words, the road to independence goes through various
stages of dependence that are consciously sought. This seems to be the
key to the skilled negotiation of adult scripts that offer as much independence as the person can take. For example, in the context of a person's
first contact with an adult agency, the negotiation may result in 'living in a
group home' (rather than at home or in an agency apartment) and
working in 'a sheltered workshop' (rather than being unemployed at
home or working in a community job at home or away from home). These
outcomes are the result of skilled negotiation if the result closely reflects
the amount of independence an individual can take. In reality, the
outcome is always a combination of common and hidden agendas, of
agencies ('we have a spot in a group home that needs to be filled') or of
families ('my son will not go into a sheltered workshop').

These sketchy life histories lead in to a consideration of some aspects of
the local model of competence in American culture. The vastness of the
country, and the capacity to overcome the inconvenience of *not* being able
to master this vastness, is very much at the core of such a model. It is here
that I understand Baudrillard's statement, quoted as an epigraph for this
chapter, that space is the very form of thought in America. This needs to
be connected with the dynamic that American lives take on at different
levels. At the level of the individual life, this is expressed in making events
occur; socially, it becomes reflected in free association and the goal-oriented nature of social engagement; culturally, it is expressed in the con-
quering of space. The dynamic is reflected in the idea of 'speed'. It is
reflected in the flexibility of making events happen, and in its radical

manifestation, violence; in the way Americans watch television, in the speed of the images, interlaced with advertisements; in 'blended' families, that are the result of living a speedy life. Lastly, it is reflected in Americans' spatial mobility, in moving and living in many different places in the United States. To stay in the same place is to stagnate.

In order to read into the meaning of incompetence, however, these life histories must be complemented. Embedded as they are in American culture, they do not serve particularly well to identify which aspects of personal incompetence can be specifically linked to key characteristics of American culture. To configure better the contours of an American concept of (in)competence, I turn now to a consideration of cross-cultural evidence drawn from my own research in African societies, and from the broader literature.

Cross-cultural perspectives on incompetence: issues in central African societies

My insights into central African models of incompetence are derived from fieldwork undertaken among the Songye of Zaïre and the Shona of Zimbabwe. I worked in Zaïre from 1983 to 1985 as a researcher for a Belgian group of flying doctors, interested in following up on their surgical work with young children with polio. The fieldwork involved intensive interviewing and participant observation at the centre for children with disabilities and in their villages. In Zimbabwe, I worked from 1989 to 1991 as an associate expert with the International Labour Organisation in a rehabilitation training and research programme for Eastern and Southern Africa. This position emphasised my role of co-ordinator and supervisor of fieldwork, involving three research assistants who worked in different Zimbabwean communities.

For the Songye, bodily faults are the expression of wronged relationships: with nature, relatives, ancestors and, ultimately, God (Devlieger 1995b). It follows that being competent is expressed in the knowledge and observance of the rules that accompany this embeddedness in a larger network of relationships. 'Competent people' are embedded people. This point is also emphasised by Susan Reynolds Whyte (this volume), who points to the social context as fundamental to personhood, with implications for notions of (in)competence. However, Tim Booth and Wendy Booth (this volume) warn that being embedded socially may be too narrow; they argue that the wider environment can only account for resiliency against the deficits that arise from the closest networks.

'Rehabilitating incompetence' is not found in the medical-technical solution of bodily problems but in the restoration of relational embeddedness. There is no linear relation between functional inability and incompetence in the African contexts which I researched. Rather, an examination of the cracks in relationships at different levels will determine whether a bodily fault can be attributed to the incompetent behaviour of the person who carries the disability, or to someone else. It is in this context that beliefs in supernatural forces of witchcraft are crucial. Witches are entities that are out there, always looking for an opportunity to harm. It is on the basis of an examination of relationships and identifying the origin of the wrongdoing that an attitude towards the person with the disability is formed. If disability is associated with the incompetence of other individuals, the person who has the disability can reckon on sympathy; but if it is determined that his or her own wrong behaviour is expressed in a bodily difference, the person will not be pitied.

In searching for the meaning of incompetence in the central African context, an examination of proverbs and traditional stories can be useful. Looking at such material among the Shona, it transpires that (in)competence is not associated with the kind of problems one encounters – for example, the functional limitations that go along with disability of any kind – but with the way individuals are creative and inventive in surviving despite their difficulties. This theme occurs in several Shona proverbs. One says 'People with disabilities are clever, they have strategies, they dance whilst leaning against the wall' (*Chirema chenmazano chinotamba chakazendama kumadziro*). Another proverb states that people with disabilities are people with ideas, that they try, like any people in trouble, to find solutions for their problem (*Chirema nodchine mazano*). The implication is that people with difficulties have hidden capabilities and could surprise one in the things they can do. This theme is very strong in some of the traditional Shona stories which emphasise that hidden skills and capacities can be revealed, provided that the person is accepted in the community. One story, of 'The Old Woman with a Very Large Knee', tells about the occult power of an old limping woman who had a very large lump on her knee. The lump proved to be magical and of great use to the community once the woman was accepted (see Atkinson 1989).

Closely associated ideas are the unpredictability of difficulties, and the moral lesson never to be too sure of your stability and security in life. A strong theme in central African – in this case Shona – proverbs related to disability is the condemnation of ridiculing people with disabilities, the logic being that situations are unpredictable and that a similar trouble can overcome anyone. Very popular in the Shona language, for example, is the proverb that says 'Laugh at disability when you're dead' (*Seka urema wafa*). The insecurity also emerges in the proverb 'One day, the wild dog will break its tail' (*Niremwe zuva gava richadimbura muswe*), indicating that the strongest person can suddenly lose direction in life.

It becomes clear, then, that in local African concepts of (in)competence one may look for issues concerned with embeddedness in a larger social network and with creativity in overcoming one's difficulties. Thus having a disability of any kind does not directly mean that incompetence is necessarily implied. It is in the way that disability is associated with either a lack of social embeddedness, or a lack in overcoming the difficulties that are associated with impairment, that one can speak of incompetence. Indications of great openness towards people with disabilities being socially embedded or integrated can be found in the following proverb: 'A person with a disability is at his place to get beer from the beer pot' (*Chirema chiripacho kucherera doro*), indicating that despite difficulties, there is a place where the person belongs. Ultimately this means an affirmation of the person's humanity. With specific respect to mental disability, there is openness towards any activity that shows the person as fitting in. This is well expressed in the proverb, 'If one has a child who is an idiot, if it dances to drums, one ululates at its performance' (*Ane benzi ndeane rake kudzana unopururudza*).

Local models of incompetence, both in Zaïre and Zimbabwe, seem to have little affinity with Western ideas of competence. Notions of personal accomplishment, independence, individuality, lead us to favour lives without much interaction; in central Africa, the reverse is true. There are some similarities, however. With respect to mental disability, my impression is that in central African countries, as often in the United States, people with mental problems are lumped together in one category. For example, no major distinction is made between mental retardation and mental illness. Instead, among the Shona people, for example, different terms describe different types of mental disability, depending on the individual's expressed behaviour. People who are 'active' are called *benzi*, those who are quiet *dununu*. However, hearing impaired people, who are quiet, are called 'dumb', which is a negative ascription of stupidity, a confusion that also exists in English. Some Shona respondents also expressed a concern that people with mental disabilities can be violent, and therefore should be separated from other people. Again, this is not unique: separation in institutions has long been a favourite solution to the 'problem' of mental disability in many Western countries, including the United States.

American culture: unity versus diversity

In defining American culture, I take a stand which emphasises its unity rather than its diversity. Although this is not very fashionable, in view of the current debates that centre around diversity, I agree with Varenne (1977: 214): 'the differences that exist among Americans are not so relevant as the differences that exist between them and people from other cultures'.

In support of his argument, Varenne compares the behaviour of Italian-Americans and Italians and argues that Italian-Americans are more like other Americans than they are like Italians. In a similar fashion, I would argue that the people with mild mental retardation are more like other Americans than they are like people with similar degrees of mental retardation in another culture.

The notion that space is the dominant organising metaphor in American culture may further support my stress on unity rather than diversity. Several scholars have contrasted American culture with European using this metaphor. Baudrillard argues that the abundance which goes together with space becomes a mode of thought (1989). Earlier, de Beauvoir commented, without connecting it to a sense of space, on the nature of American time: '[Americans] respect the past, but only insofar as it is a thing embalmed; the idea of a living past, integrated with the present, is foreign to them' (de Beauvoir 1953: 331).

'Space' became 'opportunity' on the basis that, 'the destruction of hereditary obstacles to advancement had created conditions in which social mobility depended on individual initiative alone. The self-made man, archetypical embodiment of the American dream, owed his advancement to habits of industry, sobriety, moderation, self-discipline, and avoidance of debt' (Lasch 1978: 53).

Hsu describes self-reliance, the most persistent psychological expression of which is the fear of dependence, as the core American value. He argues that, in contrast with Europe, American self-reliance is characterised by its connection to equality, suggesting that 'the inalienable right of every American is an unlimited self-reliance and unlimited equality' (1975: 384). Apparently contradictory American 'values' – freedom and equality – are, according to Hsu, manifestations of one core value. Similarly, Spindler and Spindler (1983) identified a key opposition between individualism and conformity and showed how the insecurity that goes along with individualism leads to conformity.

The person in my study on the transition to adulthood who embodies most of the American Dream is Dennis. He transcended the failures of his parents, to become someone who knows that work and money will lead to his advancement in life. His adult script is based on this simple insight and on the help of a few friends who are directly connected with work. It is not based on his parents' advice, nor on education, nor on the involvement of agencies. Dennis's academic failures and his label of incompetence will cease to exist when he walks out the school door. His academic incompetence will be completely dissociated from his capacity as a self-made man.

In a similar, though less radical sense, Mike and Tina are also self-made people. Mike's favourite stories are about his trips across the country and about the time he lived with his parents in Turkey. His stories tell of his battle with space and serve to inform the further development and construal of his own script. Mike does not intend to keep his janitorial job, but means to pack up his belongings one day and 'drive', to close to where his sister lives, and to start life over again. Tina's liberating experience – leaving home, settling in to living and work, and developing an extended network of friends, partly in lieu of a family – represents in another way the development of self-made personhood.

All of these people have rather negative perceptions of the people with whom they associated before their transition to adult life. The configuration of their network of close people, and of their social embeddedness, is somewhat limited, at least compared to African local models. It is interesting to note that Tina, Mike and Dennis all have a background of living in a trailer, an experience that adds to their sense of space and mobility. Within their perspective of self-reliance, incompetence as a cultural concept is not related to academic performance; it is much more to do with basic survival skills in a harsh environment. They do not believe in academic performance, but rather in the loyalty and protection of close friends. Tina, Mike and Dennis are the people who typically disappear as 'people with mental retardation', who are absorbed into the daily stream of life and survive against all its odds.

This understanding of (in)competence-as-survival is insufficient, however, to describe the situation of other people. This can much better be understood by reference to an erosion of individualism. Lasch (1978: 53, 59) describes an age of diminishing expectations, in which:

the Protestant virtues no longer excite enthusiasm, inflation erodes investment, and advertisement undermines the horror of indebtedness, exhorting the consumer to buy now and pay later. Self-preservation has replaced self-improvement as the goal of earthly existence.

The impact of TV commercials and credit card advertisements seems only to have strengthened the trend. As a result, Lasch goes on to argue, 'a profound change in our sense of time has transformed work habits, values, and the definition of success'.

Several people in my study fit the description of self-preservation. In Lori's life history, for example, the lack of a push for independence and an ongoing symbiotic relationship with her mother, point in that direction.

So, too, does Gregory's obsession with his security, something which his family and the agency which works with him encourage. He was extensively trained by his agency to be able to get out of the apartment building in case of a fire, and his family sees him in the morning and expects a phone call at the time he comes home to make sure he is safe. His permanent employment, with its accompanying benefits, can be interpreted in that sense. Steve's development of an agency script also leads in the same direction. His family's release of their responsibility is welcome in the context of an agency strategy which intends to take control over his life. Although functioning well below his capabilities, Steve settled into an agency culture and accepted a group home and a sheltered workshop as the initial steps of a career as a client of his agency. Sharon's clinging to home was connected to a 'cloak of competence' (*pace* Edgerton) and a mother who dominated decision-making. Legal guardianship and insurance were the means of preservation. For Brian, getting stuck in his transition, as discussed earlier, was smoothed out into vague objectives for the future.

Being competent took on still other meanings for Diane and Peter. Because of Diane and Peter's disabilities, people in their networks turned to professionalism as a major orientation for decision-making. This is most marked for Diane, whose mother and brother took on special education, as a second career and as a life career, respectively. Diane's mother felt an extreme lack of information on how to deal with a daughter with Down's Syndrome. She became convinced that the only way out of the impasse was to become a special educator. In return, Diane's life has been strongly geared towards current advances in the field and to what is acceptable according to the field. This is evident in the activities in which Diane has been involved, such as her Circle of Friends, and in her participation at national conventions on Down's Syndrome. It is most particularly evident in her language, which incorporates much special education jargon. Being competent as a person with Down's Syndrome is, for Diane's mother, being able to speak, and, in lesser degree, being able to act according to the latest developments and expectations of specialists in the field. Diane's attitude is further supported by her brother, whom she visits regularly, and who is currently a doctoral student in special education.

Professionalism as a driving force was also found in Peter's attitude of individualism. Peter's adoptive mother also shifted her career as an educator towards special education, becoming specialised in vocational coordination. This background became extremely useful in negotiating Peter's adult life script with the agency that works with him; her knowledge of supported employment impressed its workers. Supported by his mother's status, Peter became very confident in negotiating his own independence from the adult agency.

Few of the people in this study relied on the concept of competence – as the result of formal education and the increase of knowledge and skills – that is normative in American society and that, ideally, regulates career and professional development. Joyce is the only person in the study who intended to participate in post-secondary education, with the object in mind of a career in child care. Joyce's parents counteracted the advice of her school, that she should not embark on a college education – not even in two-year school – but pursue a technical skill instead. The direction of Joyce's life course can be accounted for by her parents' strong belief in education. Both of her parents are nurses; nourished by fundamentalist Christian values, they invest strongly in the moral education of their children.

A belief in education is also evident from Justin's continuous involvement in evening classes. Justin lives at home and works in the sheltered workshop, a solution that the agency that works with him agrees is incompatible with his capabilities. It results from the unavailability of jobs for higher functioning people with developmental disabilities. Justin is the only person who is born of Asian parents. Almost stereotypic of Asian-American culture, he takes classes in maths and in karate. Justin is also the only person in the study who actively takes driving classes and is determined to succeed in mastering the skill of driving a car.

Individual lives in the United States seem to be characterised by incredible mobility. This mobility is, in its original form, spatial. It is carried in essence by images which stress the vastness of the country rather than its historicity, the technological capacity that allows for mobility, and the favouring of an ever-present and renewing sense of youth. Mobility takes on dimensions of time and becomes flexibility, as reflected in the life course. This mobility and flexibility is fascinating because, as an image, it suggests that people can manage, plan and change events, social networks and cultural spaces to a degree unsurpassed in any other part of the world.

The flexibility of the life course becomes visible in its increasingly idiosyncratic character, and in the decline of the normative cultural schedules that direct the life course. These schedules, such as, for example, education, leaving home, marriage, having children, only live on as cultural ideals. Reality does not reflect these expressions of stability. Rather, change and variety in family structure, and in work and education as interchangeable stages in the life course, have become part of the everyday experience of Americans. These developments do not reflect norms, but they reflect reality. Adult life in the private sphere has turned into a lifetime of choice, instead of a period of stability reached by, and after, having accomplished permanent achievements. Buchmann (1989), for example, has drawn on a concept of the current reconstruction of the *symbolic system of love* to explain the abandonment of a conception of life-long stability, accompanied by a life-cycle-encompassing concept of identity, as the ultimate value.

These developments have profound implications for the lives of people with disabilities, and for the linked concepts of ability and incompetence. Gaines (1994) has proposed the concept of 'local ability' to indicate the extreme relativity of (dis)ability according to different environments and stages in the life course. According to Gaines, (dis)ability in modern America does not have the kind of stability it appears to take on in other historical and cultural environments. Similarly, relating to mental retardation, Edgerton (1994) has observed that decent living in the United States does not require people to be able to read or be proficient in abstract thinking, and that consequently the concept of incompetence changes with expectations in the environment. He further argued that economic criteria will be the most important in determining what mental retardation 'is'.

Looking specifically at mental retardation in a historical perspective, and at the transformation of the construction of incompetence, two contradictory forces impact on the lives of people with mental retardation. First, there are the changing expectations in American society which have been observed by several authors (e.g. Edgerton 1994; Lasch 1978). In a critical review of Edgerton's famous *The Cloak of Competence*, Gerber (1990: 19) stated, poignantly, that:

By virtue of a changing historical context and, on the part of the retarded themselves, without a great deal of the type of deliberate effort necessitated by, say, passing, these people have become more American – or, perhaps, the American people had become more like retarded people. Either way, the question of *who* and *what* should be considered normal now seemed a great deal more complex than it had at the time of Edgerton's initial research.

However, quite diametrically against this changing climate in American society is a second force which impinges on the lives of people with mental retardation. While some twenty years ago, 'we expected people with mental retardation to tie their shoes, we now expect them to maintain a job' (DeStefano, personal communication, 1994). As Edgerton has added, while people with Down's Syndrome would have been warehoused in institutions some thirty years ago, it is now quite normal for them to be married and lead independent lives (1994). It is my impression that normative cultural schedules of self-reliance and independence, which conflict with the cultural reality experienced by non-disabled people in American society, are now vigorously imposed on people with disabilities. It is as if disability advocates have taken the historical opportunity of living up to the ideal values of American society (which they were hitherto denied) even though non-disabled people's social realities do not reflect those values any more. It is in this sense that a cultural space is created in which people with disabilities can become new heroes. In some ways, they reflect the ideals of normalisation and its movements, with the only problem that 'normalisation' has become less and less clear. Some companies, such as Walmart and Mariott, still driven by a search for diversity and eager to communicate their concern for 'caring', have recognised this space; as well as hiring them as 'visible' employees, they also use people with disabilities in their advertisements. The shift is also reflected in the film *Forrest Gump* where the person with retardation is the hero while all others fail in more or less significant ways.

Individualism and avoidance: from 'stigma' to 'different'

Contemporary young people with mild mental retardation in their early twenties do not have a history of institutionalisation, but were educated in regular public school settings. This is part of their historical predicament, the mere fact that they were born after the end of the 1960s and benefited from mandated public education. Their experience runs contrary to the picture presented by those ethnographies (Edgerton 1984, 1993; Edgerton and Gaston 1991) and life histories (Angrosino 1992b; Bogdan and Taylor 1976, 1994; Langness and Levine 1986) which have highlighted *stigma* as a major descriptor of the psycho-social condition of people with mental retardation. For young people today, the stigma of institutionalisation is not the all-pervasive experience that it was for deinstitutionalised individuals. Rather, the difficulty these people experience reflects the fact that they were the test cases for their public schools in educating them alongside non-disabled students.

Enduring misconceptions of mental retardation also shape contemporary categorisation (Antonak *et al.* 1989). One such enduring misconception is the way in which people with mental retardation, and sometimes elderly people also, are seen as children (Perin 1988; Hockey and James 1993). Perin explains that, by their inappropriate behaviours

normal people are distancing themselves from discrepancy by freezing the disabled in a familiar system of meaning and conduct – the one reserved for children – in order to continue at all. Disabled people are treated like children because children are imperfect adults. (1988: 157)

Steve, for example, complained of the fact that his classmates called him names, such as 'baby', referring to him as a child. In Steve's words, 'there was a couple kids that didn't like me that much. They did not like me when I was in school that much. They'll like pick on me, call me names, and kick me, and just like grabbing my stuff and stealing it. . . . Say "look at the baby" or "look at the jerk" or whatever, call me names like that. My teacher, Miss Diana, got mad when they come right to the door and say stuff. . . . She said "you know what, I tell the principal about it." And the principal stands right in the room or in the hallway making sure people don't call me names when I go for my next class. He just like stands right there and says "hey guys, do not pick on Steve." But they kept doing it, right after lunch is over, they do it. They write nasty stuff in my yearbooks about me. Called me names in the yearbooks. It really made me upset.'

Apart from contemporary forms of stigmatisation, as described by Steve, the experience of many people with disabilities, especially in public spaces, is framed by *avoidance*. Many contemporary people choose to construct the difference of disability through an avoidance ethic. This is an expression of individualistic discourses which define personhood in one's ability to resist the surrender of one's interests to those of 'others'. In this sense, individualism entails a theory of inexorable conflict, embedded in the individualist's understanding of what it means to be an individual, as involving separate interests (Greenhouse 1992). In a more positive vein, the ultimate ethical rule is simply that individuals should be able to pursue whatever they find rewarding, constrained only by the requirement that they do not interfere with the 'value systems' of others (Bellah *et al.* 1985).

The response to the presence of people with mental retardation in many public places – their public difference – is avoidance. The group presence of people with mental retardation in public places, for example the outing of a group home to a public event, adds to this manifestation of avoidance. The avoidance ethic with respect to people with disabilities is rooted in the deep and uneasy ambivalence in relations between the able-bodied and the disabled. The person who arouses fear and loathing is made invisible (Murphy 1987). One way this can be done is by naming the anomaly and then forgetting about it (Stiker 1982). Referring to American culture, however, Murphy *et al.* (1988) explain that the rules of middle-class American culture demand that the flaw be either ignored or neutralised. This may be further clarified by the kind of perfectionism that is typical for middle-class Americans. For these 'perfect' people, imperfect people who are 'less than human' elicit a kind of culture shock. This leads to a kind of visceral reaction (Stiker 1982), or to paralysis or helplessness, encouraging outright avoidance based on their awkward 'fear of saying or doing the wrong thing' (Perin 1988).

At any rate, the difference which the people in my study represent to others is best explained by the ethic of avoidance. For better or for worse they are 'different', and their relations with non-disabled others in public spaces are regulated by avoidance, not by stigmatisation. The speed of one-to-one encounters in fast-food restaurants and in retail stores, and the degree of severity of their disability – i.e. relatively 'mild' – do not allow stigma to be constructed. There is just no time for it. Rather, in the worst cases, suspicion may arise which may delay service to them. As I witnessed the reactions of others to people with mental retardation as customers in fast-food restaurants and in retail stores, these reactions do not reflect helplessness but, rather, suspicion that 'something' is wrong. The response is to have recourse to superiors in the bureaucracy, thus slowing down the service speed.

In the case of people who are more severely and visibly disabled, relations are more likely to be limited to those people who know them, and strongly regulated by the schedules through which these individuals are rendered predictable. People with easily apparant disabilities appear in public as part of well-defined goal-oriented programmes, accompanied or coached by persons that can be held accountable for them at any time. These persons constantly assume mediation roles that make the appearance of persons with severe disabilities in public understandable and predictable.

Text, ritual and the locus of incompetence

Another aspect of American culture which greatly influences the cultural construction of difference, and of incompetence in particular, becomes clear in the notion of writing scripts, texts which involve the planning of events. I have, for example, discussed how agencies develop adult life scripts for their clients. The use of the term 'script' for these planning processes seems particularly relevant in a country which attaches so much significance to texts and words. Gorer (1948) argued that modern America is, perhaps more than any other country, actually built on words, on the words of the Constitution and the Declaration of Independence, and, behind them, the Word of God. The dependence on text, rather than tradition, is apparent in the American attachment to the law.

It is the law rather than ritual which defines competence in the individual. Ritual in the United States is closely linked with age-grading, as can be seen, for example, in the importance attached to birthday parties. While these parties are important ritual events and bestow meaning on the individual, they are only in a minor way legitimations of competence. The graduation party, which symbolises the transition from school to adult life, needs to be understood in this sense. This party, in many ways an extension of the birthday party, may imply new duties and responsibilities. As a rite of passage (van Gennep 1960), it symbolises a new identity. Almost all of the individuals in our study enjoyed graduation parties, which held deep symbolic meaning for them. However, these parties have limited implications for the allocation and attribution of (in)competence. They were largely symbolic (see also Ferguson and Ferguson 1993). Ritual and text are two juxtaposed dimensions of life transitions, but the locus of incompetence must not be sought in both ritual *and* text. The text has become the more consequential.

Edgerton argued (1994) that the construction of the difference of mental retardation has shifted dramatically over time and that the major criteria in the future will continue to be economic. Although I recognise the importance of the economic, I would also emphasise other dimensions that contribute to the locus of incompetence, such as political and societal pressures. From one point of view, the locus of incompetence has, for example, shifted from the individual to the environment (Devlieger and Hunter de Bessa 1994; Lunt and Thornton 1994: 226–7). This is reflected in the relevant legislation. In the US 1975 Education of Handicapped Children Act, the locus of incompetence is the individual; the logical remedy for the deficiency is, therefore, to provide access to education. The definition of mental retardation paralleled the emphasis on the education of the individual (Grossman 1973). In 1990 the definition was, however, revised to include reference to levels of support, thus suppressing the importance of IQ scores and attaching more importance to adaptive behaviour. In this definition, the locus of incompetence is situated in the fit between the person and their environment (Turkington 1992). The shift is made complete in the US 1990 Americans with Disabilities Act (ADA), where incompetence is located in the environment; the remediation of the environment through accessibility and new technology takes priority over personal remediation. However, the people in this study have not benefited from the recent shifts in the legislation: the ADA excludes people with mental retardation, and the remediation of the environment proposed by the ADA will, anyway, have little impact on their lives.

Cross-cultural comparison of incompetence in adult life

Despite the pioneering work of Edgerton (1970), the amount of cross-cultural information on mental retardation remains limited. Research in non-Western countries remains obscure because many of these studies are geared towards Western ideas, such as normalisation and integration, and reveal little of the local cultural understanding(s) of incompetence in adult life. In contrast to the stigmatisation and, perhaps more important, the avoidance ethic which are central to the contemporary understanding of incompetence in the United States, I would like to present some information about alternative understandings of incompetence in other countries. In exploring this information, I apply it to my study of mental retardation in the United States. The information is limited and I suggest that more work of a comparative nature be undertaken that can further support the examples taken from Britain, Japan and Zimbabwe as well as develop cases for other countries and cultures.

Great Britain

May and Hughes have reported (1988) for Great Britain that as many as half to two-thirds of all children classified as 'mentally handicapped' during their school days disappear from the official gaze on leaving school. While this phenomenon may not be unique to Great Britain, I believe the explanation they give may apply more to Great Britain than to the United States.

They cease for all practical reasons to *be* mentally handicapped. The explanation lies in the functioning of the post-war labour market. Specifically, it has been brought about by the continuing demand of western economies for cheap, unskilled labor, a demand which, until quite recently at least, was able to absorb successive cohorts of school-leavers, including a significant proportion of those from Special Education. It is an irony, not much commented on, that the self-same economic system that first created the 'problem' of mental handicap by its need for an educated and disciplined work-force should also provide the means to contain and control it. (May and Hughes 1988: 66)

Clearly, in May and Hughes's view, the construction of adult incompetence in British society is defined by economic development rather than in social terms of stigmatisation or avoidance. The same logic could be applied to the United States, where many people who were identified as 'mentally retarded' cease to be so by the end of high school, but the interpretation in terms of economic determination does not hold. This was clearly the case with two people in my study. Dennis, for example, will become a worker who will avoid having to learn by reading, but who will continue to learn throughout his life through imitating others. His family and teachers predict that he will do well as a worker, although they also predict significant personal problems. Joyce will enrol in a child-care programme and many of her deficits will be recognised as 'personal characteristics'. However, her family and her church will continue to protect her, and if her wish is granted, Joyce will marry soon. The dynamics of the life course and the speed of society do not allow us to explain Dennis's and Joyce's life courses as characterised by a system that has created the problem of mental retardation and its sustenance. Instead, while the education system may have created a problem for them, it need not be sustained. The problem may be completely resolved and even reversed.

It remains to be seen whether economic development in the United States will evolve to the point of an abolishment of low-skill jobs. For now, however, cheap and unskilled labour remains in high demand, facilitating the absorption of people with mental retardation into the workforce. Although many of the people working in low-skill jobs are not in direct contact with the public, the typical transience of contact where it occurs, and the avoidance ethic, would not, anyway, stand in the way of their social integration into the workforce.

Although economic criteria may account for much of the difference with which people with mental retardation are handled, both in British and American society, there are other dimensions of the nature of their adulthood which must be considered. For example, to return to an issue which has been discussed earlier, Jenkins, discussing court reports which involved people with mental disabilities, argues that

although they are regarded as biologically mature or chronologically adult, the individuals concerned are, in fact, regarded as non-adult in the intellectual, psychological or social senses of the word. At best, they are children. (Jenkins 1990: 141)

This argument supports the view that the semiotic structures that go together with 'childhood' are easily applied, both in the United States and in Great Britain, to mental disability. It remains to be shown whether the semiotic structures that relate to children are also applicable to mental disability in other cultures.

Japan

Okano has reported for Australasia that the act of leaving secondary school, whether to take up employment or to enter tertiary institutions, has a special significance (1993: 10). He elaborates on the ritual aspect by looking at the high symbolic significance associated with the transition, as marked by 'breaking-up parties, graduation balls, and celebrating successful examination results'. Relating to Japan, by contrast, he notes that securing a permanent position in the workforce, not necessarily leaving school itself, is a prerequisite for a youth to become a *shakai-yin* ('society person'). However, in addition, 'full' social adulthood in Japan entails marriage, not just holding a job (Plath, personal communication 1995). Japanese university students, for example, are not yet *shakai-yin*, since they are financially supported by their parents. They occupy a moratorium status, a distinctive stage between being a school pupil and full adulthood: they have learned personal dispositions associated with a 'successful' transition, but have not yet secured permanent employment. They may be competent, but they do not yet have a competence. Unfortunately, in Okano's work we learn nothing about people with mental retardation and are thus left with questions: do people with mental retardation in Japan participate in secondary education, and can they become a *shakai-yin* and under what conditions?

A moratorium status, similar to that of which Okano speaks, applies to some of the people in my study. For Gregory, Justin and Brian – and their situations should not necessarily be generalised – this period in limbo is likely to last a long time. Interestingly, while a moratorium stage may be acceptable as an interim stage for non-disabled individuals, e.g. in the case of people who travel, volunteer, or break their childhood with an experience, such practices may not be acceptable for persons with mental disabilities. Beyond the importance of moratorium, the symbolic ritual aspects of developing competence are of great importance in American culture. The persons with mental retardation in my study take stock of important gains in competence at important markers such as birthdays. Steve, for example, marked his twenty-first birthday with 'drinking beer for the first time' and 'dancing'. They are also painfully aware of some of the limitations that mark them down, 'owning and driving a car' is perhaps the most important.

Zimbabwe

By way of further contrast, in a rural Zimbabwean community, adult incompetence takes on a different form (Devlieger 1991). This can be illustrated with a case study.

Sebusile is an adult woman with a history of mental disability since birth. She comes from a family of nineteen children, of which she was born fifth. Her father attended school but her mother never went. Her relatives believe that the cause of her disability was that her tongue is too tight. They believe that it happened natu-rally and that perhaps she could be treated by a person who knows how to cut the tightened tongue. Sebusile stays on the compound with her mother, stepfather, brothers and sisters. According to her stepbrother, Sebusile is able to do every-thing she is expected to do except ploughing. He thinks she doesn't plough because her mother did not allow her to do that job. Instead, she sent her to do easier tasks.

Sebusile never went to school because she could not speak well. She stayed home playing with other children. She had friends to play with but did not participate in other activities because she could not manage. She met with her friends at the river pools where other girls fetch water. However, she would not fetch water, she would just walk with the other girls. She also did not learn how to weave as she did not like to do this. Apart from that, she does everything that she can manage. She learned what she does from observing what others do. She knows how to harvest and she makes significant distinctions, such as the difference between edible and poisonous mushrooms. She does what she feels like doing.

According to her stepbrother, Sebusile is not married because of her difficulty in communication. She does not use signs, but only produces meaningless sounds. She also does not communicate with people that she does not know. To people who know her and address her, she responds by smiling and by making sounds.

From this case study, one can learn that adult incompetence relates to family and gender roles and the ability to communicate as a condition for assuming such roles. Adult incompetence in this Zimbabwean rural area takes on very different forms to incompetence in, say, more urban, more 'developed' areas. Within the context of this rural environment, people with mental retardation are excluded from the larger world 'outside', and, in the Zimbabwean context, they are excluded from the migratory movements between rural and urban areas. But, in the case of this woman, she also is excluded from participation in schools, which do not have great importance. What seems to matter is her inability to communicate with people around her: both the cause of her disability and its remedy are sought in that direction. By contrast with the American context, however, the person in this case is not 'drawn' into some occupation, in the belief that this will ensure the realisation of the greatest potential of the person. Rather, the person is protected from the hardship of some tasks; taking on tasks is left to the person herself; she sorts out her own capabilities. Rather than being avoided, the person joins in socially. Social integration and participation develop according to capacity.

It is obvious that the information given for any country is very incomplete and merely gives a first indication of what may be different cultural notions of (in)competence. These notions develop in a cultural and historical specific context. In my approach I have brought alternative notions back to an American notion of incompetence. Although both stigmatisation and avoidance are characteristics of social mechanisms of incompetence in the American context, I considered that other elements of incompetence need to be brought in as comparative material. Looking at material pertaining to Britain, such as economic determination and the workings of the semiotic structure of 'children', this too may be an element in an American concept of incompetence. However, it would need to be described in its proper context. Similarly, the ritual characteristics, including the importance of moratorium, in the development of adult competency in Japan, plays a part in the American development of competence. Last, the Zimbabwean material stimulates reflection on the importance of family and gender roles, and communication as a condition for assuming adult roles.

Ethnographic work on incompetence and its historical situation in a particular society, in this case America, further enriched by comparative perspectives from other societies, results in a complex understanding of incompetence. Such complexity stems from the fact that an understanding of both cultural construction and relativity and historical situation is needed. Such understanding would be served well by a cultural theory of competence.

Towards a cultural theory of competence in American society

One of the most distinctive aspects of twentieth-century American society is the division of life into a number of separate functional sectors: home and workplace, work and leisure, white collar and blue collar, public and private, and so on. These developments are harmonised with the requirements of bureaucratic industrial corporations and have had profound consequences.

The organisation of society into departments as functional wholes can be compared to the situation in the nineteenth century, when functions had less distinct boundaries (Bellah *et al.* 1985). This historical trend has strongly influenced the lives of people with disabilities and especially people with mental retardation. They have been drawn into these changes. While, on the one hand, the school has become an accessible place, on the other hand they are subject to tracking into streams or layers of competence. This tracking extends beyond high school, into the wider society, where they are assigned to the lowest layers of competence, be it in sheltered workshops or community development jobs, of which work in fast-food restaurants, characterised by routine and by extreme simplification of tasks, is most typical. Association with an adult agency enhances the process of tracking. Few contemporary people with mental retardation manage their lives without the assistance of adult agencies. Those who limit their involvement with these agencies will also avoid being tracked into low competency – and hence low-paid – jobs. For most people with mental retardation, however, this is unavoidable. They share the challenge of being 'designed' to fit their organisations, and while they may not be abjectly poor, their accumulation of material assets will remain largely impossible.

Local models of competence, as they apply to individuals in the United

States, replicate deep cultural roots that both favour individualism and self-reliance, and encourage an ethic of avoidance, exemplified in the metaphor of space. It exemplifies the contrast between 'social', 'functional', 'ritual' and 'economic' models of incompetence. At first sight, one may be tempted to conclude that a 'social model' of incompetence is dominant in the American context, where integration and mainstreaming account for the play of both avoidance and stigmatisation, and the 'functional model' more dominant in the African rural context, where family, gender and communication play significant roles; a 'ritual' model in the Japanese context; and an 'economic' model in the British context. Such a conclusion would mean an over-simplification. What a theory of incompetence really needs is an assessment of all these elements in a particular cultural and historical context.

Categorisations of incompetence in the American context become society's response to individuals whose self-reliance is not obvious and demands channelling. That channelling process is historically changeable. People labelled as mentally retarded have seen society's response to them change, over historical time and in relation to their passage through stages in the life course. The labelling process of incompetence is, over time, an excellent tool for tracking some of the semiotic structures that define incompetence in a particular historical period.

The incompetence of contemporary people with mental retardation is made present and obvious in public spaces, and is regulated through an ethic of avoidance. That avoidance is transformed in a public conspiracy that ignores incompetence. In American culture, the term 'disability' refers to the evidence of ability. To support this notion, the locus of incompetence is taken outside the individual to the environment. While this is the ideal, Steve's reflections clearly illustrate the limitations of 'ignoring', and the breaking down of the avoidance ethic to outright stigmatisation. At any point, American culture reveals itself as committed to preserving self-reliance. While this is a constant in an American concept of incompetence, there is a continuous battle about the normative expectations of what the 'incompetent' should do and how they should behave. While both conservative and liberal forces are continuously present, one takes the upperhand and historically defines, in a very penetrating way, the lives of people recognised as 'incompetent'.

4   Risk, resilience and competence: parents with learning difficulties and their children

Tim Booth and Wendy Booth

Research suggests that the children of parents with learning difficulties are at risk of developmental delay, maltreatment, neglect and abuse (Schilling *et al.* 1982). This evidence has contributed to the view that people with learning difficulties lack the competence to provide good-enough parenting. Oliver (1977), for example, asserts that they 'continue to be incompetent rearers, whatever supportive treatment is offered' and Fotheringham (1980) too claims that few parents have the ability to provide 'conditions of care at the minimal acceptable level'. Accardo and Whitman (1990) argue that the only important question 'with regard to parenting failure of significantly mentally retarded adults would seem to be not whether but when'. Such blanket judgements have been challenged by critics who point out that unrepresentative sampling, poor research design and other methodological weaknesses (especially in the outcome measures used) do not allow valid generalisations to be made about the extent or frequency of parenting failure (Tymchuk 1992; Tymchuk and Andron 1990). Five limitations in particular prevent existing research from being used to support general conclusions about the parental competence of people with learning difficulties.

First, there has been no longitudinal research on the effects of being raised by a parent or parents who have learning difficulties (Tymchuk and Feldman 1991), and no attempt has yet been made to chart their children's progress through adolescence and into adulthood (Dowdney and Skuse 1993; New York State Commission on Quality of Care for the Mentally Disabled 1993). The research that has been done on developmental outcomes has mostly come from intervention programmes focusing solely on young children from birth to three years, and researchers have not followed up children outside these programmes into later life (Tymchuk 1990). Consequently, 'little can be said as yet about the long-term effects of parenting' by people with learning difficulties (Zetlin *et al.* 1985).

Second, it is not possible to predict 'the effect that a given environment, even an inadequate one, will have on a given child' (Budd and Greenspan

1984). Some children manage to thrive despite poor nurturing (McGaw and Sturmey 1993), and 'do not appear to be adversely affected' by their upbringing (Tymchuk and Feldman 1991). Catch-all claims of parental inadequacy are unable to account for these known differences in outcomes.

Third, most research does not allow the effects of deprivation and discrimination on parental competence to be distinguished from the effects of having learning difficulties. Evidence suggests that the parenting styles of parents with learning difficulties do not differ from those of other parents in similar circumstances (Andron and Tymchuk 1987) and that the problems they encounter are similar to those faced by other parents of the same socio-economic status (Unger and Howes 1986). In this context, there is a danger of falsely attributing inadequate child care to parental incompetence when it should more properly be seen as the product of poverty (Fotheringham 1980, 1981).

Fourth, research to date has adopted too narrow a view of the parenting task (Booth and Booth 1994) by tending to equate parenting with mothering; focusing on those aspects of parenting behaviour that are most easily observed, measured and quantified, such as caretaking skills, the use of discipline and the provision of stimulation through play, while overlooking the non-nurturing side of parenting; too often failing to recognise that parenting is about more than childrearing and involves more than merely practical skills; and paying more attention to parents' deficits than their strengths. Assessments of parental competence based on only a partial rendering of what parenting entails are unlikely to give a full picture and must be treated with caution.

Fifth, most research has adopted a skills model of competence. Good-enough parenting, however, is not just a matter of possessing the right skills. It is also an attributed status which owes as much to the decisions of professionals as to the behaviour of parents. It is situationally determined by the quality or poverty of people's lives and the environmental threats they face (see, for example, Chapter 9). Competence too is socially constructed in terms of the normative standards and evaluative judgements enforced by the wider society, official agencies and their front-line representatives. A skills-based perspective has led researchers incorrectly to ascribe inadequate child care or unsatisfactory child outcomes to parenting deficits when often they owe more to the pressures that bear on the families and undermine their ability to cope. In this wider context, as Feldman (1986) has commented, it is their 'adaptability and durability' in the face of major stress that is extraordinary rather than their shortcomings as parents (see also, for example, Webster-Stratton 1990).

These issues are linked: they originate from limitations in the risk paradigm that has guided most work in this field. This paradigm has focused attention on the features of parenting by people with learning difficulties that put the well-being of their children at risk. In this sense, the risk perspective shares much in common with the medical model of disability. It has tended to conceive competence as a quality of the individual, to represent incompetence in pathological terms as maladaptive or deviant behaviour, and to spotlight parents' inabilities, deficiencies and failings. In so doing, it skews our perception of people's lives and misrepresents the range of factors that shape the outcomes we seek to understand (McIntyre *et al.* 1990).

It is much easier to specify what goes wrong rather than what goes right in the lives of children at risk. Much less effort has gone into studying those 'who overcome adversity, who survive stress, and who rise above disadvantage' (Rutter 1979). Yet research by scholars such as Anthony (1974, 1987a, 1987b), Garmezy (1974, 1991), Rutter (1985, 1987) and Werner (1986) into the children of schizophrenic and psychotic parents, alcoholic parents and poor families has shown that not all are vulnerable to their situation and many demonstrate considerable adaptability in coping with lives filled with difficulty. From this standpoint, the emphasis shifts away from the nature of the risks they face to the source of their resilience.

The resiliency model directs attention to the protective factors that mediate children's response to risk and shield them from the hazards of their environment. Such protective factors are seen as critical to 'understanding why some children, facing overwhelming odds, do not succumb to the risks that surround them' (McIntyre *et al.* 1990). Three broad sets of variables have been identified as protective factors: personality or dispositional attributes, family characteristics and external supports (see, for example, Garmezy 1985). The significance of this list is that it underlines the importance of looking at the person-in-context. Child outcomes are not just a function of the skills or lack of skills of parents: they are also influenced by the factors that contribute to children's vulnerability. Equally, the level of parental competence is affected by the presence or absence of protective factors that produce resilience in children. For these reasons, the resiliency model also requires that we investigate parenting-in-context.

This chapter draws on a study of adult children brought up by parents with learning difficulties in order to illuminate the part played by protective factors in their lives, and to challenge prevailing views about parental incompetence that fail to take account of the notion of resilience.

The research study

The study[1] on which this chapter is based was designed to explore what it means to be brought up by parents with learning difficulties through the experience of their adult children. A particular concern is to investigate the longer-term effects of having been raised by parents with learning difficulties in order to throw light on the relationship between parental competence, family functioning and child outcomes.

The study used biographical methods to construct personal accounts of people's childhood and their experience of growing up with a parent or parents who have learning difficulties. Three considerations influenced this approach. First, there was no sampling frame for the focus group of adult children, and no possibility of guaranteeing the representativeness required for statistical generalisation. Indeed, the task of identifying, locating and securing the co-operation of subjects within this largely hidden population presents major logistical hurdles that have thwarted or deterred similar retrospective research in this field.[2] Generally, we used service agencies or front-line practitioners to establish contact with the parents who were then asked to put us in touch with their children. Second, more structured methods of research run the risk of over-simplifying people's stories and imposing order and meaning on lives that are 'more ambiguous, more problematic, and more chaotic in reality' (Faraday and Plummer 1979). Biographical methods provide a way of ensuring our analysis is grounded in people's lived experience. Third, our current lack of knowledge about the impact of parental disability on children (Buck and Hohmann 1983) calls for an exploratory approach. Biographical research, which offers a window into the private realm of everyday life, is perfectly fitted to the study of parenting and childrearing (Thompson 1981).

The depth interview was used as the primary method of collecting people's stories. The guiding purpose of the interviews was to produce first-person narrative accounts of people's childhoods, family lives and relationships that document their growing up and their passage into adulthood in experiential terms. An *aide mémoire* was used to provide a broad framework for the interviews (see, for example, Booth and Booth 1993) although as a rule the subject was encouraged to determine the course of the interview. Most people were seen on three occasions, for an average of ninety minutes each time. Interviews were tape recorded for transcription later. The first, introductory interview was used to get to know the informants (including their abilities as interviewees and their ways of communicating), clarify the purpose of the research and what was being asked of them, secure their consent, build up a picture of their lives in the here-and-now, and talk generally about who's who in their family. The second interview explored people's recollections and feelings about their own childhoods ranging over such topics as their knowledge of their parents' past, schooldays, family life and family crises, their perception of their parents, problems encountered as a child or adolescent (including experience of neglect or abuse), practical support their family received, time spent in care as a child, their role in the family (possibly as a primary or secondary carer), friendships and social activities, and the quality of their life as a child. Information obtained in the first interview was used to cue the informant although always the aim was to leave as much as possible of the telling of the story to the narrator. The third interview was used to return to any gaps, ask direct questions about missing details, and establish the informant's ownership of the story as told by going over it with them. A total of eight-two interviews were completed with thirty informants.

The adults who have taken part in the study have varied considerably in their capacity to reconstruct their childhood in words. Some were eloquent, others were chronically inarticulate. Lack of words alone was not an insuperable barrier to people telling their story (Booth and Booth 1996) nor was it always the reason for their reticence. Some people seemed to have scant memories of their childhood. Why this should be is not immediately apparent although Bruner (1987) provides a possible clue. He has suggested that story-telling provides recipes for structuring experience itself and for laying down routes into memory. The stories that constitute children's and young people's lives are usually told for them by others (Zimmerman and Dickerson 1994). They feature as the protagonist but someone else is the narrator. Autobiographical memories of childhood come from the sharing of such stories, primarily between parents and children. It seems likely that parents with learning difficulties engage in less 'memory talk' of this kind with their children so limiting what their children know about their own past. People who lack fully storied lives may not be able to access their own experience through memory or know they have a story to tell.

The focus group of adult children

The thirty informants (sixteen men and fourteen women) with whom interviews have been completed include fifteen people who themselves have learning difficulties (eight men and seven women). Their ages range from 18 to 42 years for the men and 16 to 37 years for the women with a median age for the group of 27 years: over half (57 per cent) were aged between 20 and 30. Eleven are either married or divorced, including three women with learning difficulties, of whom all but one have children of their own. The two mothers with learning difficulties have both had their children taken into care. Twenty-two people were unemployed at the time of interview (including all those with learning difficulties); six of the eight men without learning difficulties were in paid work. There were just three owner-occupiers in the group: twenty-two people lived in council accommodation and the remainder rented privately. Thirteen people were still living with their parents of whom nine had learning difficulties. Six people with learning difficulties were living independently in their own homes, all with some paid support.

Twenty-eight informants had just one parent with learning difficulties, usually (twenty-five cases) the mother. Although most (twenty-four) people's parents had been living together when they were born, only nine partnerships had survived death, divorce or separation. Twenty-three informants had a mother or father with learning difficulties who was still alive at the time of interview, of whom all but one remained in regular contact. Seven people did not regard themselves as being close to their parent with learning difficulties as a child, most of them women (six) without learning difficulties themselves (four). All the men without learning difficulties said they had been attached to their parent(s). Two women said their feelings towards their parents had changed as an adult and they had grown closer. Looking back over their childhoods, eighteen of the informants maintained they had been generally happy, although this figure dropped to eleven when people talked about their teenage years.

These facts aside, it was evident that the informants had in many ways experienced troubled lives. Ten people, including four with learning difficulties, had spent periods in care, during which four of them had made a determined effort to escape back home. Eleven people admitted to having truanted from school, including nine without learning difficulties, and fourteen said they had been bullied. Almost all informants (twenty-six) left school without qualifications. Twenty people reported that they or their families had been victimised within the community and made the butt of physical and verbal harassment and malicious gossip. Over half of the informants (sixteen), including ten women (six with learning difficulties), disclosed that they had been the victims of physical or sexual abuse. Some people may have chosen not to reveal the fact. In only one instance was the abuser reported to be a parent with learning difficulties. Five people accused their father without learning difficulties. Otherwise the perpetrator was named as a stepfather or stepmother, a brother or sister, or someone outside the family.

Five men and two women without learning difficulties, as well as four men with learning difficulties, had been in trouble with the police at some time. Three had been to prison. Ten people admitted to being violent, either as a youngster or an adult, and six said they had experienced mental health problems, including one woman who had suffered a nervous breakdown when her first child was taken away. Two people said they had attempted suicide, both more than once.

Domains of resilience

Rutter (1987) defines resilience as 'the positive pole of individual differences in people's response to stress and adversity'. It is not conceived as the absence of pathology but – as Devlieger shows with the Shona (see Chapter 3) – the ability to cope with lives filled with difficulty (Begun 1993; Poulsen 1993). Under high risk conditions, the resilient overcome where the vulnerable succumb (Werner 1989). Resilience is fostered or enhanced by protective factors which ameliorate an individual's response to risk (Mrazek and Mrazek 1987). This section sets out to isolate some of the protective factors in the lives of our subjects on the basis of their own narrative reconstruction of their experience as children and young adults.

Most research in this field has adopted a predictive approach, attempting to identify the protective factors leading to resilience in terms of cause-and-effect relationships between earlier events and later developments (Cohler 1987). By contrast, this study follows a narrative or interpretive approach that seeks to understand how people make sense of their past and how they reflect upon their own experience as the source of their vulnerability or resilience. These two approaches offer complementary rather than competing perspectives. The predictive approach runs the risk of over-simplifying people's lives and relationships in pursuit of statistically manageable data (Anthony 1987b). At the same time, little progress has been made in developing standardised instruments for measuring resilience (Cohler 1987). It also presupposes that lives unfold in a linear fashion and fails to allow for the way in which the changing meanings people give to past experiences shape their present efforts to cope under stress. The narrative approach, on the other hand, while putting lives in context, usually generates an unwieldy mass of data that does not lend itself to statistical interpretation or scientific control. However, as Cohler (1987) has observed, little is still known about the manner in which people reflect upon their own past in order 'to create a narrative that renders adversity coherent in terms of experienced life history'. In this paper we attempt to address this challenge by identifying the protective factors present in people's life stories that appear to have served as a counterweight to the risks inherent in their situation.

Existing research suggests that the protective factors shielding high-risk children fall into three interrelated domains: personal characteristics, family characteristics, and the characteristics of the individual's wider social environment and external support system. Werner (1989), for example, concludes that:

> Three types of protective factors emerge from our analyses of the developmental course of high-risk children from infancy to adulthood: 1) dispositional attributes of the individual, such as activity level and sociability, at least average intelligence, competence in communication skills (language, reading), and an internal locus of control; 2) affectional ties within the family that provide emotional support in times of stress, whether from a parent, sibling, spouse or mate; and 3) external support systems, whether in school, at work, or church, that reward the individual's competencies and determination, and provide a belief system by which to live.

We have used this same framework to analyse the content of our informants' narratives.

Personal protective factors

According to Rutter (1987), the available evidence suggests that 'it is protective to have a well established feeling of one's own worth as a person together with a confidence that one can cope successfully with life's challenges'. Three qualities appeared to be linked to the presence of such feelings in the personal narratives of the people in our study:

- *sociability* – as revealed through a friendly and personable disposition, good communication skills, conventional looks and manner, good physical and mental health, not having learning difficulties, a non-violent nature, and socially acceptable behaviour;
- *responsiveness to others* – as revealed through the capacity to maintain close and/or intimate relationships, expressions of love and feelings of responsibility for family members, and protectiveness towards the parent(s) with learning difficulties;
- *successful task accomplishment* – such as participation in voluntary activities, taking on responsibilities, having outside interests, being good at sports and, especially for people with learning difficulties, being able to read and write.

A few individual characteristics, not necessarily socially desirable, did not easily fit into this listing but, for some people, seemed to contribute to their resilience, including being rebellious, outspoken, independent-minded and ambitious.

The following vignette from Adam Lloyd's[3] story illustrates the part played by inner resources (especially, in Adam's case, the confidence that he could overcome his problems and sort out his life) in promoting resilience:

Adam Lloyd grew up in the family home with his mother, who has learning difficulties, and his grandparents. He was a much loved and wanted child. Although he slept in the same room as his mother, it was always his grandad who soothed him if he had a disturbed night. 'My mother used to tell me, "He'd go downstairs, sit in rocking chair, sing to you, and in five minutes you'd be gone"; and she says there were only him who could do it.' When Adam was 12, his grandfather died. He was devastated by his death. His behaviour at home became uncontrollable, and he refused to go to school. As Adam readily admits, 'I started getting out of hand.' Eventually he was put into a children's home, then another, followed by an adolescent unit, and finally, aged 18, he ended up in an open prison. While he was in the children's homes, his mother and grandmother used to ring every night at eight o'clock and visit every weekend. Losing him, he knew, 'broke their heart, aye.' In prison, Adam gave serious thought to his future. 'I thought, well, my grandma's getting old, my mother's getting old with worry and that . . . I thought, well I'm going to get out before owt happens to them . . . and I just quietened down. I thought, well, if I'd done that in first place I wouldn't have had to go in these different kids' homes like. When you get in these kids' homes, there's some in there who's in for robbery and all that, break-ins and that, and once you get mixed up with them, it all goes funny then.' He came home when he was 19 determined to make up for lost time. 'I blame myself.'

Protective mechanisms within the family

Resilient children 'are more likely to come from home environments characterized by warmth, affection, emotional support, and clear-cut and reasonable structures and limits. If parents are not able to provide this kind of positive climate, the presence of other family members can serve this function' (Brooks 1994). Similar factors were evident in the personal stories of adults in our study who spoke positively of their own childhoods, and tended to be missing in the narratives of those who did not. Three characteristics of the family and home environment in particular appeared to contribute to greater resilience in the face of risk:

- *warmth and mutuality* – as revealed by, for example, feelings of having been loved as a child, being a wanted child, experiencing fair and effective discipline, not being abused, and sharing holidays and other activities as a family;
- *stability* – as indicated by, for example, having two natural parents, one parent without learning difficulties, an absence of separations or the death of a close relative, and a parent or parents alive throughout childhood;
- *security* – as marked by, for example, having grandparents who live near,

having a supportive uncle or aunt at home, having a single parent but living in the same household with grandparents, having a large support-ive extended family, coming from a financially secure home and having parents who can manage money.

A vignette from the case stories illustrates how family supports can ensure security in the face of crisis and provide for the longer-term needs for closeness and stability:

Dennis Sutherland has learning difficulties and inherited cataracts. After he was born his mother's health deteriorated and she frequently had to spend long periods in hospital. Whenever she went into hospital Dennis and his sister would go to live with their maternal grandparents over the road. Their father, who has learning difficulties, would also stay there. Today Dennis is very close to his grandfather. He likes playing dominoes and draughts with him, and sees him every Saturday.

Protective social supports

A key feature nurturing resilience that has been noted in the literature is the presence of external supports that reinforce the child's and family's competence in coping under pressure (see also Devlieger's discussion of social embeddedness in Chapter 3). A close reading of our informants' life stories points to two aspects of the wider social environment that seem to be important as buffers against stress:

• *supportive relationships* – as shown, for example, by some combination of having a number of school friends, friends in the neighbourhood, helpful neighbours, a valued service worker, good institutional supports from agencies such as a school, church, health centre etc., and at least one supportive person outside the family.
• *participation and involvement* – as indicated by, for example, some combination of living in a small, tightly knit community, popping in to people's houses, holding and going to parties and celebrations, main-stream schooling, having a job or some sort of access to ordinary work-place opportunities, belonging to local clubs, such as the darts team, or being active in societies, like the bird-watchers, and organisations like the local church.

A vignette from Tracy Talbot's story illustrates Werner's (1989) observa-tion about the positive contribution that a school can make to the development of resiliency in high-risk children, as well as the importance of having a supportive relationship outside the family:

Tracy's father has learning difficulties and her mother is partially sighted. Tracy had enjoyed junior school, where she had a number of close friends, but she found the transition to senior school difficult. A shy child, she was bullied by other schoolchildren. At the age of 13 Tracy became pregnant. She was transferred to a small education unit for pregnant teenagers where she was taught mothercraft alongside her other studies. Tracy thrived in her new environment: 'I used to love that school. I picked up all my reading and everything from there.' Sadly, her daughter died when only a few hours old. When Tracy left school she was awarded, to her surprise, a CSE in child care: 'I couldn't believe it when certificate came through.' She had stayed with her boyfriend, the baby's father, and they married when she was 18. They are now the proud parents of three sons.

The protective factors outlined above may be missing for some people, or they may change over time, or they may be insufficient to buttress the individual against the pressures bearing on them. The balance between the stresses that heighten vulnerability and the protective factors that enhance resilience varies for different individuals and at different points in people's lives. Werner (1989), for example, notes that as disadvantage and the number of stressful life events accumulate so more protective factors are needed to ensure a positive outcome. Such a compensatory model of the interaction between resilience and risk (McIntyre et al. 1990) suggests that competence is maintained where the protective factors outweigh the risks and undermined where they do not. From this perspective, resilience, and for that matter competence, is better viewed as a process determined by the impact of an individual's life experiences than as a fixed attribute of the person. The next section focuses on the personal narratives of two people in our study in order to show this process at work in the context of people's lives.

Resilience and the life course

The following two narratives have been selected from the stories of informants in the study to represent the two ends of the continuum from vulnerability to resilience, and to show that people's destiny is not fixed by having a mother (or father) with learning difficulties.

A vulnerable life: Chris Sutton's story

Chris Sutton is 26 years old. When first interviewed Chris was living in a tenth floor council flat on the outskirts of a large city. Most days he would visit his parents who lived two bus journeys away. By the third interview he had moved in with them and his disabled sister, Kerry, owing to the sudden onset of a paralysis in his right arm. His parents live in a three-bedroomed house on a council estate in a small town. They have lived there happily for the past ten years although both of them are

Risk Factors/
Protective
Factors

Still close to family

Ill-health

beginning to find the steep hills a problem. Mr and Mrs Sutton divorced eighteen years ago and Chris and Kerry spent most of their lives with their mother who has learning difficulties. Mr and Mrs Sutton re-married last year. They also have an elder daughter, Jane, who is married and lives away. *Break-up of parents' marriage*

Mother with learning difficulties

The family is only friendly with two people in the neighbourhood: one of whom is out all day and the other does child-minding. To some extent Kerry's disability has disabled the whole family. They can't and won't go out and leave her alone and she is unable to walk far. They have no car but they are on the telephone. *Social isolation*

Disabled sibling

Lack of mobility

Chris is slim, with longish fair hair combed forward over his forehead. He has a curved spine and a disability in his right shoulder and arm. Dressed in jeans and a dark jumper, he is easy going, polite and friendly. Although unemployed at present, he has had various part-time jobs as a cleaner. He is a sensitive and caring person and helps his mother regularly with the shopping. He sometimes also does the washing, hoovering and cleaning for her. *Looks different*

Responsive to others

Sense of duty

Chris was only six years old when his mother and father separated. 'Mostly', he says, 'it were gambling and drinking that my mum and dad split up for.' He remembers his parents arguing a lot too and how his mother once hit his father over the head with a frying pan and threatened him with a meat cleaver. *Chronic family discord*

Much of Chris's childhood was clouded by violence and fear. Local children would abuse him physically and verbally in the street and at school: 'Oh they were kicking me, pulling my hair, cutting my hair . . . .Well, there were a kid and he put me through school railings . . . I mean I once got my clothes all chucked into shower and I had to go home in absolute complete wet clothes.' He was also physically attacked by his older sister who has since gone on to abuse her own five children, three of whom are now in care. *Victimisation*

Sibling with behaviour problem

Mrs Sutton recalled having lived in places where their lives were turned into a nightmare by local teenagers who used to pinch the washing off the line, bang on the windows and doors, shout abuse, and push fireworks through the letterbox. 'I got police but police wouldn't *Constant harassment* do nowt.' One night Chris had his nose broken by a gang of youths. Even after they moved house, 'all of a sudden these gangs of teenagers started on us for no apparent reason'. His mother eventually had a nervous breakdown.

Parental mental ill-health

Mrs Sutton and her three children moved house seven times, mainly in a vain attempt to escape the constant victimisation. The one place they really liked they couldn't afford: 'It were a lovely place that, it were just bills all the time because it were all electric.' All his childhood Chris recalls the family having difficulty managing on their low income. They finally moved to their present house and for ten years have felt safe.

Frequent changes of residence

Poverty

Chris began his education at a mainstream school but at the age of 7 he was transferred to a special school because of his behaviour. By the time he was 13, he was under a psychiatrist and attending a special psychiatric unit.

Segregated schooling/ separated from peers

Chris's mental health problems began when he started eating an excessive number of chocolate bars. He became 'disturbed and overactive with fits and violent outbursts'. He was given a brain scan and a body scan. 'I were breaking things, putting table upside down, barricading doors, doing all sorts . . . I spent four months in there having different tests and that, having different fluids taken out of me.' As he now quietly reflects, 'If we'd known it were Mars bars we could have stopped that years ago.' Even so he felt content in the unit and became quite attached to one of the nurses while he was there.

Mental health problems

Chris remained overactive and was given sleeping tablets as he got older. He is no longer prescribed these tablets as he once overdosed after his uncle had died. Since then he has tried other ways to kill himself by 'jumping off a bridge, trying to chuck myself in front of cars, trying to cut my wrists'. 'It's mostly with depression . . . because I get that low and I get that fed up.'

Depression

He disliked school mainly because of the bullying he endured throughout his time there. He had problems with reading and writing and found his teachers unhelpful. He left at 15. On his last day he punched a female teacher who had tried to stop him leaving. This action,

Lack of achievement/ No support from teachers

he felt, had prevented him being accepted at a further education college. He subsequently drifted into a variety of part-time jobs interspersed by long periods of unemployment.

Sporadic employment

His mother and father had started their married life with Mr Sutton's parents where they lived until after their first child was born. Both sets of grandparents were alive at this time and lived close to one another. There were also numerous uncles and aunts. However, within a few years of moving out into their own home, the marriage had ended. Chris remembers how he and Kerry took the news. 'I know she cried when they splitted up. Me, I wouldn't talk. I wouldn't do owt, you know. I used to get a fork and stick it into my belly button. . . . When they split up it seemed weird. Because, I mean, they weren't there arguing. There were only my mum there. It just seemed to be one empty shell.'

Additional caretakers

Availability of kin

Low self-worth

Father absent

Insecurity

After Chris's father left, his mother received no maintenance money and very little help with the three children. Chris did as much as he could from a very early age, washing the pots, cleaning and even doing the washing. He also helped look after Kerry, and still does. Once a year they would go to Skegness and stay in their grandparents' caravan. Chris enjoyed these times. Looking back, he never felt he had missed out on anything as a child. He thinks he was mostly happy.

Lack of support for family

Other-regarding

Family togetherness

Positive outlook

Chris moved out of the family home when he was 17, and for a while lived in a hostel for homeless young people. 'I were wanting my own space you know. But I felt really homesick for the first two months.' For the next five years he had a bedsit, and then a flat next door to a drug dealer. He left this flat to move back home. Chris feels he has always had a close relationship with his mother and recalls being cuddled by her, although that has stopped since he became an adult. He sees his dad differently, 'I mean I've never considered him as a dad. It's a bit of a relief for him to come back into the family. It's like him taking over, giving me a rest point. I mean what makes my mum happy, that's all right to me.'

Self-sufficient

Poor environment

Close affectional ties

Positive mother–child relationship

When the children were small the family had received help from the paternal grandparents who had looked after the eldest daughter, Jane, for a few years, and also

Practical support from extended family

helped them out financially. Otherwise there had been little support from elsewhere. A social worker had been attached to the family after Kerry was born but Chris feels they 'had not done owt. . . .it's just a waste of time.'

Service worker not valued

His happiest memory as a child is playing with a gang of local children: 'Playing cowboys and indians . . . . going all round back fields. . . . We used to go down to shops with a bit of spending money . . . and buy some sweets.' He was good at athletics; it was one of the only things he liked doing at school. 'I were one of top runners in our school.' He had a few close friends as a child but none as a teenager and he has made no friends since he left school. No one ever came round his house to play.

Loss of friendships and peer relationships as adult

Chris thinks of himself as being very close to his extended family: 'Oh yes, we're very close, yes. We've all got us own way of getting in touch with each other.' But the extent of contact is limited: 'Well, we do see them now and again in town. . . . We don't actually visit them, or owt like that, because it'd be a bit too much because there's that many of us.' Nobody comes to visit them.

Emotional ties with extended family

but

weak contiguous bonds

Chris has mixed thoughts about his future. Sometimes he wishes he could move south and start a new life. At other times he is haunted by a recurring dream of his own funeral. He believes he will be dead by the time he is 33.

A month after the last interview, Chris suffered what turned out to be his second stroke. The first had gone undiagnosed by his GP. He is totally paralysed down one side and both his speech and mental ability have been affected. He is sleeping downstairs at his parents' house. With his father too ill to help, the job of looking after Chris and Kerry, who has to be taken to the toilet and is still incontinent at times, now falls entirely on their mother. They are waiting to be rehoused but have been told this could take at least six months.

Lack of institutional supports for family in crisis

A resilient life: Martin Riddick's story

Martin Riddick is 42 years old. He lives in a one-bedroomed flat owned by a housing association with his elder son, Graham, aged 16. Graham has laid claim to

Risk Factors/ Protective Factors

Own home

the bedroom, while his dad sleeps on the settee. Martin is looking to buy his own house. He works shifts as a support worker for a community health project for people with learning difficulties and also does other work in his trade as a roofer. Since leaving school he has tried his hand at a variety of jobs including work as a hotel porter and voluntary work with a young man who has Down's Syndrome. His younger son, Christopher, aged 10, still lives with Martin's ex-wife who is now remarried.

Regular employment

Marriage breakdown

Martin is short and slight with longish dark hair greying at the sides. He speaks in a quiet voice and his manner is open and hospitable. His marriage ended seven years ago and for the last three years he has been friendly with a woman who herself has been married before and has children of her own.

Conventional appearance

New stable relationship

As a small child Martin lived with his mother, who had learning difficulties, and his father at his maternal grandparents' house. 'I think the reason why they got married is the fact that I think I was on the way. In them days it was the done thing.' Also living with the grandparents were his mum's brother, who remained there all his life, and his mum's younger sister and her husband. His mum also had another married sister. Martin's two brothers were born after his parents were allocated their own house.

Mother with learning difficulties

Tightly knit extended family

Plenty of attention in infancy

Eldest child

His father had held a number of regular jobs. After he left the army he worked in the steel industry, before becoming a long-distance lorry driver and later a bus driver. His mum too had worked even after Martin was born: first as a buffer in a cutlery firm, and then in a sweet factory. They had met one night at a public dance in the town hall. His father had attended Catholic schools but his mum went to special school. Unlike other families in their neighbourhood, the Riddicks had owned a car when Martin was young, although they were not on the phone.

Financially-secure early childhood

Mother in steady employment

Mobile and relatively well-off

Martin had enjoyed life at home with his grandparents and at his first school. It was when his parents moved into their own house that things became more difficult. Martin was 8 and his brother, Keith, was 2 when the family moved to the other side of the city. Four years

Happy start to life

Loss of additional carers

later a third brother, Damien, was born. From this time onwards things started to become strained at home. 'I know that my dad had had affairs because I know that I've got another half-sister who's probably a few months younger than me that lives in Liverpool.' His mum and dad would argue quite a bit and occasionally they would separate only to be reunited soon after. 'Sometimes it got really bad and my middle brother, Keith, he were starting to be very nervous.' When Martin was about 14 his parents split up for good and were divorced. 'Knowing that it weren't going to get better, it was probably the best. But saying that, it didn't help the fact that my mum were like she were, it didn't help me, Keith and Damien.' His dad disappeared out of the area for a few years and it was only later that Martin learned he had gone to live with another woman. The two of them later married and had two girls, Martin's half-sisters.

Martin's mother was devastated by the break-up of her marriage and, seeking comfort, she took up with a series of men. The neighbours began to gossip. Martin heard the talk 'not so much through them but by people at school who were their sons and daughters. I didn't like that.' Martin also did a lot of babysitting at this time when his mum wanted to go out with a boyfriend. 'I always tried to get on with them for my mum's sake. I knew that she were lonely.' These relationships affected Martin and his brothers greatly. He would occasionally confront her. 'I'd say, it's not fair for us, people gossipping. And that would probably cause friction between me and my mum.' At one point she really let herself go and ended up having a nervous breakdown. She was admitted to a long-stay psychiatric hospital where she remained for a year while Martin and his brothers went to live with their grandparents. 'We never visited my mum while she were in hospital because it used to upset her. . . . or, as my grandma said, it would upset her when we were leaving. Because when they fetched her it were a real struggle to get her in the ambulance, to take her away.'

Martin's mother received no maintenance from his father and the family suffered as a result. 'I found that when my dad did leave and money were short, my mum

Margin notes:

Children spaced apart

Family discord

Parents' divorce

Positive outlook

Loss of contact with father

Emotional insecurity

Sensitive to other's needs

Sense of responsibility

Parental mental illness and separation

Additional caretakers besides mother

Financial hardship

got help to buy uniform but, like, when it wore out, we had to buy things probably what didn't quite fit and I found then I started getting noticed, like, because I looked a bit untidy. So from 14, my last two years were a nightmare because I were getting picked on, bullied in some cases, getting into trouble, getting into fights. So it's like the only way out, to stop them talking, is probably giving someone a smack, which obviously isn't the right way of doing it, as you find out. It just gets you into trouble, it pushes you further away from neighbours. Probably the ideal system would be to have gone up and said, look, you know the situation my mum's in, do you mind not talking about it.'

Victimisation

Maturity through self-knowledge

From the age of 5 until he was 15, Martin spent every weekend with his grandparents. It was here that his close friends lived. His dearest memories are of his childhood Saturdays. They always followed the same pattern: 'Saturday was always a good time. Pictures in the morning, came home from pictures, had my dinner, then from pictures played with my mates all day and then we all went to the football match. At night, we'd come home from football match, had us tea and we used to go to pub with my grandma and grandad and my Auntie Doris. I used to sit in the corridor on a bench with some pop and a bag of crisps. It made my day.'

Close relationship with adult outside the home providing security and stability

Strong peer friendships

Martin attended three schools in his life but only suffered trouble and unhappiness at the senior school. He missed a lot of time at school by pretending to be poorly. Apart from being the butt of cruel remarks about his mother and their poverty, Martin had dyslexia. His difficulties went unrecognised by his teachers and he struggled with his lessons and failed his 'O' levels. Dyslexia was only diagnosed later on in life when he went back to college to take some GCSEs, successfully passing in maths, English, sociology and law. He says he still enjoyed some aspects of his schooldays mainly because he was good at sport, especially football and swimming.

Poor school attendance

Specific learning difficulties

Sense of self-efficacy and self-esteem

It was after his father left that Martin became aware of the extent of his mother's learning difficulties. 'We never really had to think about mum because my dad did it all anyway. I suppose we did know, but it never really dawned on us how it would affect the family if anything happened to my dad.'

His dad had even prepared meals before he went off to work ready for when the boys came home from school. Martin's mum couldn't read letters, notes from school or claims for rent arrears and she found managing the domestic budget an almost impossible task. Martin gradually assumed more and more responsibility for running the house. When she received her benefits the family would dine 'like princes' on chops and steak for a few days until the money ran out when it would be jam or dripping sandwiches or meat paste.

Loss of principal caregiver

Parent with learning difficulties left on own

Advanced self-help skills

Martin and his brothers decided they would have to do something about the situation. 'We've always been close, me and my brothers. It weren't like, "I'm taking over so you do what I say." It were like, best work together. They were really supportive.' Martin always talked things over with his brothers and then presented their suggestions to their mother. They would go shopping with her and advise on what foodstuffs to choose, suggesting cheaper meats like sausage and liver.

Shared values – sense of togetherness

'When my dad first left I probably felt, like, I'm man of house now and I probably felt I were getting a bit clever. But, I think, once I saw how it affected my mum and how it upset her . . . then my aunties said, look, man of house don't need to be going off like you are doing, get to grips. And then I realised that I were getting bad, and I thought, yes, you're not helping situation at all. I think from that time on, it were a case of we'll all pull together. So we did like grow up very quick.'

Matured through self-knowledge

Internal locus of control

When Mrs Riddick decided they should move nearer to her own parents, Martin's grandmother and two aunties provided the extra support the family needed. 'It's about ten minutes walk to any of relatives. They'd help out best they could.' His mum also knew quite a few of the neighbours 'who weren't just talking (they) were helping out a lot'. The only formal support the family received was a bundle of second-hand toys delivered by social services at Christmas.

Availability of kin

Support from neighbours

Lack of formal support

Discipline in Martin's life was fairly strict. His mum and dad would keep him in check with a swift slap on the arm and his aunties would slap him on the legs.

Fair and effective discipline

Sometimes 'if I'd been a bit clever and my dad had been on nights, I remember getting a few real hidings from him'. But afterwards 'it used to be all apologies'. Occasionally he would be kept in or sent to his bedroom. His teachers at school were much more brutal. Punishment for lateness was a detention, but for bad work or behaviour it could be a ruler across the knuckles, a slipper on the bottom (once when he was only wearing swimming trunks) or the cane on both hands. He was once slapped across the face for poor work although he now knows the problem was his dyslexia. 'What made it more painful, it were by a teacher what I really liked.' Martin, however, was treated no differently to the rest of his classmates. 'You weren't one of the boys unless you got it. If you got caught then you got a punishment. If you didn't get caught, you got away with it. It was just something you accepted really.'

Martin has only once been in trouble with the police. 'Went down town with some friends and something happened and then these lads saw me following day at the football match and it turned into a bit of a fight like. We both got arrested. I got fined £70 and a suspended sentence for twelve months on good behaviour. I got more of a reaction from my grandma and my aunties than I did from my mum. It were a case of, "What you doing, you're not like this, look at shame you're bringing your dad and your mum." It made me feel right tiny.'

Martin left school at 15 and went straight into a job. For the first time in his life, he was able to buy the clothes he wanted, and sometimes for Keith too. 'I'm not making out to be good like, but occasionally you could say, "Well I know what I went through, I'll get you a pair of trousers."' He never resented having to help Keith out: 'What I would have resented more is kids giving Keith a hard time at school.'

Martin always had close friends at school but he never invited anyone back to his house because of the sad state of the old furniture and the general untidiness. 'I didn't really want them to see it because my mum weren't a great person to keep the house tidy.' He never blamed his mother though 'because I knew it weren't down to her, I knew that she'd tried everything in her power to make

Structure and rules in household

Positive attitude to authority

Strong moral guidance and authority

No period of unemployment after leaving school

Financial independence

Responsive to others

Strong sense of loyalty and protectiveness towards mother

everything all right.' Today Martin feels, 'We've all come out of it probably better for it, me, Keith and Damien. Probably responsibility were there at an early age. Where if the money were there you'd probably think, can I have this and they'd probably let us have it. I know what it's like not to have it. So you're more responsible with your money and probably more tolerant with people that are just down on their luck.'

Positive self-concept

During his late teens his mother finally settled down with a new partner, although she never re-married. Martin's current relationship brings to mind his own feelings at that time. 'Looking back on my mum, I can imagine what my girlfriend's youngest must be thinking. And it did actually come back . . . now how should I handle this? So I had to really think hard about trying to get a friendship with her.'

Matured through experience

When he was 21, Martin left with some friends to find work in the south of England. Here he eventually met his wife and settled. When their marriage ran into difficulties, they returned to his home town to try and sort things out. Finally they parted and his wife moved back down south.

Marriage break-up

'I think I've always been lucky and I've always been able to make friends very easy. Probably the hardest time was when my marriage split up and I moved back. Where before you could always call on your friends – because they were single – to go for a pint, now it were a case of, well he's married, he doesn't live here no more and, like, you thought, I'm actually stuck for the first time. It were a case of making friends all over again really . . . nightschool, getting involved in squash and badminton, getting involved in different activities.'

Sociable

Positive social orientation

He decided to improve his education. 'If I were reading out loud, it were embarrassing more than anything else. And my spelling, I couldn't spell quite simple words. I still do roofing but I just didn't feel like doing just that for the rest of my life, and to get into what I wanted to do I knew that I couldn't do it unless I put myself out to get some qualifications behind me.' He is now reaping the rewards of that hard work and likes nothing better than 'helping people with learning difficulties to make a bit of life for themselves'.

Motivated to improve himself

Personally ambitious

Understanding of others

Martin has always felt close to his mother. 'I always loved my mum, especially when my dad left. I loved her more, well if you can love more, because she were really pining after my dad and you just wanted to hold her and say, "It's all right".' She would hug and kiss him as a child, while his father would occasionally put his arm round his shoulder. He knew his father loved him by how he talked to him and by the way he would sit on his bed at night and relate stories of his days in the army. 'He showed his affection by laughing and joking a lot.' After the break up of his parents' marriage, he grew distant from his father and didn't see him for a few years. Five years ago his mother died suddenly at the age of 62. Today he still calls round to see his father and stepmother, and enjoys the company of his half-sisters, but he is not close to his father. 'The real people in my life was, like, my mum, my two brothers, and my grandma and grandad and my aunties. I still loved him but not in a close way.

'Sounds a bit rotten but I think we've always been closer to my grandma. I know I have. I think we all have. Because, like, she were always there when we needed her. So when my mum did go into hospital, my grandma and aunties were still there. I think if we were taken away and put into care it would probably be a different story altogether. But the fact that we were living with people we loved, it didn't change a great deal. Yes, I loved my mum to death but, you know, my grandma were like the matriarch of family.

'Sometimes I think no, it weren't a happy time, especially at school. But in general, I can think of a lot more people having a worse time. It weren't like getting beatings or, you know. In general, I don't think I fared too bad. I did have a happy childhood.'

Positive mother–child relationship

Close affectional ties in early childhood

Renewal of family bonds in adult life

Mother-substitute available when needed

Secure emotional foundation

Positive attitude to life

Chris Sutton and Martin Riddick have much in common. They both come from families where the parents' marriage broke up leaving a mother with learning difficulties to cope on her own with three children. Their early lives were marked by poverty, under-achievement at school, lack of support from the services and their mothers' breakdown under the strain. On the positive side, they both had a father without learning difficulties with whom they maintained contact in later life, a close and protective relationship with their mother, a strong sense of responsibility for the family, and supportive grandparents. At this point, however, the similarities in their stories end. Where Chris is now back living at home with his parents, unemployed, disabled, lonely, depressed and suicidal, Martin is a family man, with his own home, in regular work, full of ambitions and well-integrated in the local community. Coming from much the same background their lives have taken a very different course. Looked at through the framework presented above, their stories show how the balance between risk and protective factors helped to shape these outcomes. Table 4.1 highlights some of the key biographical experiences contributing to the differences in their resilience.

The wider significance of this analysis of two personal narratives is to show how resilience (in the face of risk) and competence (in dealing with the pressures and challenges of living) are not merely natural endowments but are socially constructed in the context of people's lives and experience.

Conclusions

Parental competence is frequently equated with parentcraft: good-enough parents are endowed with the skills required to meet their child's developmental needs, inadequate parents lack these skills. By this reasoning, (in)competence is located as a characteristic of the parent which can be assessed in terms of the child's developmental progress.

This chapter has shown that no such simple link between parenting skills and child outcomes can be assumed. How children turn out depends on more than just their parents. The notion of resilience as a compensatory factor shielding children from the potentially damaging effects of parenting deficits calls for a reappraisal of the meaning of parental (in)competence itself.

Resilience is not a childhood given but 'a capacity that develops over time in the context of a supportive environment' (Egeland *et al.* 1993). From this point of view, it reflects the strength of a person's support system. Similarly, parental competence may be seen as a distributed feature of the parents' social network (see also Reynolds Whyte on the importance of 'belonging' in Chapter 7). The notion of 'distributed competence' attests to the fact that parenting is mostly a shared activity and acknowledges the interdependencies that comprise the parenting task. Chris Sutton's situation has not come about as a result of his mother having learning difficulties. Martin Riddick has made a very different life for himself while coming from a similar background. What distinguishes them is the balance of risk and protective factors within their wider social

Table 4.1

Dimensions of resilience/protective factors	Chris Sutton	Martin Riddick
Personal protective factors:		
Sociability	Unconventional looks, poor mental health and disability, past record of violent behaviour	Good communication skills, capacity to make and maintain friendships, positive social orientation
Responsiveness	No close relationships outside family, low self-esteem	Wide network of relationships (including two children of his own), matured through experience
Task accomplishment	Few achievements aside from being good at sport at school	Leading an independent life with a home of his own, successful return to further education, desire to improve himself, active hobbies
Family factors:		
Warmth and mutuality	Physically abused by elder sister, only a year between each of the children	Children spaced six years apart, brothers close to each other
Stability	Parents split up when he was aged 6, left home at 17 to live in hostel for homeless	Parents didn't split up until he was aged 14, continuity provided by matriarchal grandmother
Security	Repeated changes of residence, financial hardship throughout childhood, persistent victimisation, younger sister admitted to care	Family comfortably off until father left home, strong sense of place during childhood, lived with grandparents as an infant and again during mother's spell in psychiatric hospital
Social supports:		
Supportive relationships	Lonely and isolated	Longstanding peer friendships as youngster and adolescent, socially engaged as adult
Participation and involvement	Segregated schooling, irregular employment, few contacts in local community	Mainstream schooling, regular employment, range of outside interests and voluntary activities

environment that have influenced their capacity to cope with the challenges and adversities of their upbringing.

Just as resilience is better understood as a feature of the life course
than an attribute of the person so competence, too, is better viewed as a
process rather than a skill. If parental competence is resourced by the
family's social network, it is also vulnerable to changes over time in these

relationships. The birth of another child, the death of a grandparent, a change of school, the departure of a valued social worker, the separation of parents, the onset of unemployment or the like may all affect the capacity of the family and social network to support or sustain parents in their parenting. Both Chris Sutton's and Martin Riddick's parents encountered new problems after moving into their own house, and these became more serious when their parents subsequently parted leaving their mothers to manage on their own. In Martin's case these difficulties eased when his mother decided to move closer to her own parents. Parental competence, then, is not a fixed ability. It is crucially related to the way people live and can only be understood or assessed in the context of their lives.

Research has shown how resilient children play an active part in influencing the course of their own development. Cohler (1987), for instance, comments on how the more resilient children of psychiatrically ill parents make better use of other adults as substitutes for their emotionally unavailable parents than their less resilient counterparts. In such ways, children's coping strategies bear directly on the competence of their parent(s). As a lonely and isolated child, Chris Sutton could not cope with the troubles in his life and sank into depression. Martin Riddick, on the other hand, an altogether more outgoing and sociable lad, found an outlet through his peers. The protective factors that foster resilience in children also help to support parents in their parenting, just as their absence heightens the vulnerability of children under stress so making the parenting task even more difficult. When Martin became aware of the extent of his mother's learning difficulties after his father left home, he assumed greater responsibility for the running of the house in order to sustain his mother in her role. Significantly, until then, his mother's limitations had not registered with him. Parenting is thus not a one-way process. As Rutter (1974) has observed, parents 'help to shape their children's development but also children help shape their parent's behaviour'. The study of resilience suggests that parental (in)competence is the outcome of this sort of ongoing, everyday interaction.

Competence, like resilience, is a negotiated activity bounded by the rules and understandings that regulate family life. Chris Sutton, for example, saw himself as part of a close extended family, but these rules meant that he had only limited contact with his relatives, other than his grandparents, and derived little from them in the way of support. By contrast, Martin Riddick's aunties were sanctioned to play an active part in his upbringing, providing discipline, moral guidance, emotional security and practical support. For both Chris and Martin, the social organisation of family life had a crucial impact on their experience of growing up and on their parents' capacity to respond to their changing needs.

Parents with learning difficulties are commonly seen as lacking mastery of the skills required to ensure the well-being and development of their children. Our research challenges such a summary judgement by showing that child outcomes cannot be predicted on the basis of their parents' label alone. Some children, like Martin Riddick, become well-adjusted adults who make their own way in society and bring up families of their own. Others, like Chris Sutton, are corralled into a melancholic and shrivelled existence. Understanding their stories means looking beyond the capacities and limitations of their parents. In each case, factors over and above the skills of their parents influenced their resilience or vulnerability. This mix of risk and protective factors not only helps to shape what life holds for children as they grow into adulthood but also defines the limits of parental competence.

Notes

1 The study has been funded by a grant from the Joseph Rowntree Foundation.
2 'For us, it is difficult to find grown persons, the daughter or son of mentally retarded persons, who wanted to speak to us' (personal communication, Ursula Pix-Kettner, University of Bremen).
3 Pseudonyms are used throughout when referring to people in the study.

5 Constructing other selves: (in)competences and the category of learning difficulties

Charlotte Aull Davies

The Western medico-psychological model of learning difficulties assumes that intellectual incompetences are basic to this classification. However, on closer examination, the category of people with learning difficulties is so heterogeneous, as regards the competences of its members, how they perceive themselves and how they are regarded by others, as to appear to have no genuine basis of cohesion, certainly not in specifiable intellectual abilities and disabilities. This raises the question of whether there are other reasons for their categorisation in this manner.

This question can initially be addressed by considering how categorisation as someone with learning difficulties affects other social identities, in particular the achievement of social adulthood. The various difficulties that people with learning difficulties face in acquiring implicit recognition as adults in Western society, many of which are only marginally related to intellectual incompetences, raise questions about the relationship of these two social identities: learning difficulties and adulthood. There are very great differences between these two identities both in the ways in which they affect the lives of young adults with learning difficulties and the manner in which they are discussed and understood by people with learning difficulties and those close to them. Among the group of young people with learning difficulties whom I came to know in the course of research on their transition to adulthood, most claimed that they were indeed adults. They and their parents participated in a discourse about their adulthood which originated in a normalising philosophy of care promulgated mainly by the social services. However, their claims to adulthood were made on the flimsiest of evidence and often unsupported by parental opinion; nor did such claims result in substantial changes in their lives in terms of the acquisition of many of the widely accepted markers of social adulthood. In contrast, learning difficulties as a social identity had a major impact on their daily lives and future prospects. Yet only a handful had ever discussed it with their parents, the vast majority of whom nevertheless regarded it as the central determinative feature of their daughter's or son's life. There was a discourse about learning difficulties in the social services, mainly revolving around non-stigmatising terminology. But few of these young people participated in that discourse. Neither did they understand the commonly used terms for learning difficulties nor associate that identity with themselves, at least not at the level of discourse.

These contrasting relationships with two major social identities suggest an alternative cultural basis for the classification of people with learning difficulties, one which may be found in Western conceptions of the self and the nature of personhood. People with learning difficulties challenge Western conceptions of an autonomous and reflective individual self and for this reason may be seen as threatening to basic cultural assumptions. Such a threat is managed in the first instance by categorising and marginalising people with learning difficulties. But it may also be addressed, as in the discourse about adulthood, by trying to provide them with behavioural characteristics which make their self-presentation more consistent with Western cultural expectations. Such a programme has its pitfalls in that success in producing behaviour that projects the reflexiveness of the Western model of individual selfhood may simultaneously undermine individual autonomy.

Some of the parents and carers of the young people I worked with seemed to be taking a different route to the assertion of these young people's personhood, one which essentially rejected the Western cultural model of the self and constructed an alternative based more on a nexus of social relationships than on any concept of an internal private self. In this endeavour, they shared similar approaches to those that have been found among carers and close relatives of people with Alzheimer's disease, and they appeared to be working with concepts of personhood which had much in common with those that have been reported for many non-Western societies.

The research

I spent approximately eighteen months, from March 1990 to October 1991, in the field working with young people with learning difficulties and their parents and other carers in West Glamorgan, South Wales.[1] The focus of the research was upon these young people's experience of their transition to adulthood. In considering this transition, from the perspectives of the young people and their parents and carers, I was concerned with a complex of social identities, such as social class and gender, as well as social adulthood. It quickly became apparent that their social identity as someone with learning difficulties was affecting all of these others, while still remaining unclear or invisible to the vast majority of the young people themselves. Thus one unanticipated aspect of the research was to explore their and their parents' engagement with this social identity.

Sixty young people, and the parents or carers of fifty-six of them, participated in the study. The process of locating them revealed another problematic aspect of the category with which the research dealt. I initially contacted young people through various day centres and special needs units at local colleges. However, it was also felt that it would be desirable to interview some young people in this category who were not in receipt of services. Although it was possible to conceive of such a category, the practical difficulty of locating such people proved to be very great indeed. Upon reflection it seemed that assuming such people exist implies an ontological status for the category 'learning difficulties' which may be quite unjustifiable. Thus in the end all the young people I worked with were in receipt of some sort of service earmarked for people with learning difficulties, although the nature of such services varied widely.

The research was a combination of semi-structured interviews and participant observation. Each young person was interviewed several times, with the series extending over several weeks or months. The interviews were based on a questionnaire, but only as a memory aid for the interviewer. The order and wording of questions were varied to fit the circumstances and allow for clarification. Interviewees were encouraged to expand on a point, digress or introduce other topics. The interviews were supplemented by participant observation at the various research sites. In a few cases, with people who had very poor communication skills, this was the major source of data; it was an important supplementary source with nearly everyone. Participant observation and most interviews took place at day centres (Adult Training Centres; special needs units in local colleges; other day centres such as training houses and patch-based centres). A few interviews were carried out in other locations, for example, a workplace, café, club and residential centre. The young people were always interviewed prior to their parents or carers. The interviews with parents took place in their homes, usually in a single session lasting from one to four hours, and were also semi-structured.

The sample was not constructed as a probability sample but it did have a relatively equal distribution by gender and class. It was also selected so as to include individuals from a variety of types of day centres plus a few who were not attending any such centre. I deliberately did not select people on the basis of their intellectual abilities or communication skills. Instead, at each site, I contacted and invited to participate all individuals within the age range of 18–26. Because of the requests of several individuals to participate in the study, I eventually extended the range slightly to include one young man of 17 and another man and a woman who were 27 and 28, respectively. In the excerpts from interviews which follow, . . . indicates a longer than usual pause, . . . //. . . material omitted.

Deconstructing the category

The treatment of people with learning difficulties has been substantially de-medicalised over the past two decades. Drawing on an ideology of normalisation (Wolfensberger 1972), public policies have moved both users and providers of services out of large institutions into the community. Such relocation typically has been from hospitals, run by medical personnel, to smaller group homes, supervised by the social services. However, the process of identifying people with learning difficulties has been largely unaffected by this change in treatment, although the labels used to identify them have altered. (Thus, in education, 'special needs' replaced ESN, and the social services began to use 'learning disabilities' or 'learning difficulties' in preference to 'mental handicap'.)

There is a degree of consensus concerning the definition of learning difficulties, at least among those primarily involved in the labelling process. Learning difficulties entail both considerably below average intellectual functioning (practically taken to be an IQ below 70) and some adaptive behavioural problems. Furthermore, these indicators must be manifest during the developmental period; that is, the label of learning difficulties must be assigned prior to an individual's reaching chronological adulthood (Zigler and Hodapp 1986: 10–11).

An individual may be labelled as having learning difficulties while still an infant or as a very young child. In these cases, the labelling is done by a member of the medical profession who usually has been able to identify a specific organic cause for observed physiological and developmental abnormalities. There are known organic causes for approximately one-quarter of the cases of learning difficulties (Zigler and Hodapp 1986: 86–7). For the majority of people with learning difficulties, the labelling process does not occur until later childhood, with the greatest proportion being so identified between the ages of 10 and 14. For these individuals, diagnosis is usually made by clinical psychologists after referral for testing due to problems in school. Such problems nearly always involve perceived behavioural maladjustment in addition to apparent intellectual deficiencies (Squibb 1981; Tomlinson 1981). Persons having learning difficulties that can be attributed to known organic causes are fairly evenly distributed across social classes and ethnic divisions. But the remainder, the vast majority of people with learning difficulties, are disproportionately present in the lower socio-economic classes and in certain ethnic groups (Mercer 1973; Tomlinson 1982: 106–33). In Britain, for example, Afro-

Caribbeans are over-represented among people with learning difficulties, while Jews are under-represented.

There are several points worth noting regarding this process of labelling people with learning difficulties. First, learning difficulties as a social identity is virtually entirely determined by others; the individuals who receive it neither seek it nor participate in defining it. Second, it is assigned to a child by adults. Thus, the differential in power and authority between those doing the labelling and those being labelled is maximised. The possibility of children under diagnosis successfully negotiating a more acceptable social identity is small indeed. Nevertheless, some parents with sufficient knowledge, confidence and determination may occasionally do so on behalf of their child, and this is doubtless one factor in the uneven distribution of people with learning difficulties across class and ethnic groups. A third point regarding this labelling is that it initiates a process of socialisation of the individual into a particularly comprehensive social identity. Furthermore, in comparison to other powerful social identities, such as class, race, ethnicity or gender, socialisation into the identity of a person with learning difficulties is carried out to a much greater extent by people who do not share in that identity. Thus, its meanings and expected behaviours are constructed externally to the category of people who embody and exhibit them (Angrosino, this volume; Bogdan and Taylor, 1982; Koegel 1986; Levine and Langness 1986). Finally, although the label 'learning difficulties' is assigned to a highly variable category having a wide range of intellectual abilities and social competences (Byrne *et al.* 1988), the consequences of being so labelled are relatively uniform. People with learning difficulties have more restricted life chances than do others (Flynn, 1989; Hattersley *et al.* 1987: 40). They are likely to be segregated (spatially and/or socially) from extensive contact with 'normal' peers, and such segregation usually increases as they get older. They have very poor employment prospects. Their economic position consequently depends primarily on the level of their state benefits, which are often adequate only for basic needs. They are less likely to marry or to establish stable sexual relationships. And they are very unlikely to have children.

All of the young people I worked with were identified socially as having learning difficulties in that they were in receipt of some of the services provided specifically for this category. However, they varied enormously in the nature and degree of their intellectual, as well as physical and social competences. One way to describe this variation would be to enumerate its extremes: those who are literate versus those who cannot speak; those with full-time jobs versus those with no realistic prospects of employment ever; those who live independently versus those who require assistance with everyday activities such as eating and dressing; and so on. However, such an approach tends to suggest a simple continuum from relatively 'mild' learning difficulties to quite severe. It does not begin to portray the complexity and non-linearity of the variation in this category produced by the unevenness and unpredictability of individuals' intellectual, social and physical competences and incompetences. I will try to provide another perspective on this complex variability through somewhat fuller descriptions of a few individuals and their interactions with myself and others.

I had been interviewing and doing some participant observation in the special needs unit of a local college for several weeks before I realised with some dismay that Wesley Grant was among the students I was scheduled to interview. I had known who he was from very early in my experience there, primarily from hearing his frequent and apparently disconnected comments proclaimed in a penetrating and querulous voice. Although both the delivery and content of his speech were clear, my first impression was that his utterances were unrelated either to his surroundings or to what others said to him. Consider some of my fieldnotes from a day spent in participant observation mainly in Wesley's company at the college:

I was first aware he had arrived when I heard him saying 'silly bugger' in the corridor. He repeated this several times, was led into his classroom by one of the assistants who told him not to say that and to sit down . . . . [Later] Rees Morgan comes in and attracts a lot of attention with a new haircut. 'Get out Rees!' Wesley continues to say 'get out' several times, then 'Sue, get out' to one of the assistants who has come in and is standing behind him. He repeats this four or five times. Then 'Sue smacked John this morning' several times . . . . He says something about swearing and Sue says that we don't want to hear about that. Then 'Mrs Peters is a swine.'

My only attempt to interview him was disastrous if judged in conventional terms. However I was quickly disabused of my initial impression that he was unresponsive to his social environment. Having noted that he spent quite a bit of time looking at catalogues, I had brought along a set of pictures cut from magazines in an attempt to direct our conversation; 'bloody boring' was Wesley's verdict, interspersed in his usual running commentary. After he returned to his classroom, it was reported to me that he was repeating 'I want to talk to you' in a good imitation of my American accent.

By this time my notes were beginning to suggest the problem I was facing in coming to terms with the category 'learning difficulties', in that I was speculating about the difficulties of differentiating between specific incompetences, once a label of 'learning difficulties' was placed on an individual. Some of the comments made by staff members reinforced this impression.

One told me, 'Wesley is very unusual; it's all there in his head but all mixed up. He has a good memory; he remembers what kind of car everyone on the staff has and will suddenly say so-and-so drives a Micra months after he has been told that.' One further example of the complexity of Wesley's mixture of (in)competences that illustrates the ease with which they could be misinterpreted will suffice. I accompanied Wesley to the canteen for lunch and tea breaks on several occasions. He always had a chocolate drink, I had a cup of tea. I carried our drinks since he could not manage a tray; he selected our table, always one apart from other staff and students. On the first such occasion, he asked for sugar as we were starting for our table; I refused saying he did not need sugar for chocolate. However, the second time I did not stop him, thinking perhaps he did put extra sugar in his chocolate. Once we were seated he handed me the sugar for my tea. Thus what I had interpreted as inappropriate behaviour was in fact an expression of social competence in his anticipation of another's possible need.

These experiences contrast dramatically with my introduction to another participant in the study, 23-year-old Lucinda Alton. Lucinda's education had been almost entirely in special schools, and she had obtained her job through the support of WISE, the Welsh Initiative for Specialised Employment, an organisation funded by the All-Wales Strategy for People with Mental Handicaps.[2] On the other hand, when I met her, she was working full-time, drove her own car and had an active social life. I had arranged to interview her at her parents' house. When I arrived, she met me at the door, explained that her parents were out, that they had house-guests and suggested that we go out someplace else to talk. She was quite skilled at carrying on a social conversation as I drove us to the nearby café she recommended, and perfectly at ease with the informal interview format that I subsequently adopted.

The question must certainly be asked as to how and why individuals with such disparate competences and incompetences are included in the same category of 'people with learning difficulties'. During the early stages of my fieldwork, having been drawn into a discourse that accepted the category's ontological status, I tended to speculate about these anomalies in terms of whether or not someone 'really had' learning difficulties at all. Regarding Lucinda my fieldnotes recorded:

She occasionally made an error with time (saying two months when she meant two years) or in giving directions (mixing left and right), but she always corrected herself. Aside from being slow – she explained to me that she was a slow learner – she does not appear to have a mental handicap at all.

I eventually had to conclude that the category does not cohere, that it cannot be understood in terms of its formal definition based on intellectual and social incompetences. It must instead be seen as an artefact of a formal, but arbitrary, social process which nevertheless defines a highly salient category whose members are identifiable primarily through being in receipt of particular sorts of services.

The variety of observations that finally led to this conclusion is quite startling. Consider the following extract from an interview with Sandra Price whose days were mostly spent in an Adult Training Centre.

CD: 'Who do you live with?'
Sandra Price: 'My parents.'
CD: 'Your parents. Your mum and dad?'
SP: 'Yeah. I don't get on very well with them though.'
CD: 'You don't?'
SP: 'No, I don't.'
CD: 'What's the problem?'
SP: 'It's my mother is the problem.'
CD: 'Is that right?'
SP: 'She keeps beating me all the time.'
CD: 'About what?'
SP: 'We have a fight sometimes, in the house.'
CD: 'You do?'
SP: 'Yeah.'
CD: 'Well, all families have fights sometimes, don't they?'
SP: 'No, my mother said, I don't know what it's, well she's beating me up and she's beating me really hard and I don't like it. In the house. And it's frightening me as well.'
CD: 'Oh dear.'
SP: 'So I don't like it. So I said to my friend, I said, if it carries on I'm gonna, I'm gonna just walk out.'

Although this transcript might suggest someone a bit younger than Sandra's 21 years, there is nothing that would identify her as someone with learning difficulties. However, her self-presentation, in common with the majority of the young people I interviewed, tended to project this identity in face-to-face encounters. Only as I began to transcribe the interviews was I struck by the fact that their substance contained few markers of this identity, once they were divorced from various communicative difficulties, physical manifestations or inappropriate social behaviours. On the other hand, markers such as poor enunciation, appearance characteristic of particular conditions like Down's Syndrome, too much or too little eye contact, failure to observe cultural conventions regarding personal space, and many others, while not restricted to people with learning difficulties, served to keep this identity in the forefront of social interactions for those who were so labelled. In a few instances there were no such markers in the substance of the conversation; more commonly they appeared only in references to time or money as in the following continuation of my discussion with Sandra about her conflict with her mother.

CD: 'You have arguments with your parents sometimes?'
SP: 'Yes.' [Laughs]
CD: 'What about?'
SP: 'Some, mostly I kick the twins and my mother shouts, tempers and things like that.'
CD: 'I see. You don't like the twins?'
SP: 'No.' [Laughs]
CD: 'How old are they?'
SP: 'They were both six on, I don't know what date, but they were both nine or seven.'

In contrast some interviews could almost certainly be identified as involving someone with learning difficulties simply from their substance. In the following excerpt from an interview with James Riley, whose enunciation was poor, I have deleted a few sections in which I repeat his words to secure confirmation that I am understanding him.

CD: 'What school did you go to James?' . . .//. . .
James Riley: 'Sports.'
CD: 'Bore? Say that again.'
JR: 'Football.'
CD: 'Mm hmm. OK.'
JR: 'Baseball. Netball.'
CD: 'Netball?'
JR: 'Yes. Tennis. In the park. Play tennis.'
CD: 'Oh yes.'
JR: 'Weight lifting . . .//. . . Badminton.'
CD: 'Oh, say that again.'
JR: 'Shuttlecock.'
CD: 'Oh yes. Badminton. Badminton, is it? Oh, very good. That's what you did at school? Yes. What school was that? What was the name of the school?'
JR: 'Don't know.'

In spite of his cleverness in helping me to understand him (switching from 'badminton' to 'shuttlecock', for example), the substance of James's conversation does seem to identify clear intellectual incompetences. Thus, if one takes the substance of what is said rather than the manner of delivery as the better indicator of intellectual competence – and this is a debatable issue – then once again the variability within this category is remarkable, along a continuum from instances in which virtually every utterance appears to reflect certain incompetences to those in which there is no such indication in the substance of the conversation.

Similar variability appeared in the evaluations of parents of their sons' and daughters' awareness of or responses to their identity as someone with learning difficulties. Nor did this variability in parental attitudes seem to be associated in any direct way with the competences of their sons or daughters. Katherine Davies was the mother of Cindy Brown, a 19-year-old woman whose abilities in terms of ordinary measures of intellectual competence were very good indeed. She had good communication skills, could read and write, did some of her own shopping for clothes and could travel about by bus independently. Her mother felt that she was aware of having learning difficulties but when asked how that awareness affected her self-image commented:

I don't think it does really. I mean you would have to have a very sort of intellectual approach to think of that, wouldn't you? That sort of question, you know. You would have to be intelligent enough to say what am I missing out on.

Compare this to the following discussion with the parents of James Riley, the 27-year-old man referred to above.

Sean Riley: 'I think that the terrible thing about it is that he knows, himself, that he's different.'
Maureen Riley: 'Yes, I was telling Charlotte that.'
SR: 'If a person didn't realise they were different, different from, but James does know. And that makes it worse because you can see, many times we've seen this. Gets into a little shell, you know'. . .//. . .
MR: 'I think he's been aware from the, James was never a stupid boy. I used to watch him from the time he was a very small child, Charlotte. Because no one could give me any idea of what he was like or any help. Because of that I was observant myself and watched him. And I was hopeful with James because his eyes were always bright and you tell with the eyes, can't you? And there were one or two little things, now, I don't know how old he was, three or something, you know, kids put on their anorak and they put the wrong arm in the wrong sleeve sort of business. But James overcame that, he put the hood on first. And I thought, "Well God, that's clever".'

As these examples illustrate, the more I worked with people with learning difficulties and their parents the less confident I became in my understanding of the basis of the category. While this lack of coherence is considered herein only with reference to internal variability, it is clear that examples abound of people who are not labelled as having learning difficulties but who share many of their definitional incompetences (such as difficulties with time and money, communication problems, illiteracy or socially unacceptable behaviour). Such external variability makes the category even more problematic.

One way of understanding the categorisation is to argue that it is a way of identifying individuals who are thought to require certain forms of social provision in Western societies, that is, who are believed to be unable to function with the degree of autonomy exhibited by the majority of individual citizens of Western states and who do not have access to other social resources which can compensate (cf. Angrosino, this volume). Thus a structural (and circular) definition of this category is that its members are those in receipt of services designed for and provided to people with learning difficulties.

Such a structural definition is not without practical merit. However, I want to consider other possible bases for such a category, linked to Western understandings of the nature of the self and of personhood. Before turning to these broader questions, I will look at the construction of social identities by and for people with learning difficulties, in particular the social identities of learning difficulties and adulthood.

Learning difficulties and social adulthood

Personhood and conceptions of the self are closely linked to social adulthood. In many societies full personhood is only attained after reaching social adulthood, often marked by rites of passage symbolising a death and rebirth, and sometimes only fully acknowledged after producing children (La Fontaine 1985; Nicolaisen 1995; Talle 1995). In Western societies attainment of social adulthood is not marked by any single achievement or ceremony but is linked to a complex of attainments. Firstly, of course, is chronological age – 18 having fairly recently replaced 21 as the most significant milestone – which brings with it various legal rights (to vote, drink in pubs, drive) and responsibilities (notably for one's actions, especially criminal actions). Other achievements also contribute to becoming an adult, for example, employment, setting up independent living away from the natal home, marriage and children, but none of these alone is either necessary or sufficient for full social adulthood (cf. Jenkins 1990).

The achievement of adult status by people with learning difficulties has become a matter of great concern in the social services with the growth of the normalisation philosophy of care. This philosophy contends that people with learning difficulties should be helped to live as 'normal' a life as possible, including moving through culturally expected life stages. Thus service providers have been sensitised to the ways in which chronological adults with learning difficulties were treated like children: being spoken to in a condescending or overly authoritative manner; not being consulted about likes and dislikes ('Does she take sugar in her tea?'); not having opportunities to socialise in adult settings such as pubs; and so on. As a result, a great deal of emphasis has been placed on respecting the adulthood of people with learning difficulties in these sorts of interactions, as well as on encouraging them to develop age-appropriate behaviour.

Among the young people I worked with, this had produced a high level of awareness of themselves as adults. All but a handful of these young people said that they were adults. Many backed up their assertions by pointing to specific markers of adult status. Some noted physical characteristics. For example, one 21-year-old woman said, 'Grown-ups have periods but children don't. They don't understand about periods. But young women do understand periods.' And 22-year-old Gary Richards explained, 'I used to be a boy. But I'm not now though. If you get to be 21 or 22, you'll be a man.' Others, such as 20-year-old Kevin Powell, emphasised social markers: 'With a man he can go into a pub for a drink. And he can go into a betting shop.'

Some also showed a keen awareness of other aspects of the discourse about adulthood, in particular attempts to discourage 'childish' activities.

Gaynor Jones: 'I know it sounds childish, I shouldn't be doing it, but colouring just passes the time away.'
CD: 'You enjoy colouring, do you?'
GJ: 'Although it sounds childish.'
CD: 'Oh, it sounds artistic. You think it sounds childish yourself, do you?'
GJ: 'Yeah.'
CD: 'Yes. Why is that?'
GJ: 'I don't bother so much as I used to. I used to colour a lot. I don't bother now.'

Many parents, too, participated in this discourse regarding adulthood, with one result being that some actively tried to discourage childish activities. The parents of 18-year-old Patrick Chapman expressed the dilemma this sometimes created:

Dorothy Chapman: 'He was given quite a lot of money for his birthday. I took him to town and he spent all his money on buying things for his train set. This is a big improvement because in other years, we've just been about four years training, while I've tried to stop him buying toys.'
Lyn Chapman: 'Cars.'
DC: 'Tractors, forklift trucks.'
LC: 'Lorries and, play for hours with them, but he was getting bigger and we tried to get him out of them. But at the same time, he still goes back to them, don't he?'
DC: 'Yes, I know, he still plays with toys you see. Although we tried to learn, I mean he does adult things. He's got his train set, he's got a TV, and he's got a video, and he's got a music centre, all in his room. And he does play those things, but he also still plays with his toys.'

The emphasis placed on controlling such activities probably stems from the paucity of other indicators of adult status. Of the young people I interviewed who were over the age of 19 and not in full-time education, only five (14 per cent) were employed; fifty-two of the sixty were living at home with their parents; none was married; and only two were engaged. Thus, other more commonly cited indicators of adulthood simply were not available to the majority; those few who could refer to such positive indicators, did so. For example, Lucinda Alton explained that she was a woman,

'because I got a job . . .//. . . and a car . . .//. . . If I think I was a child, I wouldn't have got the jobs. You wouldn't be able to have a job. You wouldn't be able to have a licence.'

Parents, however, were generally much more ambivalent about the adulthood of their sons and daughters. Although fewer than one-third of parents said they regarded them as children, two-thirds felt that having a learning difficulty interfered with their achieving adulthood. Their reasons included 'childish behaviour', especially lack of responsibility for personal hygiene, specific disabilities, such as poor reading skills, and restricted lifestyles, particularly the limitations on independent social-ising. A few poured scorn on some of the activities of the social services in this respect which they regarded as window dressing and ultimately insulting. The parents of Norman Everson, a 23-year-old man with Down's Syndrome, reported that he had recently been appointed to a county-wide committee designed to bring together clients, parents and various categories of service providers.

Glanmor Everson: 'But Norman is on this committee now. Now what value it will be I don't know. I honestly don't know, because I mean to say, when you were interviewing, he told a few lies you know. [Laughs] I don't know what they expect from them really.'
Stephanie Everson: 'He came home though feeling quite pleased with [inaudible].'
GE: Yes, but it's as if again it is a little bit outside their capabilities you know. They're liking it as being accepted and . . .'
SE: 'Ah well, you don't know.'
GE: 'Well now, the fantasies they got in their mind, oh that, that brightened him up a bit. But when he gets a couple of meetings under his belt, possibly he'll be [laughs] . . .'
SE: [laughing] 'Yeah.'

Thus the adult status of most of these young people was not very secure, being dependent more on discourse than material markers, and even then not being fully supported by those closest to them. A further impediment to their claims to adulthood was to be found in the degree of control they experienced in their everyday lives, some of which was neces-sary for their own welfare, some relatively trivial. Often even so-called adult activities were controlled in ways that limited their significance as

markers of adult status. Twenty-two-year-old Gary Richards's father had pointed to the fact that 'I take him out for a pint' as one indication that he was treated as an adult.

CD: 'Do you ever go out to pubs?'
Gary Richards: 'Yes.'
CD: 'Who do you go with?'
GR: 'Well, I go with my father.'
CD: 'What do you have to drink?'
GR: 'Pint.'
CD: 'Did you ever drink too much?'
GR: 'No.'
CD: 'No?'
GR: 'Only two I'm allowed.'
CD: 'Who tells you to just have two?'
GR: 'Two pints is all right.'
CD: 'Is that what your father says?'
GR: 'Yeah.'

Clearly the relationship between difficulties of achieving adult status and the category of learning difficulties is very close. A few parents saw the two as inseparable. The father of a 21-year-old woman responded to a question about what would make her an adult thus: 'To get shot of her handicap.' Roger Hartley's mother had a similar reaction:

CD: 'How do you see Roger? Do you see him as a child or as an adult?'
Sylvia Hartley: 'I think we're apt to treat him still as a child. In many ways Roger is still a child.'
CD: 'Yes. What would make him an adult in your eyes?'
SH: 'To be normal.'

However, the young people themselves, who as already noted were keenly aware of and actively participated in the discourse about their adulthood, were for the most part unaware of the ways in which this other 'master status' (Hughes 1945), that of learning difficulties, affected their assertions of an adult identity. With only a few exceptions, namely those whose parents had discussed their 'handicap' with them, most did not have access to the cultural discourse about the category 'learning difficulties'. They were unfamiliar with the terms commonly applied to this category and they did not apply such terms to themselves. This is not to suggest that they were unaware of the social consequences of their categorisation as someone with learning difficulties, but their awareness was primarily through material and embodied experience rather than through discourse (Davies and Jenkins 1997).

One consequence of the interplay between these two social identities is that categorising someone as having learning difficulties tends to undermine their personhood in ways that are dependent upon Western conceptions of the individual self. In the first place, their autonomy is undermined by the very high level of control to which people with learning difficulties are subjected in their daily lives. But autonomy is more subtly weakened by some of the ways in which service providers and other carers attempt to assist them in laying claim to adult status. In particular, encouragement of age-appropriate behaviour and proscription of childish activities may help them to present a less ambiguous adult image. But the process of creating this image may limit its relevance, given the price that is paid in their loss of autonomous expression of individual preferences. In the second place, the very restricted access of most people with learning difficulties to the discourse about this social category undermines their self-presentation as reflexive self-aware individuals.

These two characteristics, autonomy and reflexivity, are among the most fundamental features of Western conceptions of the individual self (Morris 1994; Taylor 1986) and such conceptions form the basis of social constructions of personhood. This suggests that one way in which the category 'learning difficulties' may cohere is that it systematically, albeit implicitly, impeaches the personhood of its members. I turn now to a fuller consideration of the ways in which personhood and the nature of the self are culturally constructed. I do so in order to examine other ways, not directly related to current philosophies of care, in which some parents and carers assert the personhood of people with learning difficulties through two different means of challenging Western conceptions of the self.

Selves and persons

'If the self is an individual's awareness of a unique identity, the "person" is society's confirmation of that identity as of social significance' (La Fontaine, 1985: 124). Personhood is based in cultural assumptions and confirmed through social relationships. Attainment of personhood is thus dependent upon the interplay between the expression of an individual self and the particular cultural contexts in which it develops. However, the danger in this formulation of personhood is of failing to recognise equally the socially constructed nature of the self, in spite of its closer association with the individual. Observations that conceptions of the self are not constant but vary cross-culturally in fundamental ways strongly support the notion of the social origins of these concepts as well. Not only is the complex of social identities that combine to make up self-identity affected by, and to a large extent produced through social relationships, the very nature of the self that they constitute is also a product of these relationships and their underlying cultural assumptions. Shweder and Bourne have drawn attention to the culturally dependent nature of both individual selves and social persons in their discussion of 'two major alternative conceptualizations . . . the "egocentric-contractual" and the "sociocentric organic"' (1984: 193). The former is related to Western assumptions about the autonomy of individual selves, the latter common to many non-Western cultures which, it is argued, do 'not abstract out a concept of the inviolate personality free of social role and social relationship – a tendency to not separate out, or distinguish, the individual from the social context' (1984: 167; cf. also Devlieger, and Reynolds Whyte, this volume). While this dichotomy is doubtless far too simplistic in terms of its implied linearity, it is useful as a first step in characterising Western conceptions of the self and personhood.

Rosaldo (1984) in a reflection upon emotions among the Philippine Ilongots noted that certain responses to emotions such as anger, which would superficially appear to be common to most societies, are entirely inappropriate to the point of impossibility in Western terms: for example, Westerners cannot be paid for an anger and then genuinely forget it. The use of the word 'genuinely' is significant, in that a Western version would be to say that one could be paid off and appear to forget the insult, but that 'underneath' anger would remain. Rosaldo argues that the notion of there being a true self, which remembers its anger, underneath the public personae, which might be expected to act as if that anger had been forgotten, is in fact a reflection of a Western dichotomy that assumes an internal self, distinguishable from social roles and statuses, which actively interprets and reflects upon the external social scene.

This dichotomy, between the self and social roles which the self may choose to enact, assumes that we may act in certain ways which do not truly reflect our inner state, or true selves. D'Andrade (1987), in a discussion of a Western folk model of the mind, explicitly links this concept of an inner self to cognitive capacity. In this model, the process of thinking is controlled by the self as are other forms of action, and thought is the clearest expression of the self. If the capacity to think is impaired then one may not be responsible for one's actions. Although this cognitive self is acted upon by emotions, is the object of emotions, it usually can control its responses to emotion. Such self-control is the hallmark of the adult self and is something that children have to acquire.

Given that cognitive competences are so closely linked to Western conceptions of the self then people with learning difficulties might be expected to be in a weakened position as regards their personhood. However, as we have seen, cognitive competences, in fact, vary greatly among people with learning difficulties, so much so as to make this an unsatisfactory basis for their categorisation. However, as discussed earlier, people who are so categorised tend to experience, for various reasons, restrictions in two other respects that are closely linked to cognition in Western folk models, namely, individual autonomy and reflexivity. Both of these capacities involve a separation of social and individual selves which also is in accord with Western constructions of the self. Thus people categorised as having learning difficulties tend to transgress these expectations of selfhood in ways that undermine their personhood under Western conceptualisations.

Thus far I have discussed Western conceptions of the self and the cultural construction of personhood based on them as if they were unitary and constant. However, while they do seem to represent widely held dominant perspectives, it must be remembered that they are 'ideas, premises by which people guide their lives, and only to the extent a people lives by them do they have force' (Shweder and Bourne 1984: 193). In particular, I want to avoid suggesting that these commonly held cultural constructions are universally accepted within Western societies. On the contrary, any such constructions will be affected by social position and historical context and responsive to power differentials. An ethnographic study of Japanese identities (Kondo 1990), which examines a similar process of 'crafting' selves (both Japanese selves and the ethnographer's self), concludes that any such constructions respond to internal difference and contradiction and are sensitive to power relationships. 'We participated in each others' lives and sought to make sense of one another. In that attempt to understand, power inevitably came into play as we tried to force each other into appropriately comprehensible categories' (Kondo 1990: 10).

In a similar vein some of the parents and young people I worked with, while still operating with Western cultural concepts of the self, interpreted them so as to challenge their implicit attack upon the personhood of people with learning difficulties. There were two distinct ways in which this challenge was framed: in one approach parents developed rationales for asserting the reflexivity required by Western concepts of the self on behalf of their daughters or sons; in the second approach, perhaps a more fundamental challenge, parents and some young people implicitly rejected Western notions of an internalised individual self in favour of a selfhood based in social relationships and social actions.

As already noted, one of the reasons why people with learning difficulties may fail to satisfy Western cultural assumptions regarding personhood is an apparent low degree of reflexivity, in particular as regards awareness of their social identity as someone with learning difficulties. It should be clear from my earlier critique of the category 'learning difficulties' that I am not suggesting that low reflexivity is a defining characteristic or an inevitable result of learning difficulties; I argue rather that it is made more likely due to social practices towards, and cultural attitudes about, people who have been so categorised. For example, in Western societies, it is usually considered impolite and unkind to refer to someone's learning difficulties in their presence. In contrast:

the Punan Bah [of Central Borneo] talk openly about physical or mental impairments, and it is not considered poor manners to do so in the presence of the impaired person. Nor will the disabled abstain from discussing their handicap quite freely. In contrast is their handling of ugliness, a matter it is most tactless to bring up in the presence of the person considered plain. (Nicolaisen 1995: 48)

The parents I interviewed varied widely in their notions of how or whether their sons and daughters were aware of their identity as someone with learning difficulties: only a few had discussed it with them; the majority had not. Among the former, one mother in particular appeared to link her daughter's awareness of her learning difficulties – as well as other aspects of her self-presentation – very closely with her personhood. June Price explained that her 21-year-old daughter Sandra had been told about her learning difficulties when she first started asking questions at the age of 6 or 7.

We told her all about it. We told her, we explained that when she was a baby, she was seriously ill and that we had to rush her into hospital and that the fluid went to her brain and caused her brain to be damaged and not function right. And she accepted, she accepted it. If we'd be out anywhere, you know, shopping or something, she had no qualms about telling people that she was handicapped.

This concern about self-presentation extended to virtually all areas of her daughter's life, encompassing her dress, physical appearance, speech and much more. In describing her extraordinary efforts over many years to develop her daughter's public persona, June Price occasionally made explicit reference to her personhood:

When I, when we took her to the hospital when she was just over a year old, and Dr Jones told me that her speech and the movement part of the brain was damaged. He said, 'She'll never walk for you or talk.' So I turned round to him and said, 'You must be joking', and I walked out. And I was on the bus, taking her home, and I thought, well, no child of mine is going to sit in the corner and vegetate. And it really got to me what he said. It hurt. For him to say outright she'd never walk and she'd never talk, and I think that, that made me more determined than ever to prove that doctor wrong. And prove him wrong I did. Because, as I say, she was gone three before she walked, and she was due for a checkup . . .//. . . And when I walked in, Sandra was on my hand and she was toddling. And . . .//. . . Dr Jones said, 'Well, you've proved me wrong.' And I said, 'I knew no child of mine would, you know, suffer sit in a corner.' I could have been like other women and thought well that was it, and just stick her in a pushchair and leave her there. But she was a human being in my eyes, and she had to have the chance then, to learn these skills.

Among the majority of parents who had never discussed learning difficulties with their sons or daughters, opinions about their understanding of this identity varied widely. A few advanced the familiar cultural stereotype that not only did people with learning difficulties fail to understand or reflect upon this identity, they were happier than most other people as a consequence. Leslie Jordan commented of her 23-year-old daughter's life:

I'd change places with her tomorrow. I would! She's got a lovely life, that's all she knows is enjoying herself. She hasn't got no worries about money or anything. She gets what she wants and she's got a lovely life. Like I say, I'd change places with her tomorrow. That's all is on her mind is enjoying herself. You know, no worry. She hasn't got a worry in the world. She hasn't got a worry in the world, and I think today that's a nice position to be in, isn't it?

On the other hand, some parents attributed awareness of this identity to these young people, thereby according them the reflexivity basic to Western conceptions of personhood, without adopting June Price's approach of explicitly instilling such self-awareness in them. Parents' attribution of reflexivity to them did not depend on their intellectual competences, nor did it rely on their verbal affirmation. Instead it was usually based on behavioural observations. The case of James Riley has already been discussed. As another example, the parents of Gary Richards were convinced he had understood that he had learning difficulties from quite a young age.

Kevin Richards: 'He's sensitive, see.'
Linda Richards: 'Oh, very sensitive.'
KR: 'He doesn't like . . .'
LR: 'Because last year now there were boys down the camp making fun of him. Oh and he come home and he cried. Oh, he broke his heart, you know.'
KR: 'Because he is an intelligent lad, you know. You know, he's not like the carpets here now, listening to people talking, taking no notice. He takes it in, he understands, you see.'
LR: 'He knows.'
KR: 'And that's the worst part.'
LR: 'If they're calling him names and what have you, it upsets him.'

This assertion of reflexivity based on behavioural observation has also been reported among those who care for people with severe and multiple disabilities. Bogdan and Taylor (1989) suggest that one of the ways in which these carers engage in the social construction of humanness (what I have called personhood) for their charges is by attributing thinking to them. Other studies of the nature and treatment of people with Alzheimer's disease have noted a very similar process among their carers and family members; 'concerned others recognize that the person with Alzheimer's has feelings but cannot express them properly; and so a translation is required' (Herskovits 1995: 154; also cf. Gubrium 1986).

Translation of this sort was clearly in evidence in Rachel Thomas's discussion of her 22-year-old son Owen's understanding of his learning difficulties. Owen Thomas did not speak, apart from a few words, nor did he sign.

CD: 'Knowing Owen so very well, what do you think it means to him to have a mental handicap?'

Rachel Thomas: 'Embarrassment. He feels embarrassed.'

CD: 'Do you think so?'

RT: 'I know he is.'

CD: 'Do you feel that he is aware of having a mental handicap? Have you noticed anything, or has anything ever happened to make you feel that he has become aware of it or is aware of it?'

RT: '. . . It's other people that make him aware of it. And he blushes like.'

CD: 'Under what circumstances?'

RT: 'They speak to me. And some say, "Ohh pity". And he just blushes.'

One way of viewing these assertions of reflexivity on behalf of others is to suggest that they are illusions, perhaps even pathological, projections of the carer's wishes (e.g. Pollner and McDonald-Wikler, 1985). However, carers themselves advance these assertions based upon observations of and relationships with these others, certainly not as illusions. An alternative and preferred way of understanding these assertions of a reflexive self – one that does not do violence to carers' interpretations – is to regard them as an implicit recognition of the origins in inter-subjectivity of all subjective experience. In this light it becomes reasonable to develop a philosophy of care for Alzheimer's sufferers in which 'the key psychological task . . . is that of keeping the sufferer's personhood in being' (Kitwood and Bredin 1992: 269). Understood in this way, parents' assertions of reflexivity for their sons and daughters with learning difficulties suggest that they are implicitly working with a different understanding of the nature of the self than the dominant Western model.

Such a challenge to Western notions of a private internal self is made more explicitly by some parents, as well as by young people who promote their personhood based upon their roles within a social network, rather than some inner essence separate from their public personae. Assertions like this by young people with learning difficulties may be manifest in their assumption of the outer trappings of particular social roles to which they aspire. Two young men in particular, both of whom told me they wanted an executive position, always carried briefcases, usually dressed in jackets and ties, and made clear that their goal essentially involved the acquisition of certain other external markers. For 21-year-old Martin Hibbs, who was unemployed, this meant 'typing, answer the phones, meeting with different people, staff meetings'. For Daniel Connor, who worked full-time as an office boy, this desired executive position primarily meant 'an in-car phone'.

One of the most common ways in which parents worked to establish the personhood of their daughters and sons through their social relationships was by actively promoting their involvement in a network of extended family and friends. Owen Thomas's mother explained that her granddaughter's name had been selected because its shortened form – Car – was one of the handful of words that Owen could say. Diane Edwards, whose son Hugh likewise had only a limited vocabulary, described how she kept him involved in family contacts maintained by telephone.

Mind I do get him to speak to friends that ring up. And there's a dear old lady, she lived by my aunt and she keeps in touch with me – my aunt, the one that died in February, you know – and she rings often. So I calls him to the phone and I say, 'This is Betty. Come and speak to Betty.' And he do and he'll say 'hello'. But mostly mind, I got to tell him what to say. He'll say 'hello' and then he don't know, he's just holding the phone. And I'll say, 'Tell her you been doing, just say "jigsaw".' And he'll say 'jigsaw' and then he'll say a few words, and I'll say, 'Say goodbye now, goodbye.' And then he'll say 'goodbye' to her. But you know what I mean, I got to get him to talk. As I say, when people phone up I do get him to the phone sometimes. When my cousins ring up, and he'll say a few words, see.

Many parents also took great pride in their adult children's social skills; meals in restaurants were frequently invoked as evidence of their full participation in social life. As Helen Miller said of her 21-year-old son David:

I've never had this feeling that I've got to be sorry for him. I don't. I mean, as far as I'm concerned he's one of the family and he does things the same as us. And I can take him anywhere. And if we go to a posh restaurant, I'm quite sure that he's able to conduct himself because he always has. It's expected of him and he does it.

As they reflected upon their relationship with their sons and daughters, parents often implicitly challenged prevailing Western assumptions about personhood in their recognition of the socially embedded nature of selves. Several mothers clearly found that their lives were constructed around their sons or daughters with learning difficulties, not primarily because of any increased responsibilities, but rather as a result of their relationship which they valued highly. The mother of 26-year-old Jennifer Farley expressed this not uncommon sentiment in a way which acknowledged both her daughter's personhood and the contribution she made to her mother's life:

I knew between 12 and 18 months it was Down's Syndrome. Oh, very shocked. And very upset, at the time. But, of course as time goes on, of course, I think she's wonderful. Really wonderful. And I don't think of her now as being any different to a normal child, you know. Perhaps as she's so good in what she does, and what she says, even though she doesn't say a lot here, and I don't think of her as being any, a great handicap then. I consider myself very fortunate to have her.

Furthermore such relationships with these young people were not always primarily based on psychological need and companionship. There were also instances of material dependence. Elizabeth Thomas acknowledged her own dependence as well as the full and unambiguous personhood of her son Paul Warren in the following exchanges.

CD: 'Does he contribute to the family budget?'
Elizabeth Thomas: 'Oh yes. I wouldn't be able to live without his. . .'
CD: 'Without his allowance?'
ET: 'Without his allowance.'
. . .//. . .
ET: 'I don't have any hard feelings or regrets about having him, especially in the circumstances are now, as they are now, you know. To me, well, Paul was born for a purpose in life and the purpose in life is now to help me. Other than me helping him, you know. Maybe I'm, maybe I'm looking at it a selfish way, I don't know.'
CD: 'But you feel that, at present, having Paul is more of a positive thing for you?'
ET: 'Yes, yes.'
. . .//. . .
ET: 'He's my only . . . my only support then, in a way, you know. He's my ally. We're great friends, you know. I mean, as I said, if he was an awkward child then things, I might feel differently about it, but he's not. He's no trouble at all, actually, he isn't.'

Conclusions

The category of 'learning difficulties' superficially appears to be based upon intellectual incompetences. However, the process of assigning individuals to this category is more ambiguous than its formal definitions suggest and quite open to the influence of other social and cultural factors. This results in a category which to all intents and purposes fails to cohere when its members are considered individually. Such categorisation of these highly disparate individuals can be explained in structural terms in that they are all in receipt of services specifically provided for those labelled as having learning difficulties. Another way of understanding this category is by recognising that its members, because of both cultural attitudes regarding 'learning difficulties' and associated labels and social experiences that are consequent on receiving this label, often undermine Western concepts of an autonomous reflexive individual self. Such considerations make the category highly problematic and strongly suggest that it needs to be conceptualised quite differently, particularly so in order to avoid implicitly impugning the basic humanity of those assigned to it. As the category is presently constituted, people with learning difficulties are often seen to challenge Western cultural notions about the nature of the self and as a result may be denied full personhood. Service providers working within a philosophy of normalisation attempt to develop age-appropriate behaviour, particularly to promote the transition to adult status of people with learning difficulties. But this process may in subtle ways further discredit their personhood, for example through limiting their autonomous expression of individual preferences. Parents and other carers often take an alternative approach to asserting the personhood of their sons and daughters in which they implicitly challenge Western notions of the self and promote an understanding of the selves of people with learning difficulties as constructed through and within social relationships. In this, they share developing philosophies of care with those who work with people with severe and multiple disabilities as well as those with Alzheimer's disease. And it is these perceptions which are most likely to offer a way forward in providing a basis for reconceptualisation of the category 'learning difficulties' that would be both socially and analytically more desirable.

Notes

1 This three-year project was supported by the Joseph Rowntree Foundation and the project director was Richard Jenkins. For further details, see Davies and Jenkins (unpublished).
2 The All-Wales Strategy was set up in 1983 by the Welsh Office to develop services for people with learning difficulties. It was funded for ten years and provided both new money for services and new ways of delivering them. In 1993 the Welsh Office renewed its support for the Strategy but restricted its role to policy rather than implementation.

6 Work, opportunity and culture: (in)competence in Greece and Wales

Sylvia van Maastricht

'Competence' and 'incompetence' are categories defined culturally as well as by individual ability or disability. Culture here means the combination of social organisation (institutions) and norms and values characterising a particular society. Culture influences who is classified as (in)competent, and the consequences of that classification. These consequences may be far-reaching and extend to many areas of everyday life. Ultimately, the personhood of people classified as (in)competent is influenced by both their individual ability/disability and by their cultural classification. In this chapter I will look at:

• Who are the people classified as (in)competent and how and why does this classification take place?
• What is their place in society?
• In what ways does culture influence their selection and their lives?

The historical record is clear that 'mental retardation' – what is also known as 'learning difficulties' – has existed in all cultures and societies in one form or another, though its definition, diagnosis and treatment have varied according to the philosophical, political and economic climate (Edgerton 1970; Manion and Bersani 1987: 231). To explore this variety further I studied two societies, Greece and Wales: the island of Ániksi and the small town of Ffynnon.[1] These communities differ from each other in a number of ways; I have concentrated on economic and social structures, and norms and values.

Ániksi and Ffynnon

Ániksi is an island off the coast of Greece. A car ferry makes the journey to the mainland four times daily. From the island's airport there are daily flights to Athens, and during the summer to and from northern Europe. Of the 30,000 inhabitants, one-third live in Ániksi town, the rest in small villages spread throughout the island. The standard of living is, by European standards, quite low. The main source of income is tourism. Due to local structure and planning regulations, most accommodation is in small hotels, pensions and rooms built and owned by local families. Most rural families have a garden in which they grow flowers and some vegetables. In addition, they usually own a small plot of land with olive trees and/or grapevines. Except for some employment in the state sector, such as banks, schools and transport, work in Ániksi is seasonal and small-scale. Irregular hours and more than one occupation are the rule. Ániksiots work to earn a living: those interested in a career will, more often than not, have to leave for the mainland, usually Athens. However, as in other countries that have experienced a sudden rise in income and exposure to luxury goods through tourism, materialism has caught on rapidly in Ániksi. Despite this change, values and social structures have not changed dramatically.

Most people on Ániksi are Greek Orthodox Christians. Although many only go to church occasionally, religion is still important: most children are baptised, women bless themselves passing a church, houses often contain ikons. Except for the baptism and wedding feasts there isn't much social life connected with the church; priests are not seen as people who offer a lot of support to the community. Family ties are still strong. The mother is the strong one inside the house, the father the person of authority in matters outside. A man's obligation to his family, defined as those who eat and live together and who are protected by the same ikons, is absolute and categorical (Campbell 1983). Brothers should look out for their sisters and are responsible for them until they get married. Children should look after their elderly parents. The men go out to work or to sit in the local tavernas drinking coffee and *raki*, playing backgammon, watching television and discussing the news. The boys go around on their motorbikes, or play football and basketball. The women stay at home; even the young girls are not allowed out often and then only with their fathers' or brothers' permission. Times are changing, though, and more and more girls rebel against these old values.

Unless young people leave the island to study or work on the mainland, they stay at home and live with their parents until they get married. If a girl marries someone from another village she usually moves to her husband's village (cf. Campbell 1983: 200). This often means that she will have relatively little contact with her parents, brothers and sisters. Her own new family becomes the centre of her existence, especially when children start arriving.

The Borough of Ffynnon in South Wales – with a population of 75,000 – is very different. Ffynnon, the main industrial and commercial centre of the area, is a busy town. It has good bus and train links to the rest of Wales and England. Until recently the majority of the male population was employed in tinplate mills, steelworks, foundries and engineering works.

The closures of many industries, particularly the mills and steelworks, created a serious unemployment situation from the late 1970s onwards. Most people in the area have one source of income, their regular employment. The unemployed are dependent on state benefits for survival. The local authority and other agencies are trying to bring back some industries into the area and to develop tourism. Despite these efforts, unemployment stays high. The state-run Job Centre provides advice and incentives for training, retraining and job seeking. People with learning difficulties are not part of these schemes. They receive disability allowance or attendance allowance, rather than unemployment benefits. This indicates that they are not seen as unemployed (i.e. as eligible for employment). Agriculture in the borough takes the form of small family farms, which do not employ a large number of people. Besides industry and agriculture people work in commerce, service provision, education and health.

In the Ffynnon area, strong family ties exist. There seem to be many large families, and many family members tend to live close to each other. For young families, this often means involvement with granny for baby-sitting and frequent visiting. Some young people stay in the parental home until they marry. Others leave to work or study in other cities. Others again leave when they are able to support themselves and live in flats or share a house with friends. Social life and leisure are centred around the family and/or going out. 'Going out' means the pub or a disco, the cinema or theatre, a meal. Facilities in the area include a leisure centre and a bowling alley. Despite the fact that most people do not own their houses outright – they are tied to mortgages or rent – the standard of living is reasonably high.

Church or chapel play an important role in Ffynnon. People belong to the Baptist or Wesleyan chapel, the (Anglican) Church in Wales, or the Roman Catholic Church. Many people meet friends at church services, at choir practices or at special social functions. In general, it seems that in Ffynnon, work and social life are highly organised (even to the extent that there is a befriending scheme for people with learning difficulties).

Two institutions

Ániksi and Ffynnon each have a Day Centre for people distinguished from other adult members of their society by their 'incompetence'. In Ffynnon these people are said to 'have learning difficulties'; on Ániksi they are called 'disabled people'. It is in these institutions that I undertook my research. I chose institutions because of their double function. Institutions are part of the social organisation, of the social order; they are not only a product of human activity, but also precede any individual development (Berger and Luckman 1967: 69). Institutions are set up by people and are thus influenced by the norms, values and structures of that society; at the same time institutions influence the lives of individuals. In the discussion which follows of two institutions for 'incompetent' people – the Day Centre in Ániksi and the Social Activity Centre in Ffynnon – I focus on the relationships between their foundation and purposes, the kind of people selected into them, and local economic and social structures.

On Ániksi the Centre 'for disabled people' is the first institution of its kind. Until 1983, when the Centre opened, there was no provision for children or adults who, for whatever reason, did not fit into the regular structures of education and work. The only schools and large institutions for children and adults with special needs were in Patras or in Athens. Most children attended regular schools. If they were not able, or the teacher refused to continue teaching them, they stayed at home. The only other alternative parents had was to send them away from home. The result was a group of people who had received little or no education and, because they were not able to find or to keep a job, spent their days at home. Especially in the case of the more severely disabled people this could be a heavy burden on the family, a burden not made easier by the absence of support or information within the community. For specialised medical or psychological care parents had to travel to Athens with their child, all paid for out of their own pocket. Even then, whatever help or advice they received did little to make their daily lives easier.

Local government became aware of the needs of this group of people through two sources. First, all disabled people in Greece are entitled to a small sum of money every month and a list exists of the people receiving this benefit. Second, in Ániksi village councils play an important role in liaising between individuals and local government. The establishment of the Centre was a joint initiative by local government (particularly the mayor of Ániksi), the Department of Health, and the European Community. It was an experiment, together with five similar centres in other parts of Greece, made possible by the coming together of different forces. The pending admission of Greece into the EC made people aware of standards of social provision in other parts of Europe. At the same time the EC's Social Fund made it possible to attempt to live up to those standards. The Centre for disabled people is one such attempt, which also addressed a need that was slowly becoming recognised within the local community.

Wales has a longer history of services for people with special needs. The state has assumed a responsibility to provide education, training and day care for those who do not fit in with regular education and the labour market. The day centres for adults with learning difficulties, in this case the Social Activity Centre in Ffynnon, are expressions of that responsibility. The Centre was set up and is managed by the County Council's Social Services department, and fulfils the requirement to provide day care for adults with special needs. The day centre has been part of the local structure since 1976. It provides a follow-up service for young people who have been in special education, and a safe haven for people who, because of their 'incompetence', are not able to find or hold a place in the labour market.

On Ániksi, children with special needs and their parents have been left to their own devices to find solutions to their problems. In Wales, children are taken out of regular schools as soon as a diagnosis of mental handicap or learning difficulties is made. Special education, day centres, leisure facilities, clubs, hostels, hospitals, parent organisations and even friendship schemes are waiting. These institutions reflect the notion that these children and adults should be catered for in a special way in every area of their lives. One of the major differences between Greece and Wales is in the 'efficiency' of the classification processes that label children as having 'special needs' (in Wales and the UK) or as being 'disabled' (in Greece). In Wales, if only because of the existence of better-resourced medical and educational systems, children are more likely to be formally classified, and will be classified earlier. Nor is this all: the consequences of classification – in terms of being drawn in to a system of institutionalised provision – are altogether more substantial in Wales than in Greece.

Each of the Centres has official objectives. The official purposes of the Centre on Ániksi, according to its manager, a psychologist, are:

- (a) To provide occupation for disabled people.
- (b) To teach disabled people the social and technical skills that would enable them to make some money in work appropriate to the area, i.e. in the tourism sector, particularly in arts and crafts.
- (c) To help to find disabled people work outside the Centre and to create job opportunities within the Centre.

Aims (a) and (b) were the original ones, and correspond to those of the other five Greek Centres set up at the same time. It is only in the last couple of years, in co-operation with the Horizon Programme (another EU initiative) that efforts are being made in regard to (c).

The designated purposes of the Social Activity Centre in Ffynnon can be found in *Into the Nineties*, a report by the local planning group. This group includes representatives from social services, the health authority and voluntary bodies. Their report is based on the principles set out in the *All-Wales Strategy*, a policy established in 1983 by the Welsh Office, for the development of services in Wales for people with learning difficulties. These general principles apply to all people with learning difficulties:

- Mentally handicapped people should have a right to normal patterns of life within the community.
- Mentally handicapped people should have a right to be treated as individuals.
- Mentally handicapped people require additional help from the communities in which they live and from professional services if they are to develop their maximum potential as individuals (Welsh Office 1983).

The aims of the Social Activity Centre, Ffynnon, try to incorporate these basic principles, in that:

- (a) The needs of the individual, not their handicap, should be the prime criterion for attendance.
- (b) The programme should cover all aspects of the individual's needs and not be concentrated on repetitive and mundane tasks that have no relevance to daily living or the encouragement of independence.
- (c) Maximum use should be made of all the resources in the community.
- (d) The service should develop the ability and confidence of a person in his/her daily life.
- (e) The running of the Centre will be achieved through regular meetings of the manager, staff, consumers and parents.

The manager told me that, in his view, the day-to-day reality is that, 'We should provide a service that is caring and responding to the needs of staff, parents and users.'

There are similarities and differences in the aims of these Centres. First, both communities have identified or recognised a group of people who, for reasons of 'incompetence', are not taking part in the normal day-to-day activities of other members of their society. In Greece these people have dropped out of school and/or experienced difficulties in finding work. They have often been at home for years. People attending the Day Centre in Ffynnon usually have gone through special education; for them the Centre is the usual follow-on from school. Both Centres also reflect ideas that parents should be supported in caring for their handicapped children, and that these people themselves have a need and a right to be occupied during the day within a special institution. The Centres offer parents a break and their children a place to go, people to meet and things to do.

It is in their programmes and their ultimate aims that the Centres seem to differ significantly. On Ániksi, the ultimate aim of the programme is to enable people eventually to find work and make some money, towards maintaining themselves. In Ffynnon, the programme aims at the overall development of the person. The ultimate aim is to teach people to live a life that is as independent, and as 'normal' as possible. Independence here is mainly understood as social independence, especially in areas of personal and home care, and not – as in Greece – as economic independence: 'overall development and independent living' as against 'work'. The difference between the two aims, and its sources, becomes clearer when we look at the economic and social structures of both societies.

The Centre opened on Ániksi during a period of economic optimism. Tourism was booming and bringing in money. Everyone could have a cut of the cake, so why not disabled people? Simple craft products could be made by nearly everyone and visitors would buy them as souvenirs: beadstrings (*kolombi*), plastic flowers, wood paintings, leather address books, and embroidered table cloths, could be – and are being – sold during the six-monthly exhibitions at the Centre. However, it was not just this that seemed to offer disabled people a chance to find work. The structure of economic enterprises on Ániksi is very small-scale: family or one-person businesses. This is as true for the tourism sector as for agriculture and commerce. There is no need for intensive training, qualifications or employment procedures. All that one needs to start a business is a building or even a room.

In Ffynnon, where unemployment was and is high, experience had shown little success in the employment of people with special needs. As the Centre manager put it, 'If normal people cannot find a job, what chance do people with special needs have?' Originally the Centre had been more like a workshop. It moved away from this model under the influence of the economic situation. However, there was also another influence which resulted in the Centre becoming a place for 'individual development'. In the field of 'mental handicap' – as it was then known – the idea of 'normalisation' had really caught on (Wolfensberger 1972). Originally meant to promote the rights of people with learning difficulties to a life filled with the same kind of meanings as other members of society, it became interpreted to mean that everyone should live as independently as possible, and do the same things as 'everyone else'. The *All-Wales Strategy* drew upon the principles of normalisation, and the focus shifted from employment, work and occupation, to individual needs, and personal, academic and social development. This is worthwhile and humane, but there is an irony to the reasoning. The insistence on *teaching* people with learning difficulties skills for independent living means that a group of people who are not independently 'competent' are, in the Centre, constantly in a situation of inequality and dependence. On Ániksi, independent living is not seen as important or worth striving for. After all, people on Ániksi usually stay at home, living with their parents until they marry or find work on the mainland. At home, the mother does most of the housework, so there is no need to teach this to people attending the Centre.

Another consequence of 'normalisation' is the encouragement of people with learning difficulties to use the same communal facilities that others do. In Ffynnon, efforts are made to take people into the community: to shop, for example, or to use the swimming pool. To a lesser degree, the same thing happens on Ániksi; the difference is that it is not an official aim. Perhaps the underlying idea in Ániksi is that the people attending the Centre differ from other members of their society only in the fact that they do not work to support themselves, whereas in Ffynnon the need is felt to address nearly all aspects of a person's life. But another factor also plays a role here. In Ffynnon, leisure for all members of the community is more formally organised than in Ániksi. Leisure centres, as opposed to a swim in the sea; all sorts of teams, as opposed to a game of basketball with one's friends. In Ffynnon young people go to the pub or disco to meet each other, on Ániksi they go for a walk or a spin on the motorbike. Young women on Ániksi hardly go out at all; neither do most other people in winter, they just watch television, sleep and talk. In Ffynnon it seems harder than on Ániksi for people with learning difficulties to join in with the leisure activities of other members of their community.

A final difference between the aims of the two Centres lies in the efforts made on Ániksi to find work for people attending the Centre. Once again, this can be related to economic structure. Because enterprises on Ániksi are small-scale and often family-run, conditions for the employment of disabled people seem to be more favourable than in Ffynnon, where the labour market is more formal and there are standard procedures for acquiring work. Greater demand for formal qualifications, interviewing and strict rules for starting up one's own business do not favour the employment of people with learning difficulties.

The people

Comparing the people attending the Centre on Ániksi with those attending the Centre in Ffynnon, I found similarities and differences. To start with the similarities, both groups of people show a variety of abilities and disabilities. Although the Centre in Ániksi was meant for all disabled people, the majority of clients are what would be called 'people with learning difficulties' in the UK. In addition, a few people with multiple disabilities and some people with mental health problems attend the Centre. Physically disabled people seem to be a different group:

Helena is a young deaf woman; she does not attend the Centre. However, when a course linked to jobs in the community was organised under the Horizon programme, offering an opportunity to learn skills, one of which was using computers, she did join in. When a member of staff asked her if she would attend the Centre daily, and join in the activities there, she explained that the Centre was not really the place for her. She told us that she was engaged to someone and would probably find a job soon.

On Ániksi, two things separate 'normal' people from 'incompetent' people: the abilities to find a job, and to get married. This young deaf woman did not see herself as among the group of people who would attend the Day Centre. This question of a 'hierarchy of handicaps', for want of a better expression, has also been recognised by Dybwad (1970), discussing the mixing of people with learning difficulties and people with mental health problems.

The Centre in Ffynnon also caters mainly for people with learning difficulties. However, as on Ániksi, we also find some people with psychiatric problems. These two categories are, it seems, seen as more closely related to each other than physical disability and learning difficulties (Devlieger, in Chapter 3, documents something similar).

There is great variety in the ability/disability of the people attending both Centres. In each group there are people who have severe problems, not only intellectually, but in their social adjustment, communication and ability to look after themselves. At the same time in both groups we also find people who are well able to communicate, to look after their own basic needs, and to carry out a variety of activities more or less independently:

Théra is 27 years old. She has suffered from severe epilepsy since birth and her abilities are greatly affected. She has attended the Centre on Ániksi since it opened. Théra is barely able to communicate except for making some noises and taking your hand when she wants something. Her walking is unsteady, she likes to hold your hand whenever she goes outside. Most of the day she sits at a table packing and unpacking her bag. Sometimes she does some colouring in a book that she brings in this bag. The other people of the Centre pour her lemonade at breaktime, or put the straw in her carton of juice. At home she is like a toddler, constantly seeking attention, and her mother has to occupy and look after her all the time.

Socrates is a young man in his twenties. He has been at the Centre on Ániksi since leaving primary school. He is quiet but friendly and, if you take the time to sit down with him, enjoys a chat. In the Centre he has, with some help now and again from a member of staff, been making leather wallets and covers for address books. For two years he has been working in a kiosk in the grounds of the Centre, where he sells ice cream, sweets, cigarettes and lemonade to people from in- and outside the Centre. He works out the bills on a calculator and his family help him with stock-taking and ordering goods.

Tom is a man in his forties who has Down's Syndrome and is partially sighted. He has attended the Centre in Ffynnon since leaving special education. A quiet, gentle man who only talks in whispers, much of the time, unfortunately, even his mother cannot understand him. Tom needs considerable help looking after himself at home. At the Centre he is able to do simple activities such as making Christmas decorations and some weaving. Once he begins an activity he likes to stick at it, hour after hour and day after day. He enjoys making things and shows them off to all who are interested. He spends his days in the craft area and does not join in with other group activities.

Mary is in her thirties and she too has attended the Centre in Ffynnon since leaving special secondary education. Mary likes to keep herself to herself, but will talk to you if you make the effort. At the Centre she is popular with her own group of friends. She is active and joins in with many activities. Her speciality is sport: she is a member of the Special Olympics team at the Centre and spends a lot of time running. She is also good at, and enjoys, the more complicated craftwork. Once a week, Mary helps out at a local mother and toddler group organised by the Salvation Army, as part of a work experience scheme.

Neither in Ániksi nor in Ffynnon are the people classified as 'incompetent' a homogeneous group, something which corresponds with the findings of the other contributors to this volume.

Finally, people attending the two Centres also have in common the absence in their areas of other facilities catering to their needs, and their difficulty in joining in with the activities of other adult members of their community, e.g. study, work or marriage. For both groups, coming to the Centre means more than just learning a skill or making something. The social aspect – a place to go, a structure to their days, a chance to meet people and make friends – is at least as important.

Having looked at how the groups of people attending the Centres resemble each other, let us now examine how they differ. First, while around 100 people attend regularly in Ffynnon, plus 25 in the Special Care Unit, the Centre on Ániksi has 28 people on its list: approximately 0.2 per cent of the population of Ffynnon, compared to 0.1 per cent of Ániksi. There are several possible explanations for this difference. On Ániksi, some people cannot attend due to lack of transport: the area is large and some of the villages barely accessible because of poor roads. The Centre has one bus, compared to the four that are used to transport people to and from home in Ffynnon. Another reason for the difference in numbers seems to be the relative absence of more severely disabled people in the Centre on Ániksi. Many of these people have been sent to special schools and larger institutions on the mainland; until the opening of the Centre there was no alternative day care.

According to staff on Ániksi it has not always been easy to persuade parents to send their child to the Centre. In many cases their child would not have attended a special facility before; going to the Centre would be the first public admission that there was something 'wrong'. There may still be shame about such matters:

One day I went into the bank to change some money, and began talking to the lady behind the counter, who asked me what I was doing on Ániksi. When I explained, she told me about a lady friend of hers, a doctor. This woman had a child who was mentally handicapped. The child was five years old and sat at home in a chair all day. The doctor was too ashamed to admit this openly. She could not take the child anywhere for advice or assessment, or even out to school or playschool, because of this shame. According to her friend, the bank employee, this was made worse by the fact that she was a doctor herself.

Herzfeld (1980) has discussed the importance of the concept of shame (in Greek, *timi*) in Mediterranean countries, and its social component, the failure to live up to expectations. In the literature discussing the experiences of parents of children with learning difficulties in countries such as the Netherlands and the UK we also find the concept of shame to be important, as a sense of personal and social failure (Janssen 1982; Zevenbergen 1986). However, among the families I researched directly I found little evidence for this notion of shame. In Ániksi, for example, parents' primary concerns were practical and economic, as well as a fear for the future. They did not hide their children; in fact many were taken out regularly into the community, for walks, swims and outings, by various members of their families. One Ániksiot, mother of a young woman with severe impairments, said that she had always made a deliberate point of this: 'They [the brothers and sisters] take her out a lot for walks. And I do. From when she was a baby. I said, that's the way it is. We go out, no hiding. We went for walks, we went visiting. And we still do.'

The fact that parents on Ániksi did send their children to a public institution could be seen as a sign of, and a step towards, coming to terms with shame. In Wales, because of the information available to the general public on learning difficulties (for example through the media), having a child with learning difficulties seems to be more accepted, a matter for grief rather than shame.

There is also a gender difference. In Ffynnon, an equal number of men and women attend the Centre. On Ániksi, however, there are only six women to twenty-two men. This may reflect the strong differentiation in gender roles in Greece. On Ániksi, most women stay at home; being 'slow', or having a learning difficulty, is less of an obstacle to doing simple jobs in the house, than it is for a man who is supposed to go out, work and make money:

Lambrini is a fairly capable young woman in her early twenties. She has attended primary school and has been at home for a few years. She now works at weaving carpets in the Centre in Ániksi. Her mother was initially reluctant to let her go: 'I did not want her to go at first. I did not want her to work. Now, I see she likes it. She has her friends there. I would like her to marry one day. A working boy. She is healthy, she could have children. She does not know her letters but she is very out-going.'

The next difference is where the people attending the two Centres live. On Ániksi, twenty-three out of twenty-eight people live at home with their parents. The other five live in the nursing home which shares the same grounds as the Centre. The parents of these people are dead, ill or live on another island. On Ániksi, young people live at home; the only difference for people with learning difficulties is that they are less likely to leave home because of marriage or employment on the mainland. By contrast, many people attending the Centre in Ffynnon live in hostels, foster homes or group homes. A high value is placed on independent living for all members of the community and efforts are made to provide opportunities to do so for people with learning difficulties. However, despite this, the majority of those attending the Centre whose parents are alive and well still live at home.

Finally, there are age limits to membership. In Ffynnon the youngest people in the Centre have just left school, at 18 years of age. On Ániksi the official minimum age is 16; however, due to the lack of alternative facilities, exceptions are made. The youngest boy admitted was only 12. For both Centres, retirement age is the upper age limit.

I have discussed only briefly the differences between the client groups of the two Centres, and related them to differences in local – especially social – structures. I will now focus on what these people do in the Centres and how this compares with what other adult members of their societies do.

Incompetence and work

Work is one of the main adult activities, of great value to the individual as well as to society as a whole. Work, in its widest sense, is a basic condition of the existence and continuation of human life, it is independent of any particular form of society (Parker 1983). The fact that work is important, indeed necessary (even if only to secure human survival and reproduction) does not mean that it takes the same form or has the same meaning in every society. 'Work' is not a straightforward category. What is understood by work and how it is valued is not self-evident, but culturally and historically constructed. The value attached to work has not always and everywhere been positive. In Western societies people of high social status have often looked down upon work, in particular manual labour, as the lowest and least of human activities.

The widespread influence of Protestant morality, with its emphasis on the virtues of work, and the introduction of the large-scale machinery that made the new discipline necessary, resulted eventually in the belief that people actually need to work (Sayers 1988: 734). This need goes beyond economic imperatives: work plays a crucial psychological role in the formation of self-esteem, identity and a sense of order (*ibid.*: 724). Socialism itself is based on the importance to the human individual of social, productive labour. Organisational structures and the values attached to work are interrelated. The literature on work offers a number of different definitions of work. Most of these reflect different types of social organisation.

Brown (cited in Parker 1983: 56) distinguishes between the basic activity of work, and work as an occupation. Work is:

a very general, all embracing term, used to refer to all those physical and mental activities which are intended to transform natural materials into a more useful form to improve human knowledge and understanding of the world and/or to provide or distribute goods and services to others, in whatever context such activities are carried out.

An occupation is:

a socially structured and socially recognised set of work activities, the carrying out of which produces goods and/or services for which others would be prepared to pay.

According to these definitions, all occupations are work but not all work is an occupation. An occupation is work socially structured, recognised and valued in particular ways. Employment, which implies an employer, employee, pay and specified conditions of work is occupation formally organised; it is a relationship specific to a capitalist economic system (Harding and Jenkins 1989). Work in modern, Western society is often equated with employment. Employment is not only a narrow definition of work, it is also a relatively new one. It was only in the late eighteenth and nineteenth centuries that the modern Western world saw the rise of the male breadwinner in employment, as opposed to the household production and economic strategies of pre-industrial times (Pahl 1988). The narrower the definition of work, the more sensitive it will be to cultural and historical influences and the more activities fall outside the category. An example of this is housework. Once seen as important work, carried out by a complete household, it became an activity that was 'outside' the economy, and the people responsible for it became 'non-working', housewives.

A common notion about 'incompetent' people is that they do not, and/or are unable to, work. It is not as simple as this. Whether people are able – 'competent' – to work depends on the social definition, form and structure of work. In this section I look at two questions. First, do 'incompetent' people in Ániksi and Ffynnon work or not? Second, is there a relationship between the answer to that first question and local structures and values? These issues require a definition of work. The form and meaning of work vary between and within societies, suggesting that no universal definition of work is possible and that comparison is difficult. Wallman's framework (1979: 20) offers a solution to this dilemma:

Work is the production, management and conversion of the resources necessary to livelihood. . . . These resources are identified as: land, labour and capital, time, information and identity. Each resource may be assessed in terms of its economic, social or personal value and that resource value is by no means a measure only of utility or material worth.

Work is thus a process, with various aspects or dimensions. Cultural differences do not change these basic aspects, only the way they relate to each other. It is in the form and emphasis of the relationships between the aspects of work that local structures and values become apparent. For example, Wallman (*ibid.*: 4) defines work as involving the application of human energy to things, within a structure of time and place. It is thus important to know not only what is done, but where and when.

Work is not done for its own sake, there are economic, social and personal incentives (*ibid.*: 4–6). The most obvious incentive for work is sustenance; humans need to work to keep themselves alive. For some authors this is what makes work 'a general category of economically-oriented transformative activity' (Harding and Jenkins 1989: 12), undertaken 'as a means to satisfy our needs' (Sayers 1988: 723). Within each society work is necessary to ensure the survival and reproduction of its members, whether directly – hunting, gathering, farming, caring, etc. – and/or indirectly, by earning a wage. However, there is more to work than material reward. Work is also seen as 'man's "calling", his craft, his means of self-expression' (Ronco and Peattie 1988: 716), the way to self-development and fulfilment, necessary for self-esteem, identity and a sense of order. These are the personal incentives. Closely related to the personal are the social incentives. Identity gives a sense of self, but always in relation to the other. The social incentives for work vary from interaction with fellow workers, to relations with society at large, to status and social identity (Sayers 1988).

The economic, personal and social incentives to work, and its nature and structure, are the dimensions along which I will compare the activities of 'incompetent' people in the Centres in Ániksi and Ffynnon.

Ultimately, the question is whether 'incompetent' people can be said to 'work' within the society in which they live.

Work: Ániksi

When I asked the people attending the Centre in Ániksi why they came, nearly all said, ' Work', 'To go to work', 'To do work'. When asked, 'What do you do here?', the answer again was, 'Work'. The official purpose of the Centre is to teach clients a skill, to give them the prospect of earning a living on the island in work that is appropriate for that area. In the Centre that means making things that can be sold as craft objects or souvenirs, mainly to tourists. Here is an economic link with the future, and, in fact, there are people – six out of thirty – who have left the Centre and are now earning money. However, only two out of those six people found craft-related work; the others are providing services for tourists within hotels and tourist information, or working in kiosks (small shops selling newspapers, sweets, cigarettes etc., to be found on nearly every street corner in Greece).

The economic links are not only with future prospects. There is the fact that products made in the Centre are sold twice a year during an exhibition. The money this brings in goes back into the Centre for outings, day trips and holidays. There is the money which the clients receive once a month. This money is not enough to give them economic independence, but at about £50 a month it is more than pocket money, especially considering that they work part time (only mornings), that they receive free breakfast and dinner, and that a 'teacher' is paid about £200 a month. A small number of people work outside the Centre too, helping their parents in the vegetable store or woodwork shop, or in part-time jobs in hotels or restaurants. This fits in with the rest of the community on Ániksi: few people have only one well-defined job; most jobs need no qualifications, application or interview; they are often advertised by word of mouth; they may be created by other members of the family. The economic situation for people with learning difficulties is poor, even if they work in the Centre and have a job on the side. But they are not the only ones in that situation. Full-time, regular paid jobs are scarce, many people are more or less unemployed, and there is no unemployment benefit. Money is a big worry for most people in Ániksi. Economic dependency on the family is high, for people with learning difficulties and for 'ordinary' people.

The social aspect of working in the Centre is very important; 'meeting' and 'making' friends was the other main reason that clients gave for attending the Centre. For many people this was the first place outside their homes that they had visited regularly. It is a place where they are accepted as they are, and where some attempt is made to meet their particular needs. Most had either spent their days at home before they came to the Centre, or attended ordinary schools without ever having been able to keep up with their peers.

It is a relatively small group, twenty-five on average, that comes together in the Centre nearly every day. They know each other well and usually seem to enjoy being together. A lot of laughing and joking goes on. They also help and teach each other. For example, when I interviewed Nikos, who is not able to speak very well, Markos interpreted for both of us. And when Helena has a dirty nose, Demi runs after her with a tissue and helps her to wipe her nose.

Outside 'working hours', the staff organise day trips or holidays on and outside the island. A considerable effort is made by Centre staff, especially the Manager, to encourage integration with the rest of society. People are encouraged to leave the Centre when the opportunity for work outside arises, and clients are helped to find suitable employment. A recent project is the opening of a kiosk in the Centre grounds, which is currently run by two Centre clients and supervised by their families. The kiosk is used by people in the Centre, people from the nursing home, and people from outside the Centre. The next project planned is the opening of a car wash, again in the Centre's grounds, to be used by people from inside and outside the Centre. The driving force for these projects is the Horizon project, funded by the EU and implemented in co-operation and co-ordination with similar centres in Belgium, Germany and Denmark. However, it is only the more able people who participate in these programmes. The more severely impaired people remain making things within the Centre, with no plans or prospects to move outside.

What of the nature and structure of the activities in the Centre? The Centre's purpose – to teach skills that can be used to earn money – is reflected in activities such as: working with leather (making purses, diaries, folders for letters, etc.); needlework (cushion covers, tablecloths, scarves); decorating wooden and metal pictures; and rug-making. A teacher used to visit the Centre to teach a few of the more able people literacy and numeracy. However, these lessons were discontinued when she found a job in another part of Greece. They are not part of the official programme, depending on individual and voluntary initiatives. Another example of this is sport. A local physical education teacher visited the Centre one day and offered to take the clients twice a week during the winter time to the sports stadium for exercises and games such as basketball and volleyball.

The day starts early; the bus to collect everyone leaves before 7.30 a.m.

After lunch, the Centre closes and the people go home to rest and spend time with their families. This corresponds with many a working day on Ániksi, where, in the summer, the afternoons are too hot to work. There are some leisure activities, mainly sport. They take place outside, in the grounds or the stadium, and are completely separate from work. This structuring of activity, in terms of place and time, is comparable to elsewhere on Ániksi.

The work is done in three large rooms, each devoted to particular activities. Clients spend most of the day in 'their' room doing their own 'work'. However, people are allowed to wander about to a degree. Only in the carpet-making room did I witness people being sent out, back to their own room. It is routine for people to move around and have a chat here and there. Sometimes they try a different activity, often helped by other clients:

Nikos, who is normally based in the large room where he strings beads, walks into the middle room. Socrates is there, working with copper. Nikos watches him. Socrates, without saying anything, shows him how to do it. Nikos wants to try and Socrates holds his hand, guiding him. Finally Nikos, concentrating, does it on his own. Suddenly he gets up and leaves. Socrates calls after him, but Nikos does not come back.

The clients work at their own speed and are allowed to do just that. There is little interference by the teachers, and no instructions or encouragement to work harder (with the exception again of the carpet-making workshop). There, the instructor likes to remind people that they come to the Centre to do something:

'It is nine o'clock now, you are supposed to work by now. If you do only one row a day it will take you two years to make a carpet. If you do four or five rows, it might be finished in six months or so.'

Help is offered when asked for in the middle room and routinely at one table in the large room (needlework). Like her colleague Maria in the carpet room, instructor Emilia often works together with 'her girls':

Maria is setting up a new carpet. She tells Manos to come over and to start working. After a few minutes, Maria takes over from Manos again, to show him how to do the flower pattern: 'Ella (here you are).' Manos gets on with it. Now and again Maria takes over or works beside him.

Emilia is helping Anna with a wool collage for the wall. Emilia glues the background while Anna sticks on the wool.

At the other table in the large room, clients do very little; their ability to work, and their teacher's ability and motivation to stimulate them, are limited.

Although people are generally left to function at their own speed, and are often slow, there is a productive element in what they are doing. This is the way they see it themselves. They show off their work if one shows interest; they seem to enjoy what they are doing, and are proud of the results. There is room for freedom; for the individual client to switch activity now and again; to work at his or her own speed, when he or she wants; freedom for a walk and a chat. On the other hand, this means that there is little encouragement to do better, there is little expectation on the part of the teachers.

In conclusion, these people do work: at the Centre, at home and outside their homes. They are productive though slow; sometimes they need help. They enjoy their work and find satisfaction in it; they enjoy and engage in social interaction with each other. Although they cannot sustain themselves with their work, this is also true for many other people on Ániksi. The Centre is located close to the centre of Ániksi town and people on the island know about it. Although the clients see it as their place of work, most outsiders and even members of staff call it a school. Thus, working in the Centre lacks the status of real work in the eyes of other islanders. But it does offer some opportunity for people with learning difficulties to enter 'normal' channels of work.

Work: Ffynnon

Most of the people I interviewed here, when asked why they came to the Centre, answered that they came there to work. This is despite the fact that the Centre in recent years is moving towards providing educational and leisure activities, and away from the idea of providing training in basic skills, to be used in workshops and doing contract work. There may be various reasons why its users see the Centre as a place of work. Perhaps it is a remnant from the days of contract work or an identification with other adults they know, who are going to work. The Centre as a follow-up to, and something completely different from, school could mean for them the difference between childhood and adulthood, between education and work. Whatever the reasons, for the people I interviewed going to the Centre meant going to work.

Closely connected with this notion of work is the money that people receive at the end of every week they attend the Centre, which both staff and clients refer to as 'pay'. This brings us on to incentives, in this case economic. The amount is very small, miniscule in comparison to average wages (between £0.50 and £2.00 weekly, depending on when the person first started attending the Centre). But to the clients it represents real pay. It is money that enables their access to things like snacks from the shop at breaktime, during the week in town, or during their evening out at local clubs like the Gateway Club (which organises social events for people with learning difficulties and is attended by a majority of the people attending the Centre). So, although remuneration is very small, to the people in the Centre there is an economic aspect to their activities. Not nearly enough to sustain themselves, it still offers them some access to things such as snacks and leisure. From society's point of view, whatever the people at the Centre do, it is not seen as sufficiently valuable to demand 'proper' remuneration.

Another important reason for attending the Centre mentioned in the interviews is to be with other people, to make and be with friends. Since the biggest part of their time spent outside the home is spent at the Centre, this is the main place for clients to meet people other than their family. Many have known each other for years, even from school. They also meet at local, mainly special, clubs, during outings and holidays organised by the Centre or by Mencap (a charity for people with learning difficulties), and at events organised by the Centre, such as Christmas parties, etc. In fact, most of them have little contact with 'ordinary' people outside their families. This social incentive is part of 'going to work' at the Centre. Even if the feelings of friendliness seem to vary – sometimes on a daily basis – clients often refer to each other as 'friends'.

However, meeting and being with other people is not the only social aspect of 'going to work' at the Centre. There is also the place of people with learning difficulties within Welsh society to consider. Despite the fact that people with learning difficulties are often able to do particular jobs – from woodwork to contract work, helping in a playgroup to washing cars, gardening to toy-making – they are doing very few of them. Most people attending special schools go on to the Centre; few end up in 'ordinary' jobs. In documents on the purpose and policies of the Centre, and in conversation with its Manager, the difficulty in finding suitable work for people with learning difficulties, especially, but not only, in times of high unemployment, was emphasised. The expectation seems to be that when it is hard for an 'ordinary' person to find a job, people with learning difficulties should forget about it altogether. This is also expressed in the Centre's day-to-day policy, where very little attempt is made to train people for, or find them, work outside.

A few people are on voluntary schemes, only 6 per cent of the Centre's client group. One of these is Peter, a man in his early twenties who has been at the Centre since he left secondary special school. His big interest is cars and buses, and he loves washing and looking after them. For a while he has been washing the Centre's bus, and cars belonging to the staff. Recently his social worker has arranged a job for him at the police station, washing the police cars and doing odd jobs. Only one morning a week, this was due to be increased to two mornings shortly. To Peter his job, washing cars, is very important in terms of his self-esteem and his place in society. But he is also aware that there is no economic reward:

I come here to work. I wash the bus first thing in the morning. If I have nothing else to do I wash a few cars, and buses maybe. The bus is shining today. Social Services leave it all to me. I enjoy coming here. If people work, they enjoy it. . . . I wash all the cars. They should pay me but they don't. I like washing cars, I like to do them all. I work hard for it. I should get money. I wash the staff cars too. A lot.

The Centre is not completely isolated from society; in the area of work there is some interaction with the 'outside world'. In addition to the voluntary schemes I have mentioned, in the part of the Centre called the workshop many clients produce seasonal presents and decorations around Christmas time. These products – dried flower arrangements, bags of potpourri, découpage pictures, Christmas decorations, cards etc. – are sold on the local market at a special stall. Clients seem to enjoy this work and are proud of their products. The découpage was a particularly succesful project. One young woman, who has great skill and patience, is continuing to do this work.

Until a few years ago, Christmas was not the only time that products made at the Centre were sold to the general public. There used to be a woodwork shop where garden benches and stools were made; in the other workshop the clients made soft toys. Both were very popular with people outside the Centre. Clients, staff and parents express regret that these projects have been discontinued:

We used to do a lot here. Soft toys, bins, soft Chrismas trees etc. Every six months we would have an exhibition and sale here. It stopped because of the Safety Act. We needed labels and we did not get them. Things changed. Safety regulations on toys. We were told not to bother any more. It is all education now. Don't get me wrong, I am well for it. But, they need this too. To do something and have something to show for it. We all need occupation, we all need to feel we have done something. To learn about money and transport is important, but this is too. (Instructor)

'Mark isn't quite satisfied with the Centre. There was a change. Probably the costs. When he went to the Centre first it was an Adult Training Centre. He was making plenty. Woodwork. Wooden benches. We bought one for the garden. Basketmaking. Now it is a Social Activity Centre and they are confined to social activities, I see them around town. Mark would do a good job, in a restaurant for example. He knows how to lay the table and he is quite capable of doing little jobs.' (Father of client)

Much of what happens in the Centre depends on the individual Manager and the instructors. There has not been a consistent structure or pro-

gramme over the years, partly due to staff turnover, partly due to changing values and policies. With respect to changing values, years ago the
Centre undertook contract work of various kinds; subsequently this was
seen as exploitative and discontinued.

Centre policies have adjusted themselves to this trend, as can be seen in
the document *Into the Nineties,* referred to earlier:

The emphasis from a work-orientated environment to a service which looked to
develop the ability and confidence of a person in their everyday lives would be signalled in a positive way and Adult Training Centres would be known as Social
Activity Centres. . . .The Centres' programme should be organised to cover all
aspects of the individual's need and not to be concentrated on repetitive and
mundane tasks which have no relevance to daily living and encouragement of
independence.

Some activities in the Centre can be called 'work', because of the meaning
clients give to what they do, the pay at the end of the week, the sale of
products on the market at Christmas time, the contribution to society
through the voluntary schemes, and the social aspect of meeting people in
a regular place at a regular time. How do the other activities in the Centre
compare to the notion of 'work' in Welsh society?

The activities taking place in, or organised by, the Centre include: personal care and skills; cooking and housework; shopping, numeracy and
literacy (some of which take place outside the Centre); woodwork, arts
and crafts; and swimming, running, bowling, yoga, etc. These activities
can be categorised thus: *education,* the main purpose of which is the
further development of the client's skills; *sports and leisure,* with the
emphasis on the process and on individual enjoyment; and *work,* where
the end product or result of the activity is at least as important as the
process. There are, of course, problems with this categorisation. Looking
at the notions informing the categories, they are simply those most commonly accepted in both Wales and Greece. In each country there seems to
be a rough division of labour along the above lines. But there is overlap
between the categories. In some sport, for example within the framework
of the Special Olympics, it is arguable that the result is as important as the
process or the enjoyment of the activity.

Another problem is how to decide which activity comes into which category. Whose description of the activity and its purpose to use? I will draw
on what the clients themselves said or showed me, my own observations,
and what the instructors and Manager said. The following activities can
be described as 'work'. Woodwork, activities carried out in the workshop,
especially around Christmas time, housework, cooking and shopping all
count as work. So do the voluntary schemes: some clients spend time
outside the Centre, helping in a mother and toddlers group, helping to

supply lunches for the elderly, and, as we have seen, washing cars for the police. In all of these cases people 'labour' to achieve a 'product' that would be seen as 'useful' or 'valuable' by the majority of local people.

Some of the sport and crafts are borderline areas. In the latter case, there is often an end product involved, important to the clients – who frequently showed it to me with obvious pride and satisfaction – and sometimes to the instructor (depending on its quality). The quality and usefulness of a product are important criteria in its appreciation by people other than the clients themselves. Instructors would show me bags of potpourri, Christmas cards or decorations. However, no one but the clients would show me an undefinable painting.

So, part of what the clients do at the Centre in Ffynnon is work: labour to produce an end result or product that is generally seen as useful. This brings me to the last aspect of work I will discuss here, its structure. For work to be really seen as work it has to have some kind of structure: time, place and discipline. These elements can to some degree be found in the daily activities in the Centre. Some of these correspond with the structures organising work in the rest of society: the five-day week, the spatial location of the Centre within the town, the identifiable areas allocated to the various activities, the expectation that people stay within a certain area during the set period of that activity. These are all general features of work organisation.

There are also differences from the world of work. The time structure of the various activities during the day at the Centre, especially since the 'one-hour period' system started, means that clients do an activity for one hour and then move to a different area, a different instructor and a different activity. This is more like school than a workplace. The instructors experience this system as positive; it forces them to structure time as productively as possible:

You have to be more structured. You need to structure it more so that all get to do something. But sometimes one hour is not enough. We skip break then and have one and a half hours. (Instructor)

For the clients this seems – to an extent – to prevent distraction and boredom. On the other hand, it makes clients very dependent on the staff, as few of them know their programme for the day. They have a written programme, but most cannot read. So situations constantly occur where, at the start of a period, clients are wandering around and instructors are looking for them. The problem appears to be finding a balance between the needs and rights to respect and relative freedom of choice and independence of the client, the 'given' factors such as the size of the Centre and the number of clients, and the staff's need for structure.

Typical days

Let us now look at a 'typical day' at each Centre for two individuals, one on Aniksi, one in Ffynnon.

Sofia is a woman in her forties, who lives with her mother in a village ten miles out of Aniksi town. At the age of five she contracted meningitis as a result of which she experienced serious delay in her development. She has attended the Centre since the day it opened and works in the hand production of rugs and small carpets.

07.45 Sofia is picked up by the Centre bus, arriving at the Centre just before 8.30 a.m. She goes straight to the room where she works and meets up with her three fellow workers and the 'teacher,' who makes some coffee on a hot plate in the room. They drink coffee and chat about anything from weekend outings to friends who are ill and did not turn up for work. Sofia likes the chat at least as much as her work.

09.15 Time for work. The four people and the teacher take their places at the large wooden looms. The teacher moves around from one place to another, helping and showing the others what to do and making sure they follow the right colour patterns. Sofia stops now and again to chat with Manos, another worker, or with someone entering the room. Progress is slow but with the help of the teacher who will often do a few rows before the others come in, or while they are rolling the wool into balls, a new rug is finished every few months. ·

10.30 Breakfast time. Manos and Sofia have collected the rolls, meat and cheese from the kitchen and put them on a table in the largest room. Everyone takes a roll with some meat and cheese. One of the teachers helps with the distribution of the rolls and hands out packets of fruit juice. Most people go outside, standing around chatting in the shade or sitting at the tables of the kiosk. The younger ones play ball. Sofia sits on a bench in the shade with two other women. They eat, laugh and chat.

11.00 Back to work. One by one everyone goes back inside. Sofia continues her work on the rug. She is happy to show me how to do it, everyone smiles and praises me when I do my first row. Maria, the cleaner, comes in to sweep the floor and empty the bin. Ari, a young man who is usually in the large room and likes to do little jobs, follows her and carries the bins. He shows Sofia the money he received for doing jobs in the kitchen. Maria, the teacher, urges everyone to get back to work. She is setting out the colour scheme for Sofia and tells her to pay attention to it.

12.30 Dinner time. Clients, teachers and the children who live in the orphanage, all eat together in the big dining room. There are two large tables: one for the children, one for the people of the Day Centre. For them the food is already laid out on metal trays on the table by the kitchen staff. The children's food is put on plates in a press to keep it hot: they all come in at different times during the next hour. Sofia complains about the children making noise.

13.00 Sofia gets on the bus and waits for it to take her home. The bus fills up slowly. Two girls of the orphanage come for the ride and one of the teachers sits in the front beside the driver. It is noisy and the radio plays loudly. When the bus leaves the driver puts on a familiar tape and everyone sings and claps. Another day at the Centre is over.

Suzy is in her late forties. She lives in a special hostel about two miles away from the Ffynnon Centre. From the time she first went to school she found it hard to keep up with the other children and she was transferred to the Junior Training Centre, from where she continued on to the Adult Training Centre (later to become the Social Activity Centre).

08.30 A Council minibus picks Suzy up from the hostel. A few minutes later she arrives at the Centre, where she meets up with Maggie. Suzy and Maggie have been at the Centre for many years and get on very well together. Today their group meets in the Hall with their Key Worker, D. From 9.00 until 9.30 they chat about the news of the day and any other topic that comes up, personal or having to do with the Centre.

09.30 Suzy has Education with Sam this morning. Suzy follows Sam, who has come to the Hall to 'round up' her group, to a room off the Art Room. It is 'sums' today and each of the six people in the group receives a paper with simple sums on it. Sam explains the first two and then they must do the others by themselves. Two people finish after ten minutes or so. Sam helps two others, who manage with a bit of encouragement. Suzy finds it very hard and Sam goes through each aspect of the sum with her until she gets it. I help Mary, who manages each sum with guidance. Sam, the instructor, tells me it is hard work: 'You have to keep at them, and then if they do not do it for a few months it is all gone again. Not with all, there are the ones who are very good. But with some of them.'

10.30 Tea break in the Hall. Everyone gets their own cup of tea, made by the group who have 'tea duty' this week. Suzy sits at the same table most days, with the same people. They talk, laugh or complain about each other. A young man at the next table is crying. Suzy goes over to him and puts her arm around him. When I ask what's the matter, she answers for him: 'Oh he's alright, he often gets like this.'

11.00 Homecraft this morning means cooking lunch. Suzy makes her way to the Staff Room where there is a cooker and a sink. Three people out of the group of eight have not turned up yet and Annette, the instructor, goes looking for them. When all are present, it is decided what to cook for lunch. Some people make suggestions. Suzy favours chips, someone else fancies trifle. Annette says chips would be okay, and what about tinned fruit and cream for afters? Annette goes to the kitchen to get the potatoes, she sends Suzy to the flat to ask for a tin of peaches and cream. The other members of the group wait around. When all the ingredients are there, the work is divided. Some people volunteer for tasks. Suzy offers to peel the potatoes, someone else wants to cut the chips, others get jobs assigned to them, for example washing up or opening the tins. Annette cooks the chips and when it is ready all eat their lunch. After that they join the other clients who are eating their lunch in the Hall.

13.30 Suzy has Craft in the Art Room. Fiona, the instructor, decides they will make designs today. There are nine people in the group. They make designs with a ruler and pencil on big sheets of white paper and colour them in. Suzy enjoys this, she makes a clear design and is very precise in her colouring. She shows me her work when it is finished. Fiona makes the design for the people who find this difficult; they just colour in.

14.30 Teabreak again. More chatting around the table where Suzy sits.

15.00 Instructor Norma rounds her people up for Self-Help Skills. Suzy, Tracy and Liz are washing each other's hair in the special washing area. After that Norma dries their hair and puts make-up on everyone who wants it. The others sit around; Mary is doing her nails and Ann is having a doze.

16.00 Everyone gets ready to go home. Suzy is looking for her coat. When she finds it she waits in the Hall until the bus is ready to take her home. It has been a long day but she tells me that she likes coming and 'would not miss a day'.

Comparing Wales and Greece

Pahl (1988) and Ronco and Peattie (1988) consider actors' perceptions of what they are doing one of the foremost criteria with which to distinguish work from non-work. The majority of the people interviewed, in both places, consider what they do at the Centres as work. The justification for this notion of work for them is in the nature of the activities, and in the economic, personal and social incentives attached to them. In the programme of both Centres I have identified activities which can reasonably be called work. The emphasis of these activities is on their product. On Ániksi these activities take up most of the day, as opposed to only a small part of the day in Ffynnon. Work used to be a more important part of the activities within the Centre there, but a combination of factors changed this: the interests of the individual managers and instructors, and the notion that work, especially contract work, judged to be boring and monotonous and done for less pay than 'normal' workers, is exploitative. This illustrates the influence of local values – values that do not seem to consider the views of the people themselves – on the activities of 'incompetent' people. Some, for example, told me that they missed the work they were doing before, especially woodwork and toy-making.

   In both Centres there is some financial reward for working. Some of the products made at both Centres are sold into the community, at local markets or exhibitions. The proceeds of these sales go back to the Centres and thus, indirectly, to the producers. However, the money received as 'pay' is, in both places, unrelated to productivity; it also differs greatly between the two Centres. In Ániksi it is a much more 'realistic' sum than in Ffynnon. It is clear that both groups of people enjoy productive activities, find pride and satisfaction in them, and are often quite skilful. The less able people might not produce things that the majority of people would rate high in quality and usefulness, but this fact does not seem to affect the positive experience of the workers themselves. The social incentives for the people attending both Centres are to be found in the opportunity to socialise with people outside their own families and to make friends. Spending the day doing something similar to what 'competent' people do, makes it easier for both groups to identify with other adult members of their society.

The main differences between the two Centres are in their links to the wider community. On Ániksi it seems to be easier for people to move on to work outside the Centre, and active efforts are made by the Manager to achieve this. Some people attend the Centre in the morning, while working somewhere else in the afternoon. There is also the semi-independent work carried out within the Centre's grounds, i.e. the kiosk and, soon, the car wash. In Ffynnon people engage in so-called 'work experience', but the boundaries between this and the labour market are much more fixed. Work experience takes place in the community, but it is voluntary and unpaid, and no one moves on from it. In reality, it is more like an extra sphere of work *between* the Centre and employment.

This difference between the two places seems to be strongly influenced by the structure and definition of work within both societies. The majority of jobs on Ániksi do not require formal qualifications, they are often self-initiated or obtained through family contacts, it is routine to hold several jobs at the same time, and everyone struggles to make a living. There is no such thing as unemployment benefit. The structure and organisation of work on Ániksi is fairly informal. In contrast, in Ffynnon it is much harder to get a job; qualifications and a formal interview and selection process are usual. The boundaries between working and not working seem less flexible.

This contrast, between formality and informality in structure, is the second major difference between the Centres, particularly in the structure of time and place and, to some extent, the roles of staff. On Ániksi clients work more or less at their own speed and when they want to. They can walk around and have a chat with other clients in the same or another workroom. The clients appear to be happy, relaxed and quite independent within the framework of the Centre. In Ffynnon, where the Centre is much larger, and thus harder to come to terms with, the structure of time is stricter and difficult for the clients to grasp. This makes them much more dependent on instructors. While time is more structured in Ffynnon, activities move around more, adding to the clients' confusion.

So, although on Ániksi things appear to be less organised, this seems to suit the clients better and offers them greater independence. It also means they are on a more equal footing with the staff members. Staff members on Ániksi do not interfere much with what the clients do and spend a large part of the day just sitting around and chatting together. In Ffynnon, however, instructors spend a lot of time telling clients what to do and when.

This 'created' dependency in Ffynnon raises questions about the Centre's aim to offer clients a variety of experience and opportunities in order to develop a broader range of skills. This results in a 'student–teacher' relationship, without much room for individual spur-of-the-moment input by clients. In a more one-sided approach, where people do one or two things more intensively, and are comfortable with it, they might not reach their full potential in *various* skills but they might experience more independence. Davies, in Chapter 5, sees this loss of autonomy as the price to be paid for the creation of an adult image for people with learning difficulties. It is a price which may limit the meaning of such an image. Again, we see here the influence of policies – ultimately reflecting local norms and values – on the daily lives of 'incompetent' people and on the degree to which they are treated as adult members of their society.

'Incompetent' people are able to work and do work. That the emphasis on the various dimensions of work varies, between 'incompetent' and 'competent' people, and between societies and cultures, should not obscure this. Some dimensions of work are more problematic for 'incompetent' people than others, in particular the economic incentives and the structuring of time and place. And local values and structures matter. Contrasts between formality and informality, and between large-scale and small-scale, make access to the local structure of work easier in Ániksi than in Ffynnon.

Pahl (1988) signalled a growing awareness in the more developed Western societies of the need to redefine work, in particular as a consequence of rising unemployment. Perhaps looking at work through the experiences of 'incompetent' people may contribute towards a better understanding and development of the concept of work and ultimately to a more humane society. A society in which work means more than the mere satisfaction of basic needs; where people of all 'competences' and 'incompetences' are allowed to work.

Conclusion

In Wales and Greece there are people who have been classified as 'incompetent' in the society in which they live. In Wales, classification takes place earlier, is more or less permanent, and leads to segregation in many areas of the adult person's life. In Greece, where classification is more *ad hoc*, segregation is not a direct result, but is, rather, based on individual abilities and circumstances. Segregation on Ániksi is neither inevitable nor necessarily permanent; it is possible for incompetent people to join in with the activities of other adult members of their society, both within and outside their own institution. Cultural variation in the segregation of incompetent people is also documented by Reynolds Whyte in Chapter 7 (Uganda) and Nuttall in Chapter 8 (Greenland).

There are links between these differences and local social and economic structures. Particularly important in this respect is the formality of social organisation and economic opportunity in Wales, and their informality in Greece. There is, however, an additional link, with the cultural model of competence in each place, i.e. what is locally expected of a competent adult.

In Wales, intellectual and personal development are valued and rated highly on the scales of adulthood, exactly those areas in which incompetent people, by definition, experience the most difficulties. They thus have little chance of ever reaching adulthood, as locally understood. Highly organised services for people with learning difficulties, however well-intended, do not change this. Early diagnosis and segregating institutions merely emphasise the weakness of incompetent people and place them outside society.

In Greece, the successful adult contributes towards the upkeep of his or her family and, if possible, marries and starts one of his or her own. It is sometimes possible for 'incompetent' people to live up to these expectations. We thus see, ironically, that in a country where formal interest in, and care of, incompetent people is minimal, incompetent people, because of local social and economic structures and a different model of competence, do have a chance to be a part of their society.

I began this chapter by asking if, and to what extent, the position of the person with learning difficulties, in the society in which he or she lives, is influenced or even determined by 'culture'. Rather than local norms and values – i.e. what we usually mean when we talk about culture – it seems to be local social and economic structures of opportunity that enable or disable people with learning difficulties to participate in and contribute to the society in which they live.

Note

1 Both of these names are pseudonyms.

7 Slow cookers and madmen: competence of heart and head in rural Uganda

Susan Reynolds Whyte

In the introduction to a classic study of mental incompetence, Walter Goldschmidt wrote:

Of all the attributes of man, mind is the quintessence; to be found wanting in mental capacity – in general intellectual competence – is the most devastating of all possible stigmata. (At least this is manifestly true for American culture; perhaps there are other cultures in which the self is less closely tied to intellective potential . . . (Edgerton 1967: vii)

In this paper I explore the meanings of mental competence in eastern Uganda, by considering people in whom it is found wanting. In describing individuals who are slow or foolish or mad, I shall suggest ways in which local notions of personhood, agency and self relate to competence.[1]

Let me begin by making a distinction that is blurred in Goldschmidt's phrasing – that between intellectual and mental capacities. Intellect is generally defined as the ability to reason, perceive or understand relations or differences (the Latin root means to gather or choose among). Intelligence has to do with the ability to learn and to use reason in solving problems. In contrast, mental capacity refers to abilities of mind, a broader term that includes will, intention and feelings, as well as intellect. And mind is also a verb that means to attend to, apply oneself, care or feel concern about. This wider notion of mind and mental capacity is the more relevant for understanding the situations of 'incompetent' people in everyday life.

The term competence refers to ability, skill or fitness. It encourages us to ask: for what? Competence and its inverse point towards tasks and actions, the application of abilities. Intellectual competence may be measurable by tests, but mental competence and its lack can only be studied in the context of daily life. Indeed, two of the best-known anthropological monographs on mental incompetence in the United States have been inspired by symbolic interactionism (Edgerton 1967; Estroff 1981), an approach that emphasises the social construction and

153

manipulation of meaning and personal identity – or, in these cases, the consequences of spoiled identity – in ordinary social life.

As Richard Jenkins concludes in Chapter 10 of this volume, the most basic competence of human beings universally is probably the capacity for sociality. Because the ability to respond to others is so fundamental, mental incompetence is seen as particularly devastating, as Goldschmidt argued and as Marshall (1996) suggests in underlining the gravity of incapacities for social and moral responsibility. But sociality takes different forms. One of the goals of this chapter is to provide an ethnographically rich description of what sociality entails in eastern Uganda. Thus I begin with a discussion of the elements involved in mental (social) competence as Nyole people understand it. The other goal is to illustrate that competence is a property of social relations, not just of individuals. As Jenkins puts it, mind exists not only in the individual, but in 'the social spaces, the mutuality of interaction, between embodied individuals'. In eastern Uganda this means that mental (in)competence is always embedded, or 'distributed' as Tim and Wendy Booth (Chapter 4) suggest, in kinship relations. Families can enhance the competence of individuals; mental incompetence need not be devastating. But if competence is distributed, perhaps incompetence is as well. The inability of a family member to extend the lifeworld of social relationships is also a loss for the family as a whole.

The body of this chapter is a series of examples of persons in whom mental competence is found lacking. In presenting them, I hope to convey the Nyole appreciation of individuality, while emphasising the qualities of sociality that are problematic in each case. In describing people who are slow or wild or unable to converse, I want to show what (in)competence means in terms of a local lifeworld where relationships to kin and neighbours are basic. Mental disorders in eastern Uganda are often dealt with in an explanatory idiom that posits spirit and human causes for misfortune (Whyte 1997). Because the focus here is incompetence, I have not dwelt on these aspects. Instead I emphasise the implications of mental disability for social interaction.

Personhood and social competence

In Bunyole County, as in much of rural Uganda, to be a person is to have a place in a nexus of kinship relations. Everyone, even an 'outside' child (born to an unmarried mother) takes the clan of his or her biological father. The word for clan in the Lunyole language also means kind, and every person is a kind of person. In this agricultural economy, relations of production are largely kinship relations. Men inherit land from their fathers, women have access to land through their husbands. Families are

large – completed fertility for a woman is between seven and eight children – and polygyny is common. Since brothers divide the land of their
fathers, groups of male agnates and their wives tend to be neighbours. But
relationships to and through women are also important. People have close
ties to their mothers' relatives, and women come home to their parents
and brothers for visits or in case of divorce. Because kin terms are
extended to members of the same clan, even strangers often find that they
are related somehow. But the importance of kinship is existential, not just
terminological. To be a person is to be a child and a parent, a sibling and
an in-law. In a version of Jack Goody's observation that in lineage
systems, people are wealth, the Lunyole word for poverty, *obutahi*, also
means being without relatives.

   This fundamental principle of personhood has implications for notions
of (in)competence and for the situation of individuals who are impaired
in one way or another. Even people who in medical terms have grave
mental deficits are social persons in that they belong to clans and have
parents and siblings.[2] All of the children and adults I know, live with, and
are recognised as, relatives; that includes those who are deaf, foolish,
lame, mad, drunken, blind, barren and impotent. They are all persons in
the sense of having social identities as kinsmen (Ingstad 1995a). Some of
them, however, are unable to extend the wealth of family through marriage and children. People whose abilities to care for themselves and
others are impaired get help from their families and expect little assistance from government (except for a dispensation from paying tax). One
can say that their individual competence is supplemented and extended
by that of their relatives. More radically, one can put the individual perspective aside and say that competence is distributed.

   But this is only a first and programmatic statement about personhood
and competence. People are always more than kinship identities.
Managing as a social person involves a variety of skills that individuals
display to a greater or lesser extent. As we shall see, these abilities overlap
and facilitate one another. But for the sake of simplicity, we may distinguish five qualities relevant to social (in)competence.

1. Advisability

A fundamental ability of persons is understanding in the sense of social
awareness and willingness to accept guidance. Nyole speak of child
development using a verb – *ohulabuha* – which means to understand, to
take advice, and to mature. Etymologically, this word is related to the verb
'to advise' and it suggests being advisable, being receptive, being sensitive
to people's wishes, being able to discern and accept the needs and counsel
of others and to respect older people.

   This quality of receptivity is similar to the ability to listen described by

Devisch (1990:139) for the Yaka of south-western Zaïre. But whereas Devisch describes listening as the means by which children develop their hearts as centres of inner understanding, Nyole tend to speak of advisability in terms of its effect on a person's conduct. 'Selima is not yet old enough to understand (*ahirihulabuhi*); if I ask her to bring me drinking water from the pot, she does not do it.' A person who understands the counsel of others shows it in social life. A child shows understanding by obedience and helpfulness; an adult by willingness to follow reasonable suggestions.

A stubborn person (*ow'ehyeju*) refuses the instructions or advice of those who are trying to offer guidance. The word implies intractability and obstinacy in relation to other people rather than individual tenacity of purpose.

2. Intentionality

Nyole speak of the heart (*omwoyo*) as the seat of intention from which action springs (Whyte 1990: 57; Lienhardt 1985: 146). The abilities to plan, to decide what to do, and to act as a subject are associated with the heart. A hard worker (*omutambi*) concentrates on the task with single-mindedness or 'with one heart' as Nyole would say. A person with a good heart is loyal and sincere and does not tire of her obligations. Beyond steadfastness, agency involves seeing what has to be done and doing it without having to be told. It is not simply a matter of taking advice; a person should be able to organise and plan on his own.

Sometimes people speak of feelings and dispositions in terms of the heart as well. The heart may be afraid, or may be well disposed towards someone. You can thank someone 'for having that heart' when they show you kindness. Other qualities of subjective experience are expressed in terms of thoughts, as: 'Since her husband died, she has many thoughts' or 'His thoughts are so so' (*Ebilowoso bibye bityo bityo* – literally, 'like that like that'. 'Having many thoughts', a phrase occurring in other Bantu languages including Swahili, can be translated as depression or anxiety. Saying that thoughts are 'like that like that' or 'here and there' seems to imply unsureness of purpose or disorientation.

A woman who does not stick in any marriage or a man who leaves work at home and wanders about shows a lack of that fixity of heart and thought necessary for social competence. The indolent person (*omugayafu*) does not bother to work, or does things reluctantly, because he does not care (*atafaayo*). Here we come close to the sense of the English verb, to mind.

3. Civility

Courtesy and attentiveness to others are qualities prized in social interaction. Courtly greetings and formal politeness (women kneel to greet men and older women) are common expressions of respect. People thank each other for working and welcome each other from the night, thus constantly recognising others and their activities. Courtesy implies formality and restraint. Respect (*eng'ono*) belongs to those who show respect, who behave circumspectly and gently (*oheneenekeresa, ohwedemberesa*) and restrain themselves (*ohweng'omeha*). A dignified person does not shout at people, or show anger, or cruelty.

The emphasis on courtesy and control must be seen in terms of the concern about envy, malice, treachery and anger that may lie hidden in other people's hearts. Suspicions about sorcery and secret malicious acts are not uncommon. It is therefore particularly important to show courtesy and avoid any indication of aggressive feelings.

4. Conversation

The skills of conversation involve the ability to turn about (as the Latin root suggests) or exchange, in a flow of listening and speaking. Conversation has a specific sense of trading talk and an extended one of living together in a rhythm of social exchange. People chat with their family, visit with guests, keep company at funerals, discuss affairs around pots of millet beer, and gossip in the kitchen. Talking too much and too eagerly is undignified in adults, but being articulate and attentive in conversation is a fundamental skill in social life. Bringing news, telling the story well, injecting the right amount of humour, making implications, understanding the subtleties and replying in kind – these are the essential practices of sociability. For older men, rhetorical skills including the use of proverbs are prerequisites for leadership. For everyone, greetings, visiting and casual conversation are the stuff of social intercourse.

5. Cleverness

In addition to these socially fundamental abilities, people value liveliness and cleverness. A child who is too docile is not a healthy child. Children should play and laugh, just as humour is appreciated in adults. The word which could be translated as intelligence, *amagesi*, seems to me better rendered as cleverness. Children who do well in school are clever. But so is a child who makes 'pictures', that is likenesses – a radio out of mud or a lorry out of bits of old wire and rubber. Clever people are ingenious at solving problems. The word has overtones of creativity and sometimes of cunning. People who find ingenious ways of cheating or stealing may also be said to have *amagesi*. A person asking advice or wanting to make plans may ask someone for their *amagesi,* their cleverness, that is for a plan. In Lunyole, doubling the root intensifies the meaning of the word. *Omugesigesi* is thus a very clever person; sometimes this term implies cheekiness or being a show off. Cleverness in itself is not necessarily socially valuable. Respect is given to the civilised person, *omugunjuhi,* who is sociable, cultured, wise and refined. He shares good ideas with others and has the ability to lead people; in other words, his qualities bring social and not just individual benefits. In his rich discussion of Chewa perspectives on intelligence, Serpell (1993: 24–74) makes a similar point and cites other studies to show that social responsibility is seen as an important dimension of intelligence in many African cultures.

'School smarts'

Education is highly desired in Bunyole. Schooling is a means to knowing about and participating in the nation and the wider world. To be a modern person one must be a 'reader' (*omusomi*) which also implies being an adherent of one of the religions of the book (Muslim, Roman Catholic or Anglican). More than that, education still holds out the hope for a good job and a salary that can help the whole family towards a more comfortable life (Whyte and Whyte 1998). The hope persists despite high unemployment among school leavers, and miserable salaries for those who manage to obtain the civil service positions for which education used to be the key. School fees are prohibitive for many rural families, especially because most have many children. (P1, the first class in primary school, cost about 12 US dollars in local schools in 1996.) The drop-out rate is high, and class size declines steeply in the upper grades. About half of children between ages 8 and 18 are in school.

In schools, intellectual competence and incompetence are measured numerically and parents are well aware of the numbers on the school reports that children bring home three times a year. Children are tested at least every fortnight. Each child has a progress chart that shows marks and class rank. At first, exams are internal, but later examinations are set for the zone, the county and the district. The Primary Leaving Exam is a national one, in which children from poor rural schools seldom do as well as those from elite urban ones.

The emphasis on scores and rank is an index of the highly competitive nature of Ugandan education. Teachers with whom I spoke valued competition as a way of motivating pupils. Bright children struggle to be among the first in their class. As one experienced P1 teacher explained:

Even a dull child can come up. You tease him by showing that younger children are brighter. 'How can this small one know when you don't know? Aren't you ashamed?' Then he will come up.

(Because many children have to repeat classes and may start late or stay home a year because of lack of school fees, the age range in any given class may be large.) Constant testing is a way of checking how much the children have grasped and following their progress; it also provides a basis for grouping the often large classes into categories based on ability.

In rural schools there is a high rate of failure and repetition. In 1995 at Mulagi Primary School, only 60 of the 99 children in P1 passed into P2. Some children fail to pass year in and year out. A teacher gave this example:

Hasahya's son and daughter have failed the first grade three times. They're very dormant. You teach, they look at you. You ask a question, they look at you. Even copying from the blackboard is a problem.

Some children, even from good homes, just do not learn. As one headmistress remarked of a 14 year old who had failed P5 again, 'That one doesn't get cooked.' Just as sweet potatoes in a pot get soft at different rates, so pupils on the pedagogical hearth take the educational heat differently. Sometimes teachers promote such slow cookers to the next class even though they are doing poorly. 'She is weak but let her try P6,' as a teacher wrote on the report of a child I know. Some parents insist that their children be passed; others point out that this practice simply pushes the problem forward instead of dealing with it.

Teachers readily describe the characteristics of dull and bright pupils. Bright children are quick in understanding. They are able to reason and explain (*ohunyonyola*) and they can answer correctly. They finish their work quickly. Such children are sometimes cheeky and proud because they know things. Then you should give them extra work, make them monitors, or assign each one a dull pupil and let them compete as to whose dull pupil manages best.

Weak pupils are slow to finish their work; they wait to copy answers from a friend. Those need more help if they are to learn at all. The headmistress of Hahoola Primary School says that the teacher should try to find out why the child is slow. Sometimes children have problems at home; the parents neglect them, they have no decent accommodation, they work hard at home and do not get enough sleep. Hunger may be a reason for not concentrating in school. (Most rural children come to school without breakfast and do not eat until they go home at the end of the school day. From 1996 the Ministry of Education is requiring that all parents pay for lunch to be prepared at the school. For P1 this means a 100 per cent increase in school fees.)

But even this definitive sorting of children into bright and dull does not preclude the recognition of other aspects of social competence in school. A good pupil should have good conduct as well as high marks.

Pupils should learn how to respect and help the teacher, carry his books, take his bicycle and put it away for him when he arrives. They should greet visitors courteously and ask the teacher's permission if they come late or need to leave the class . . . Discipline is important. In the upper classes they're stubborn. If you aren't strict with a stick, they can walk on you.

In school, as at home, the social virtues of advisability and control are important.

Slow cookers

With their constant testing, schools efficiently produce intellectual incompetents in a way that ordinary social life does not. Outside of school there is no way of unambiguously categorising people according to mental ability. And there is no need to do so, just as there is not in the Greenland community described by Nuttall (Chapter 8). Therefore, it is tempting to think of 'school smarts' as totally distinct from 'life smarts' – the qualities I have suggested are the basis of social competence. It would follow that dullness in the classroom (not getting cooked in the pedagogical pot) is irrelevant to one's qualities as a member of the family. Especially in a setting where there are no books or newspapers to read, and where writing is for sending brief messages or listing contributions to a funeral ceremony, school skills are not a part of daily life.

However, school problems sometimes do provide the occasion to remark upon a child's general capacity for understanding. It was because of school failure that I came to learn a lesson by causing offence. I was trying to work through the vocabulary of competence with the help of an older man and two of his sons. We had come to the term *omung'aiyi* and they were explaining that it meant someone who is a dullard, slow in understanding, who does not grasp the import of what he is told. I needed an example and without thinking I asked whether the old man's 18-year-old grandson, nicknamed Teddy, was a dullard. Teddy came to mind because we had spoken of him earlier as someone for whom school was a waste of time and money, since he did so poorly. They all agreed:

Ah, yes, Teddy's a dullard. You tell him to sweep the compound and he says okay but doesn't do it. He has a field of millet ready to harvest, but just leaves it. You tell him, 'let's go harvest', and instead he goes to work for others. He's been to school and he still can't write his name.

The boy's grandmother and father's sister overheard this exchange and were offended that I had written down that he was a dullard.

He's just a quiet, polite person (*omung'oleeri*). But he works and he helps us. He even started trading – he bicycled to Tororo and bought bread and sold it. Is that a dullard?

Later I told another of his fathers that his grandmother had been offended that we had used the term. He held to it, though.

That boy was in P5 and could hardly write his name. He used to hide his school reports. He just forced himself to advance from class to class.

'But wasn't he trading?' I asked. 'Did he know how to make change?' smiled his father, disparagingly. Teddy's fathers went on to complain that he neglected to help around the home, disappeared without saying where he was going, earned money and used it for drinking and going with women. 'You can explain to him about the dangers of playing sex these days,' said one, 'but he doesn't understand. He won't listen.'

Teddy was compared to John, another boy in the family, just a few years younger, who also had to repeat classes. (He was the one whom the headmistress had called a slow cooker.) 'But John is a bit fair. He always helps his parents. Didn't we just see him on the path going for water?' One father explained that John did poorly because he had been sick so much – in fact, divination had finally revealed that the spirit Seja had chosen him as its medium. Also, his parents sent him on errands so he frequently missed school.

Teddy's slowness in school was taken as symptomatic of his general lack of understanding and indifference to the counsel of his elders. He could not plan or set his heart on a task and do it. They called him a dullard because he would not listen and did not grasp the import of tasks and advice. Yet that epithet is a matter of opinion, unlike the label 'last in the class'. My insensitive questioning, noted by his grandmother, showed me that.

Slow ones cannot easily (or perhaps like stubborn ones, they will not easily) understand and be taught. But you can engage them in conversation and they know what is happening. There are other people whose mental capacity is more deeply flawed.

Those who were passed over

'Those whom something passed over' (*abahyabitaho*) are described as people who cannot talk properly and whose brains are spoiled. Deaf mutes are not 'passed over' – their families communicate with them in simple sign language and they understand and follow advice. I saw a man warn his deaf mute younger brother to avoid prostitutes in the trading centre because of the danger of AIDS; the deaf man, Charles, signed his agreement and I am convinced he understood perfectly. In fact Charles, far from refusing counsel, seems extra alert to the emotions and wishes of companions as he intently watches first one face and then another.

Tito Wamudanya, the psychiatric nurse at the local hospital, gave five or six examples of passed-over ones who had been born normal and had their brains 'spoiled' after serious illness with high fever, such as measles and malaria. One of these is well known in the trading centre Busolwe; drooling and smiling, he comes up to beg from me every time I go there.

Manuel is 13 years old, the son of a woman who works at the hospital. His birth was normal, and as the child of a health worker, he completed his immunisations. But from the age of one and a half, he fell sick from time to time with malaria and pneumonia. Sometimes he had convulsions. After one grave episode, described as cerebral malaria, 'his brain was spoiled'. After that he could not talk and his behaviour became a problem. According to his mother, he has a voracious appetite. He fights with his brothers and sisters over food, and wanders in the trading centre, begging leftovers in the 'hotelis'. He forcefully grabs food from other children and many have complained to his mother about his snatching. Sometimes he does not come home, and his mother must go looking for him. She tries to keep him clean and dressed, and she takes him for treatment when he gets fever. But there is no treatment for his general condition, and there is no institution to care for children like him. As she says, 'I have nothing to do.'

Manuel's social incompetence is massive. He can neither care for himself, take advice, nor converse with others. His family compensates as much as possible for his deficits by caring for his personal needs; and the neighbours in the trading centre keep an eye on him. Therefore his quarrelsomeness and grabbiness are particularly worrying; he offends those upon whom he is dependent.

Not all those who are called 'passed over' are as incompetent as Manuel. Tamiti is a man in his 50s who lives with his mother's sister Lakeri, a widow, and her old sister-in-law, Kabite. (Both Tamiti and Kabite are poor people in Nyole terms in that neither of them has ever had any children.) Lakeri's daughter-in-law, who lives in the next home, says:

> Tamiti's thoughts are just there – so so. There's something that passed over him . . . He just sits quietly; he doesn't have friends or converse with people. He does what he's told to do, but just one thing at a time. He can't remember a list of things to do. He doesn't know the difference between a bill of 100 shillings and one of 50 or a thousand. Sometimes children tease him about that.

Tamiti can speak for himself when I ask him about his work. Slowly he tells how he was taken to the district town of Tororo by his mother's brother to work as a 'houseboy.' He washed plates and clothes, and, he adds with pleasure, he used a cooker to cook food. After Amin's coup, they went back to the country (where it was safer), and he continued to do the same kind of work. But they made him work too hard, so he came to stay here with his mother's sister. Now his work is to fetch water, do errands, and keep the home when others are gone. He is not strong enough to manage heavy tasks like clearing fields, and riding a bicycle is too difficult.

Sometimes people tease him about his bachelor status, saying, 'Tamiti, I've given you a woman.' Or a woman tells him that she wants to be his wife, and he comes home and tells his relatives that so and so loves me. One neighbour adds that a woman joked with him that she wanted him and he should meet her at a certain place. When she came, she found he had already undressed! Tamiti can talk, but he has difficulty conversing. What his neighbours seem to imply is that he does not recognise humour or irony.

But everyone I ask in the neighbourhood agrees that Tamiti is a good person. He has a kind heart. People like him because he does whatever you ask. You can send him for water or ask him to carry something to Busolwe for you. Sometimes he is sent to Busolwe several times a day. In that respect, he is like the deaf man, Charles, whom people like because he is 'soft', that is, always willing to help. But there can be a time when Charles refuses. Tamiti never does. He is advisable in the extreme.

The concomitants of fits

In Bunyole, as elsewhere in East Africa (Whyte 1995), falling and convulsive jerking are considered grave and dangerous symptoms. The word which is usually translated as epilepsy, *efuwu*, is so damning that it is not lightly used in discussing the conditions of people who fall regularly. Convulsions (*ohwesika* – to jerk, sometimes translated 'to fit') are more tactfully related to spirit possession, for small children, especially possession by the spirit called Omuhyeno. For our purposes here, however, what is most important is the way that fits are related to competence in daily life. Like the Ganda (Orley 1970: 47–9), Nyole sometimes say that the brain gets spoiled (*obongo ohuonoonoha*) in some people who have repeated fits. Although this is not inevitable, the families of people who 'fit' are concerned about these long-term effects. While the convulsions themselves are dramatic and frightening, what is most worrying are the consequences of fits for socially competent behaviour.

Hassani had his first convulsions at about 18 months when he fell sick with high temperature. Despite attempts with biomedical treatment and 'tying' the Omuhyeno spirit, he continued to 'fit' several times a month.

When I first visited Hassani in 1995, he was an extremely lively five year old. His mother was worried about his behaviour.

His thinking is not good. He doesn't understand – when I look at his eyes, I know that he doesn't understand. When I tell him to do something, he sometimes does it, sometimes not. His manners are bad – he beats other children. He used to chase the other children away from the food, but when we beat him for that he learned. He started wandering off and couldn't find his way home. Once someone brought him back and he lied that he had been to his aunt's.

Six months later, I visited Hassani's home again. His mother was more positive about his behaviour since she had started giving him valium from the local shop. Phenobarbitone (the drug of choice for epilepsy in rural Uganda) was available too, but she preferred valium because it calmed him down and made him sleep.[3] He did not beat other children so much, and he ate nicely with his mates and politely thanked his mother for cooking. 'Yes he's still stubborn sometimes,' she said, 'but if he gets medicine, he'll leave off that stubbornness.'

In interviews with two other families of epileptic children, the same concerns were expressed about their behaviour. One seven-year-old boy fought with his brothers and then ran off to hide fearing a beating from his parents. He threw dust, stones or plates at his friends, sometimes hurting them. 'When sent for something, he does the opposite. He does not help at all. So he is a problem in the home.' Thus parents are worried about stubbornness and disobedience, the failure of that quality of social competence that could be translated as advisability. And they are concerned about aggressive behaviour, not only because a child should not hurt others, but also because of the repercussions this might bring for the family and the child. At first, other parents may complain, as they do when Manuel snatches food from children in the trading centre. But the real danger is that an aggressive person will be given summary punishment by neighbours or strangers. In this respect, there is no difference between mad people who behave wildly and people who become aggressive in connection with convulsions. The anxieties about the development of aggressive behaviour in children must be seen in the light of reactions to frightening, wild men to which I shall turn shortly.

Over-protection of people with convulsive conditions may also contribute to social incompetence. Abubakali is a 16-year-old boy who developed convulsions in connection with fever when he was small. He has been treated with phenytoin off and on, but gets frequent fits because the drug is not readily available. His family reports that he gets confused but not aggressive after a fit, is 'social' to his brothers and sisters, and much loved by them. He does some light work around the home, but spends most of his time making models of cars out of old bicycle spokes. He is not allowed to dig or ride a bicycle for fear he might fall and hurt himself. He is thus excluded from a man's most important work, farming, and from cycling, a man's practical and pleasurable means of enlarging his geographical scope of sociability. Abubakali had been sent to school and did well up to P5, but when his fits became more frequent, scaring the teachers and other pupils, he was withdrawn by his family. Earlier research in Tanzania documented the tendency to withdraw epileptic children from school, sometimes at the request of the teachers, but often in order to protect the child who might fall where there was no family member to help (Whyte 1991: 101–2). This too has the consequence of narrowing a young person's scope of social activity; of course, many children have the same limitation in that they do not attend school, but they ride bicycles and get involved with others through work.

The social competence of persons is not primarily determined by whether or not they 'fit', but by their total character and situation. There were many similarities between Tamiti, the slow one, and Sam, another bachelor of about the same age, although Sam had been diagnosed as having epilepsy[4] and Tamiti never had any convulsions so far as I know. I heard both referred to as *omung'ubebe* because they talked slowly, seemed foolish, and had never managed to marry. Sam stares vacantly (*ohutaangala*) and answers questions only after a long pause. Like Tamiti, Sam had worked as a houseboy, and could only do light tasks. Both men were staying with maternal relatives. Two other people who regularly had convulsions, had more in common with the mild and wild madmen to whom we now turn.

Throwing bricks

In East Africa a distinction is commonly made between mild and wild forms of madness (Edgerton 1966). Wild madmen shout, throw stones and beat people. Uncontrolled aggression is a matter of urgency and people respond to such madness by attacking the aggressor, overpowering him, tying him up, or locking him in.[5] In Bunyole too, people sometimes distinguish between two kinds of madmen: *abalalu* are maniacs – people who shout and strike people; *abasiru* are peaceful, but foolish. They may talk nonsense, do peculiar things, or just withdraw from social interaction. (Sometimes 'passed-over' people are also referred to as *abasiru*.) Not everyone distinguishes in this way – there is no orthodoxy about nosology. But there is no doubt that violence is marked; whether or not a madman beats people is a key way of characterising him. It was the salient fact about an unhappy man named Musaja.

Musaja started to fall as a child, but he was given amulets to protect him from the spirit Omuhyeno, and his fits were not so frequent as to prevent him going to school. He did well, completed teacher's training and managed to become a deputy headmaster in a rural school. By 1988 his fits had become much worse; he frequently fell in the classroom and finally had to stop teaching. He began to have periods of violence and his condition deteriorated. Now he is 36 years old, sharing a house with one brother (a lame man nicknamed 'Chairman' because he has jokingly been declared head of the neighbourhood bachelors), and being fed by another brother's wife.

People call him mad (*omulalu*); he is fierce/wild (*omukambwe*) and causes fear (*atiisa*). His sister-in-law says: 'Sometimes he's cool, sometimes he's wild. He chases us, says he's going to kill us.' Musaja has convulsions several times a month. (His brother says he does not have epilepsy because he does not usually urinate during fits; he has never been biomedically treated for epilepsy.) He wanders off and gets lost; occasionally he refuses to eat. ('Is it loss of appetite or because his brain does not know that this is food?' mused his brother.) He stands for hours until his feet swell, and cannot be persuaded to sit. He is ever gloomy and alone. In conversation, he gets annoyed and abusive when he does not understand.[6] He used to earn a little money making charcoal and working for a neighbour, but now he does not work at all. However, none of these problems is as grave as his violence.

His family says that he becomes violent in the week before he falls in a fit. And when he gets violent, he is incredibly strong. (There is agreement that he is so strong because he eats a lot; his brother wonders if there is any medicine they could give him to weaken him. They would like to feed him less, but he gets angry when he is hungry.) When he begins to shout and throw stones, or snatches a panga (machete) and chases someone, the women of his home run away to the neighbours. If his brothers are around, they catch and subdue him by tying him or locking him in the house. His sister-in-law, the one who cooks for him, declares she is going to leave because of Musaja's wild episodes. Her husband, his brother, worries about his marriage and the safety of his wife and children. But at least the immediate family accepts him as sick and they try not to hurt him when subduing him. More distant relatives and neighbours are angered and annoyed by his behaviour. The last time I visited Musaja's home, he had slapped his brother, 'Chairman', then rushed out and attacked the neighbour's calf. They locked him in his house, but he escaped through the window. Next day, he went to where his 'cousin-brothers' were preparing to fire bricks and knocked down the pile. When he started throwing bricks, they began to beat him and he fought back. When they finally overpowered him, he asked them to lock him in his house 'because you want to kill me'.

In a society that values civility and restraint, Musaja's social incompetence is extreme. It spreads to other members of his family. 'Chairman', the brother with whom he stays, pours out his woe. He is personally and socially handicapped by having to share quarters with a madman. Musaja disturbs him during the night by lifting him out of bed, or urinating on him. When Musaja is wild, he cannot stay in the house, and when Musaja is annoyed he locks Chairman out. People who know the situation avoid visiting Chairman at home, because of the wild man. Sometimes he lies and says his brother is drunk when strangers arrive. It is clear that Chairman will remain a bachelor until he can get Musaja moved into another house. Even the older brother Paulo is struggling to persuade his wife to accept the situation. Paulo shakes his head in resignation. 'My neighbours get annoyed. When Musaja threatens someone's child, are the owners of the child happy? Or the owners of the calf that he nearly broke? Of course they beat him if he attacks them. I have nothing to do if they beat my brother. He gets wild.' Given the worry and inconvenience Musaja causes, the patience and fortitude of his family are striking. It is only because of their competence in trying to coax or drag him away from trouble that he has not been seriously injured.

Off the topic and out of the conversation

Mad people may have a short period of 'wildness' and then live peacefully but without the fundamental social skill of conversing – 'turning about' a given topic, participating in the social exchanges of daily life.

Rosa was 30 years old and the mother of five children when she began to act strangely, as her father had before her. When her condition worsened, her husband sent for her family to come and collect her. It is not unusual that married women go home to their natal families when they are seriously ill (though I know of one husband who cares for his mentally ill wife). 'It depends on the husband,' explains Rosa's sister. 'Some are weak and say, "Come get your daughter, she's defeated me."'

When they brought Rosa home, she ran mad. 'She got spoiled.' Tito, the psychiatric nurse, was called and found her dirty and dehydrated, tied with ropes, her wrists swollen and chaffed. For the next six months, he treated her with chlorpromazine and stelazine. She was seeing things, and talking to herself. After some months, she began to improve so that she could speak to others, 'but she kept going off the topic' (*ngadobiyamo*). She has been home for some years now, and she works with her sister and mother weeding and harvesting. But according to her sister, 'Her health is still so so – her head – and her body too . . . She forces herself to work, but sometimes she gives a start as if her heart is afraid.' Her mother says that Rosa cannot plan for herself: 'She can't think what to do.'

Rosa's participation in the exchanges of social life has been severely curtailed. Funeral ceremonies are a primary social activity for women, but Rosa only goes to mourn in the immediate neighbourhood, and only after the burial, since she was advised not to look into graves. As a special treat, she and her mother went to Kampala at Christmas to stay with her brother. But she became confused by all the traffic and by her brother's television. When they were ready to come home and went to the city railway station, she was so terrified she urinated in her clothes. Rosa not only goes off the topic, but in a larger sense she is being excluded from social conversation beyond that of her mother and siblings. Her husband and children do not come to see her, nor do her old school friends. She remarked sadly that 'When you have such a problem, your friends forget you.'

In an even stranger way, the conversational capacity of another young woman is inhibited. Maria has been hiccuping for seven years. Her hiccups come in spells – when she is happy or annoyed or wants to talk. When you ask her a question, or she tries to tell you something, her mouth pulls to one side, her pretty face twists, and she is racked by hics that seem to exhaust her. Maria had fits as a baby that have continued all her life. She startles and trembles, falls and jerks, runs as if possessed, and she does not know what is happening. Explaining the difficulty of conversing with her, one of my neighbours told how she used to visit her. 'Maria would ask me if I saw all those people dressed in white. Then she'd go into her room and cry. Or she'd run off and fall down.' But on the three occasions when I have visited Maria, there were no digressions or unexpected topics like these – only the painful hiccuping as she struggled with and eventually gave up her part of the conversation.

The angelic construction project

With Obutu, the problem is not so much that he gets off the topic, but that he insists that you accept his topic, which is not just a topic, but an entire world of his imagination. On the edge of the trading centre, Busolwe, Obutu has built a royal centre (*ehibuga*), a heavenly city of the future where all of us, men and women, black and white, Muslims and Christians, angels all, will enter into a life of harmony and ease. As he tells it:

There we will do no work of digging or grinding grain; we'll press buttons and food will come through pipes. Airplanes will bring us everything we want. We'll be isolated and self-sufficient. No one will come and say, your father is sick, your mother is sick. When you want to talk to your relatives, you'll switch on a picture and see them. But they won't come in person. Now we are in punishment, but in the future we'll be free. Now your father beats you if you've been wandering in town; your brother abuses you. But in the future we'll be free of abuse and punishment. It is heaven, not earth. Things are changing. These are heaven houses. No one can understand what we're saying – no beating, no quarrels. There'll be no day or night, no sun. The idea comes from God. Now we are angels building these high houses, but when the building is finished, we'll all enter, and we'll become people instead of angels.

Obutu has twice guided me on tours through his city, which covers several acres. To my eyes, it consisted of wide ditches and pillars of locally made bricks, stacked four to six high, balanced without mortar. But Obutu told of great buildings, storied houses, towering to the heavens, or reaching deep into the earth in many levels. ('It's an underground movement,' he chuckled.) He showed me the playing fields and the pavilions where we will sit to watch the games. (Later when we went for a cold drink at Busolwe's 'first class' hotel, he assured me that the football game on the television was from his field.) There was a landing field for the airplanes that fly over and see him working. And there was the mosque where he knelt to pray in Arabic. As he did so, I noticed the uprooted groundnuts and maize plants scattered about. Obutu said his brother's wife had planted them, but the angels tore them up because they did not want her to use their house. I was reminded that Obutu's heavenly city is on land that other people think is for growing crops. And his storied buildings are constructed of other people's bricks.

Obutu belongs to a large and respected family. He has seven brothers, who occupy valuable land on the growing edge of the trading centre. They are active in Busolwe's Muslim community; the brother with whom he stays is a Haji. Obutu himself attends the mosque and local ceremonies regularly in the company of his brothers. Both of his wives have left him, but he has five children. His clan identity is important enough to him that he calls his construction project, City Buguna, after his clan.

Obutu does not look mad; there is nothing exceptional in his gestures and movement. His manner is mild. 'He doesn't beat people – so no one disturbs him,' remarked one neighbour. In fact there was a time (around 1975) when he ran mad spectacularly, bothering his family, wandering away, and even attacking people. His brothers put him in the national mental hospital, Butabika. When he escaped and came home, they treated him with African medicine to cool him – effectively it seems. Even now, however, he gets upset if anyone disturbs his buildings. Children fear to tease him, and once when someone knocked down a stack of his bricks, he chased the offender to the next village.

Obutu is seen as 'a social man' – he greets people and seeks out company and conversation. But the topic he loves is his own and he keeps bringing it up, which many people find bothersome. He was pleased at my interest, confiding to a friend: 'They say I'm mad, but now even a European has come to see my work and write it down.' Now he seeks me out whenever I come to Bunyole, anxious to tell me about radio announcements and fund-raising ceremonies for the wonderful city. The respected man in whose home my husband and I stay could not understand why we troubled to visit Obutu. Did we expect to find something of value there, from a man who tells lies and goes on disturbing people? One of Obutu's brothers used the same term: he just disturbs (*adambyahudambya*) people. He added with finality: 'His head is spoiled.'

Obutu's head is spoiled not only because he sees things that others cannot see, but because he steadfastly lives according to his view of reality, inconveniencing others in the process. His brothers are hindered in using several acres of farmland, and in selling off the prime plots along the road, because angels have constructed storied buildings and sports complexes. Obutu is a strong and hardworking man. He labours long hours in his city, digging trenches and carrying bricks. But he cultivates not at all, nor does he contribute to the family economy. He is an educated man, having finished two years of secondary school, and he once had a job in Kampala, working on mosquito control for the Public Health Department. There was a time when he earned a bit hawking fried cassava chips (calling out, 'Obutu', which means 'nice little things' – hence his nickname). Now he just eats the food prepared by his brother's wife – the same woman whose maize and groundnuts the angels had uprooted because she dared to plant in their home.

The anatomy of personhood

Through the examples above run implicit dichotomies between head and heart, mind and body, individual and social person. They bear reviewing; as descriptive devices they help to elucidate some of the material presented here. But ultimately they bear dismissing in an approach that focuses on (in)competence.

Nyole speak of people who are slow as having 'weak brains' (*obongo bunafu*) and of mad or foolish people as having 'spoiled brains' or 'spoiled heads'. One can carry the anatomy and physiology of personhood further by noting the way feelings and intentions, agency itself, seem to spring from the heart. Although I have never heard it said that a heart can be spoiled, I have often understood that people can be weak in intention and concentration. Or, as in the case of alcoholics, their minds can fix on one thing alone so that they neglect the essential tasks of their lives. Confusion and the worries that Europeans might associate with anxiety and depression are often expressed in terms of thoughts, as in the case of Rosa who could not 'think what to do'. Yet whether Nyole think with their hearts or their heads, whether mental functions should be divided or united in an ethnopsychological scheme, is not the analytical question here. It is not the 'anatomical structure' of personhood, but the application and consequences of combined abilities that count.

Mental ability is essentially social; it is manifested in receptivity and conversation. In the examples above, it appears to fail along one or both of these dimensions. Mental ability is deemed insufficient when individuals are not tractable, when they do not follow the counsel of others. This can happen because a person is stubborn, or confused, or simply incapable of concentrating on or grasping what is wanted. Tamiti was compliant, but limited in his competence in that he could only remember one request at a time; you could never send him for more than one thing.[7] In extreme cases, people not only failed to concur with the wishes of others, but actively attacked them. Mental ability is also found wanting when someone is unable to participate in conversation – because they cannot follow it, because they change the topic or talk nonsense, because they hiccup, cry, or fall, or because they withdraw from interaction.

In some contexts Nyole distinguish between body and mind (if we think of the mind as including the heart and the head) as Rosa's sister did, when she said that Rosa was not alright in the head or in the body. Such a distinction seems to be operative in the way people refer to disability. The most general term for disability, *obuleme*, refers primarily to physical problems, and is probably best translated as lame. By extension, a blind person is lame, since her movement may be affected. But a deaf person is not *omuleme*, nor is a mad or foolish one. When the first organisation of disabled persons in Bunyole (Bunyole United Disabled People's Organisation) was formed a couple of years ago, only those with limb impairments and a couple of blind people joined. (Even the national organisation does not in fact represent people with mental disabilities.) Yet in other contexts, all kinds of impairment are referred to as 'sickness' (*obulwaiye*) including blindness (Sentumbwe 1995: 162–3) and strange behaviour. They are all considered misfortunes amenable to treatment in the explanatory idiom and the same kinds of agents are said to cause both 'physical' and 'mental' disorders. The 'divinatory gaze' does not analyse dysfunctions within individuals, but sees them synthetically in relation to spirit and human agents.

In terms of social competence and consequences, the distinction between physical and mental impairments fades. The ability to identify and perform tasks requires an embodied mind. People fail to work because of weakness, laziness, lack of concentration, or lack of understanding that a task needs to be done, just as they may fail because of the sequelae of polio. Tamiti was agreeable but lacked strength; Teddy was strong enough, but lacked the will to work. Obutu was a diligent worker, but he devoted himself to the wrong task.

A final dichotomy that runs through discussions of personhood is that between individuality and relatedness, sometimes phrased as a distinction between egocentric and sociocentric conceptions of personhood (Shweder and Bourne 1984). In considering social competence in Bunyole, it is possible to distinguish those qualities that are most relevant to individual functioning from those that are in essence social skills. Advisability, civility and conversational ability are all capacities for relating properly to other people. Cleverness and the ability to carry out intentions are at first glance capacities of the individual in relation to tasks or problems, rather than interpersonal abilities. But individual effort and talent are the hopes of families, just as deficits of individuals are their burdens. All of the capacities for interaction are embodied in individuals; but in practice competence is always a function of the social situation.

The relational nature of personhood in rural eastern Uganda is reflected in the fundamental significance of interpersonal skills as evidence of mental ability. In practice, the social character of personhood compensates for many deficits of the head and heart. In his analysis of the competence of the people he studied in California, Edgerton ranked them according to their relative independence, defined loosely as the ability to live without the assistance of others. The vast majority of the people in his study were not able to manage on their own, and depended on benefactors to do everything, from setting their alarm clocks to filling in their income tax forms. Indeed the benefactors did more than solve practical problems. By helping them to 'pass', they were involved in a benevolent conspiracy to maintain the cloak of competence with which these people tried to cover their discrediting identity as mental defectives. From the Nyole point of view, this is indeed an exotic culture. Most of the benefactors were not related to the people they helped; they were employers, landladies and social workers; there was not a single brother mentioned (Edgerton 1967: 202). In Bunyole, relative independence would not be a basic criterion of social competence. Individual achievement is valued, but largely because successful persons will be able to help relatives (Whyte and Whyte 1998). Benefaction implies charity, which suggests a gift that you did not have to give. When Nyole family members care for their less competent children and siblings, they do not do so as charity, but because those are their people.

Conclusion

Ultimately, the social incompetence of mentally disabled persons lies in their inability to extend and strengthen their families through social activities and relationships. Those who are unmarried are unlikely to find a spouse, so they cannot contribute to family growth through relations of affinity and procreation. Existing marriages tended to break down with the onset of mental disability. Individuals, like families, should develop through work, social activities, relationships of exchange with others, and accumulation of people and resources. Instead of reaching outward to extend the social competence of their families, impaired individuals tend to be restricted in their scope of action. Their incompetence is compensated by their families.

One may ask, as Jenkins (1991) does, whether the incompetence of an individual affects the overall social situation of the family. Certainly there are families in Bunyole, as there also were in Tanzania (Whyte 1991), that are hard stretched by the burden of caring for a mentally incompetent person. But the consequences depend heavily on the size of the effective family. Where many relatives can be mobilised in the effort of care and compensation, the social and economic consequences are not as heavy as they are for the smaller families of European or North American society.

Social competence, I have argued, is played out in relation to family and neighbours, but their evaluations of mental ability are not the only ones that exist in rural Uganda. There are also school standards characterised by competition, ranking in relation to peers, and numerical indexes of success. Incompetence in school does not have implications for one's value in the local community, though it may be associated with other qualities that do. But success in school may expand one's range of opportunity, even beyond the local community. In a sense, 'school smarts' give competence in a wider world by enlarging the scope of social interaction. Social incompetence has the opposite consequence, narrowing a person's lifeworld to the household and immediate neighbourhood.

In countries of the North, some kinds of mental incompetence permit (or impose) involvement with disability programmes and institutions. Such programmes can also be seen as a way of enlarging the scope of one's world or of extending the competence of the individual and family. In Uganda, as in many countries of the South, such programmes reach few rural people (Ingstad 1995b). In 1992, there were only 275 children in special education programmes in the entire country (Okech 1992: 17). In its new constitution, Uganda explicitly affirms the rights of persons with disabilities, and various donor-supported efforts to address mental disorders are underway. For the time being, however, resources are so slight and so skewed towards urban centres that few people in eastern Uganda benefit from them. In the absence of any state welfare benefits, 'independent living' is out of the question. For these reasons, mental incompetence remains a family and neighbourhood matter.

Mental incompetence is social incompetence. Psychologists or other authorities may devise tests of mental (or intellectual) ability, but these isolate capacities from the social contexts in which they are relevant. Likewise, analyses of cultural models of personhood risk fixing upon 'anatomy' to the exclusion of actual social practice. Instead I have tried to show the value of focusing upon the competence of people within their families and neighbourhoods, and of seeing them in relation to local expectations about sociality.

Notes

1 This paper is based on discussions in 1995 and 1996 with fourteen individuals and/or their families, who were thought to have mental problems. The work was carried out in collaboration with Tito Mudenya Wamudanya, a psychiatric nurse and local resident. I am very grateful to Tito, whose thoughtfulness and engagement were invaluable. The chapter builds on fieldwork in Bunyole County, Tororo District, first undertaken from 1969 to 1971, and continued for shorter periods since 1989. Most of the fieldwork was done together with my husband Michael A. Whyte, whom I thank once again for collaboration, discussions and suggestions.

2 The only suggestion I have ever heard that humanity (and therewith personhood) might be doubtful is the reference to 'creatures' born so deformed ('like a chunk of meat') that they were not human and had to be placed in a pot in the forest for Seja, the spirit of cripples. I have never heard of this actually happening; 'it was something of long ago'. The term for this monstrosity, *ehisabadana*, is used as an insult to a stupid child.

3 This information induced me to make a round of the drug shops in the trading centre to enquire about sales of phenobarbitone and valium. Several shops carried both. All reported that these two drugs were sold to people who were unable to sleep because of pain. Valium was sometimes administered for convulsions; that is the first treatment given for fever convulsions at the hospital. No one was buying phenobarbitone as a continuous treatment of people prone to regular convulsions. Since the weekly mental health clinic at the hospital did not dispense drugs either, it seems that practically no one was being treated for epilepsy in a systematic treatment programme. I came across one boy who had been to a treatment programme at the national hospital and been put on phenytoin. His family had been able to buy this drug in Tororo (30 miles away), but they did not give it continuously because it is costly and difficult to get. Another man, who was related to a medical doctor, had been given a number of prescriptions for phenobarbitone, but in every case, the prescription was for two weeks, and the man would finish the medicine and go without for months or years. The Uganda National Standard Treatment

Guidelines of 1993 recommend maintenance on phenobarbitone for a minimum of two years.

4 Sam's sickness started in 1952 when he was 12, and was bitten by dangerous flies where he was staying, in Bugosa (an area where there have been several outbreaks of sleeping sickness). But the problem of falling first became serious ten years later. He had to leave his job in Mbale, but managed to get work in the trading centre of Busolwe. While cooking for himself at his workplace, he fell in the fire and set his clothes alight. He sustained serious burns and spent many months in the hospital.

5 Men tend to become mad in this way more frequently than women and admissions to mental hospitals are disproportionately men who are violent or manic (Vaughan 1983; Wood 1970: 104–5).

6 When I asked whether Musaja understood what had happened to him, his brother Paulo was doubtful. He does not show his thoughts; his understanding is not normal. But Musaja knows and is constantly reminded that he was a teacher, a respected person. He likes his nickname which is the name of the Teacher Training College where he trained. He was delighted when his brothers gave him new clothes: 'I should look smart, I'm a teacher.' He wants to read, but according to 'Chairman': 'Books strain his brain, so when he starts to read, we leave because we know he will fall.' Similarly he gets annoyed when he cannot follow a conversation. I think that Musaja senses how much he has lost – socially and intellectually – and that he understands enough to be angry. His family did not explain his furies in this way, but they emphasised that he had been a brilliant student and an excellent teacher, especially in mathematics.

7 In his study of mentally retarded people in California, Edgerton (1967) found that the inability to deal with space, time and number was deeply incapacitating. Not being able to read, fill in a form, tell time, or deal with prices in a shop made it impossible to manage independently. In rural Uganda many perfectly intelligent people cannot read or write, and do not know the year in which they were born. Still, it is discrediting not to know the difference between bank notes, and not to be able to figure change. The derogatory way that Teddy's brother spoke of his attempt to sell bread contrasted with the praise I heard for blind Gamusi, who travels to Jinja alone to trade. He can tell the denomination of a bill by holding it taut and snapping it next to his ear. Children tease Tamiti about his incompetence with money; they beg Gamusi to show them how clever he is. But what is important about numeracy is that it allows or hinders practical activities.

8   States and categories: indigenous models of personhood in northwest Greenland

Mark Nuttall

In recent years the medical anthropology of the Arctic has focused increasingly on cross-cultural encounters and conflicts between indigenous peoples and non-indigenous medical practitioners. As O'Neil (1989) has pointed out for the Canadian Arctic, Inuit dissatisfaction with medical care often originates in contexts where medical practitioners misunderstand or ignore the social and cultural experience of the patient. Furthermore, patients are often made to feel responsible for their own illnesses while the socio-political complexities of contemporary Arctic villages are not considered relevant for an understanding of health and illness. In this way, doctors, nurses and others account for illness as a result of a patient's ignorance or lack of formal education (*ibid.*: 340). So in this way, for example, a patient's illness can be attributable to their ignorance of personal hygiene or lack of knowledge about nutrition and diet, or to their abuse of drugs and alcohol. Similarly, Young (1993: 73–84) argues that health problems afflicting Alaska's Native peoples can only be understood with reference to what he calls the politics of pathology, that is by focusing on linkages between social, economic and political conditions in Native villages and the increasing problems of mental illness, suicide, drug addiction, as well as other health problems. Rather than the individual being made to feel responsible for their condition, Young calls for Western medicine to understand the processes of social change and dependency.

More generally, however, throughout the Arctic the cross-cultural encounter is one where indigenous knowledge about human well-being is subverted and replaced by dominant forms of Western medical knowledge. For example, medical practitioners are accused that they often 'trivialize aspects of patients' culture that are not easily understood' (O'Neil 1989: 340), so that activities such as trapping, fishing and hunting are not regarded by outsiders as something that circumscribe and define local culture and underpin cultural identity. A clash of world-views results when Western medical science is unable to consider indigenous cosmology and O'Neil (*ibid.*) has argued that there are serious problems with the communication and interpretation of indigenous understandings of human–environment relationships as explanatory accounts for illness. As will be shown in this essay, an understanding of the status and content of this knowledge in a lived everyday context is elusive to medical practitioners because Western medical knowledge appears to people as a dominant form of knowledge. As a result indigenous knowledge becomes muted.

This essay considers how non-indigenous definitions of intellectual incompetence affect local models of humanity by exploring ideas of personhood and social identity in Kangersuatsiaq, a small, remote Inuit hunting and fishing settlement in northwest Greenland. Here local understandings of what it means to be human, and thus to be a member of a close-knit community, are challenged by dominant non-indigenous (primarily Danish) models of normality and incompetence. Non-indigenous ideas of mental disorder, which include mental handicap and learning difficulties, do not reflect or take into account indigenous definitions, explanations and treatment. When outsiders to Greenland Inuit society, such as Danish doctors, health workers and teachers, categorise Inuit as 'socially and intellectually incompetent', or as 'mentally ill', this categorisation has implications for the achievement of full personhood. Similarly, non-indigenous models of sickness and health also disrupt indigenous ideas of treatment and physical and cultural continuity. Being categorised as intellectually incompetent or as mentally ill by those in authority, and then being subjected to treatment or a special education outside the village, separates a person from a vital network of social, psychological and emotional support and places strain on indigenous models of personhood and humanity. Furthermore, such categorisation is, from a local perspective, also seen as a reinforcement of political and cultural power by dominant outside interests, feelings which are accentuated despite Greenland having achieved Home Rule from Denmark in 1979. People who would ordinarily care for relatives who have been sent away from the village are themselves left feeling incompetent because their knowledge and abilities to care have been challenged and eroded.

The setting

Kangersuatsiaq has a resident population of about 200 and is situated in the southern part of Upernavik district, the most northerly district in West Greenland. In common with other Inuit communities, identity and a sense of place are expressed with the suffix -miut, meaning 'people of'. The people of Kangersuatsiaq are thus known as Kangersuatsiarmiut, but refer to themselves as Kangersuatsiarmiit (-miut becomes -miit in the Kangersuatsiaq dialect). This essay follows the use of the vernacular.

Historically the population of Kangersuatsiaq has subsisted mainly by the harvesting of seals. Despite the recent beginnings of a small-scale inshore commercial fishery throughout Upernavik district (Nuttall 1992), seal hunting continues to underpin the cultural fabric of Kangersuatsiaq. Hunters rely on catching ringed seals during winter and spring, and to a lesser extent in summer. Harp seals and hooded seals are more important in late summer and autumn.

Since Boas (1888) described the specific ecological conditions of subsistence in *The Central Eskimo*, the literature on Inuit subsistence hunting has stressed the close cultural, ecological and economic relationship between humans and animals. Studies of contemporary seal hunting have continued to emphasise specific environmental (Nelson 1969), ecological (Wenzel 1981a), ritual (Fienup-Riordan 1983) and gender-related aspects. Yet, Borre (1994) has pointed out an obvious lacuna in ethnographies of seal hunting – the importance of the seal for human health, beyond the obvious dietary needs. While sealing remains of vital importance for Inuit nutritional and dietary requirements, it cannot be separated from social, ideological and cosmological elements. Seal meat and seal products are vital for physical, mental and spiritual well-being, and are also used to treat and cure illness. As Borre illustrates:

Inuit health is maintained primarily through the consumption of seal and other country foods which keep the body warm. Body warmth allows one to achieve strength and endurance and maintains good mental health. When one has a healthy body and soul, he or she can then contribute to the production and distribution of country foods to help others maintain their well-being. In this way the health of individuals is directly tied to the maintenance of the hunting relationship with the animals and with social relationships within the community. (*ibid.:* 12)

In Kangersuatsiaq seal hunting not only forms part of a larger cultural system, it provides the foundation for both a secure kin-based network and a sense of community. Hunting encapsulates relations which are posed in ideological, natural and cultural terms. Reciprocal rights and obligations towards the environment which from a local perspective is, following Bird-David (1990), a 'giving environment', and towards animals are underpinned by customary rules and regulations. Animals and some inanimate objects are said to be imbued with potent spiritual power, manifest in a spirit owner or guardian known as *inua* ('its owner'). Human action within the natural world involves a dialogue and moral interplay with various *inua* and as a result hunting is viewed as a complex of relations between humans, animals and spirit owners. In setting out to hunt, the hunter (*piniartoq*, lit. 'one who wants') requests that *inua* release the animals in their care, but in return must ensure the correct treatment of the animal during death and subsequent butchering, disposal and consumption. Central to subsistence hunting in Greenland generally is the sharing and distribution of meat, which expresses and sustains social relationships and reaffirms fundamental values towards animals and the environment.

In a sense, it is the subsistence lifestyle where we find boundaries between the competent and incompetent. In order to survive and to be able to provide for his family, a hunter requires skill, prowess and knowledge. Distinctions are made between the *piniartorssuit*, 'great hunters', and the *piniarteqanngitsut* and *pilersuisoqanngitsut*, people who do not have the means (whether physical, intellectual, skilful, economic and so on) to hunt for themselves and their families. Yet networks of kinship and sharing ensure that an inability to hunt does not result in the marginalisation and starvation of the less competent. This is particularly vital during periods of lean hunting in winter. Through sharing and giving meat, what was an individual success in hunting becomes a distinctive statement of community.

Social relationships in Kangersuatsiaq are defined in terms of being either kin or non-kin based. Kinship in Kangersuatsiaq is bilateral and the term for personal kindred or immediate family is *ilaqutariit*. The root of this word, *ila-*, means 'a part' or 'a companion', and a member of the personal kindred is called an *ilaqutaq*, 'someone who belongs'. All those who share this relationship with others form an *ilaqutariit*. One important feature of Greenland Inuit kinship networks is that kin relationships can be created if individuals choose to regard a non-kin relationship as something similar to a genealogical or affinal link. This is most commonly expressed by the use of kin terms for both reference and address. A genealogical relationship, however, can also be 'forgotten about' if a person regards that relationship as incompatible or unsatisfactory (Nuttall 1992: 82–3; see also Guemple 1979). In most situations of daily interaction personal names tend to be avoided and kin terms are used as a form of address instead, usually in the possessive, for example, *ataataga* (my father), *paniga* (my daughter). This use of terminology is not only a statement of kin relationships, denoting actual genealogical and affinal relationships but, as will be shown, also acts to denote continuing relationships between the deceased and the living.

Being human: ideas of the person

For the Kangersuatsiarmiit, being 'normal', in a Western sense of the term, is not a prerequisite for being human. Indeed, it is doubtful that they could describe exactly what is meant by a state of 'normality', either physical, social or environmental, in the first place. The people of

Kangersuatsiaq live in an environment which demands from them a respectful understanding that constant change and surprise are a part of everyday life, be it in the weather, the shifting environment of the sea ice, in a person's behaviour, or in personal relationships. As Jean Briggs has illustrated vividly (1986), Inuit 'expect the unexpected', and childrearing patterns emphasise that throughout life theirs will be an 'experimental lifestyle'.

But the Kangersuatsiarmiit not only have to contend with an unpredictable physical and social environment. They live in a world where the souls of dead people can inhabit an animal's body for a few days, where a human foetus can change sex in its mother's womb, and (as will become clear below) where children can be the grandparents of adults. Stories about strange experiences and happenings attributable to spirits and ghosts are also common. If hunters return to the village claiming to have seen a shaman in a flying kayak, or to have encountered small people living under rocks, or giant babies living in the mountains, or if someone sees the spirit of a deceased relative drinking coffee in the kitchen of their house, then their stories are listened to by other members of the community rather than judged by them. And it is not uncommon for a person to experience sudden seizures or fits, or to display 'hysterical' behaviour such as screaming and running wildly around the settlement. As people in Kangersuatsiaq constantly remark, '*inuunneq tupinaqaaq*!' 'Life is very surprising!'

Without risking contradiction, having claimed that the people of Kangersuatsiaq could probably not define 'normality', they would not consider everything mentioned above to be 'abnormal' either. Outsiders, on the other hand, probably would. Anthropologists and psychologists have long sought explanations for what they have categorised as specific forms of mental disorder found only in the Arctic. What has been called 'Arctic hysteria' is often identified in the literature as a psychopathological disorder attributable to the effects of the long, dark polar winter, the extreme cold and a lack of vitamins in the Inuit diet. For example, anthropologists have identified hysterical seizures as *pilluktuk*, or *pibloktok*, a classic form of mental illness found in many parts of the Arctic where the afflicted person runs around uncontrollably, eats faeces, sees ghosts and generally acts in an irrational way (e.g. see Parker 1962). While Parker regards hysteria as an institutionalised way of releasing hostility and also sees the origins of mental illness in the close-knit social organisation and patterns of childrearing characteristic of Inuit society, Wallace (1961) attributes hysterical behaviour to calcium deficiency. In contemporary Greenland, mental disorders and learning difficulties are also considered by medical practitioners to have social, economic, environmental and dietary origins (Marschall and Hjelt 1988).

And there are also fundamental differences between these non-local 'expert' explanations and indigenous accounts. In Kangersuatsiaq, a person who claims to enjoy regular visits from their dead grandmother, who sees strange figures in an otherwise uninhabited landscape, or has the occasional outburst of hysterical behaviour, is not dismissed as someone who has hallucinations or is otherwise disturbed in some way. Wenzel (1981b) has argued that Inuit ideas of health and illness can be described as continuous. By this Wenzel means that individual states of health and illness can only be understood with reference to the relationship between person and environment. An illness or period of misfortune is diagnosed and explained by examining the afflicted person's relationships with his or her social, spiritual and physical environments. In Kangersuatsiaq, much of daily life is underpinned by an elaborate system of beliefs and moral codes that act to regulate a complexity of human–environmental relationships. For the people of Kangersuatsiaq, the environment is one of risk, fraught with danger and uncertainty. To a considerable extent, part of this danger is due to the fact that lack of success in hunting, illness, misfortune, famine and bad weather are all understood to come about because this elaborate code has been contravened in some way, resulting in a violation of the relations between people and the natural world (Nuttall 1992). Indigenous healers attempt to build up a complete picture of a person's actions with and relationship to the environment, animals and other people. In this way the process of healing is one of reintegrating the person with his or her social, physical and spiritual surroundings.

Lending support to Wenzel, ethnographic evidence from many parts of the Arctic and sub-Arctic suggests there is an indigenous model of personhood which emphasises continuity along a range of personal behaviour, rather than any rigid boundary marking differences between continuous and disassociative states. For example, Vallee (1966: 61) has described how, for the Inuit of the Hudson Bay region, 'the natural and the supernatural are not clearly distinguished'. Conditions 'which would be regarded as delusional, and therefore, pathological, by psychiatrists', such as seeing and hearing spirits, are regarded as credulous and benign by the Inuit (ibid.). In such a cultural context, people become human beings and participate as social persons despite instances of what, in other cultural contexts, may be defined as intellectual incompetence, mental illness, manic depression and so on. This is not to deny that Inuit do recognise that there are individuals who are more or less competent, whether socially or intellectually, than others. But if someone is born deaf and dumb, or has epilepsy, or exhibits convulsive behaviour, they may inspire feelings of pity in others but they are regarded as a person none the less, someone to be included in all aspects of social life, not excluded because of what is regarded as a *state* (*-neq*) rather than a category of person.

By contrast, a Western disassociative model of health and illness has secularised the indigenous continuous model by paying less attention to how a person's behaviour or actions cause illness. And by being removed to hospital the person is also separated further from the social, physical and spiritual environment which is necessary for a return to human well-being.

The Kangersuatsiarmiit see the person (*inuk*) as consisting of body (*timi*), soul (*tarneq*) and name/name soul (*ateq*).[1] The body (*timi*) is subject to disease and decay, while the soul (*tarneq*) is a person's life force and is affected by the state of health that the body is in. Physical sickness can result in the soul becoming 'ill with depression and malaise, risking death to the individual' (Borre 1994: 5). The name is one of the most pervasive features of daily life and is regarded as both a social and spiritual component of the person. When a person dies his/her name soul leaves the body and is said to be 'homeless' until it is recalled to reside in the body of a newborn child. Once named a child has become a full or proper person and throughout the Inuit area the importance of the name for according the status of social person on the child has been remarked on by several scholars (e.g. Balikci 1970: 148; Guemple 1979). A person who is named after a dead person is called an *atsiaq* (pl. *atsiat*), but the first same-sex child to be born after the death of another person is called that person's *ateqqaataa*. The dead person, who can have more than one *atsiaq*, is known as the *atsiaq*'s *aqqa*, which is another word for name. Throughout many parts of the Inuit area the name is not tied to either sex, and a child can receive the name of a deceased male or female. But in Greenland all personal names are gender specific and generally a child can only be named after a person of the same sex. Furthermore, the *atsiaq* does not necessarily have to be born into the deceased's community. It is quite common to find *atsiat* in other villages named after people from Kangersuatsiaq.

As an *atsiaq*, a child enters into a multiplicity of relationships with the surviving relatives of its *aqqa*, who will all address the child by the kin term they would have applied to their dead relative. The child grows up to use corresponding terms of address, which means the actual use of kinship terminology diverges considerably from the use of terms that denote genealogical and affinal relationship. For example, a dead woman's *atsiaq* will be called 'mother' (*anaana*) by that woman's children, and 'wife' (*nuliaq*) by her husband. In addition to her *aqqa*'s father calling her 'daughter' (*panik*), she will be called 'daughter' by her genitor.

Furthermore, it may be that an *atsiaq* belongs genealogically to his/her *aqqa*'s family, which complicates the use of terminology further. For example, an *atsiaq* who is named after his maternal grandfather will address his mother as 'daughter', his father as 'daughter's husband' (*ningaaq*), and his grandmother as 'wife' (*nuliaq*). In this way children learn the identities of those they are named after and acquire a knowledge of the various relationships that link them to an intricate pattern of genealogical, affinal and fictive kin. As the child is named after people who had previously occupied positions in the kinship network, to some extent roles and interaction between *atsiat* and the family of the *aqqa* are prescribed.

People in Kangersuatsiaq, through their names, do not disappear from the social map at death. They remain part of the community and continue to extend their network of social alignments. Naming illustrates one of the most outstanding aspects of Inuit culture: the emphasis on continuity, rather than finality, of both person and community. The link between person and name is inseparable; it is not an arbitrary association which is severed at death but a bond that integrates each and every person, both living and dead, present and absent, in a social and psychological network of interpersonal relationships.

The naming of a child means that the social and spiritual essence of the deceased person is reincarnated in the newborn. To some extent, people choose to believe or deny that personal characteristics are also reincarnated. For some people, children simply receive the name of a deceased relative and do not assume any of a person's qualities or behaviour. Others, however, believe that personal characteristics are also reborn and relatives often look for signs of these when a child is growing up.

Approaches to health care: indigenous and non-local 'expert' models

The significance of this rich network of family and social relationships is evident when a person falls ill, or is born with a disability. Not only does a sick person's family take an active part in caring for them, as they may be aware of the causes of the illness, the community (including the relatives of the *aqqa* for whom the person is named) as a whole provides material and emotional support for both the sick person and the family. Thus, if the sick person is the sole or main provider, then others will give shares of seal meat and fish to the family, who are now *pilersuisoqanngitsut*, people who lack, either short or long term, the means and ability to hunt for themselves. It is vital that the sick person continues to eat the meat and other parts of the seal, including the liver, blubber and blood, as health depends on the body being warm, which only seal meat can make it. Both body and soul must be nourished by the meat and blubber of the seal and Borre (1994) lists a number of ailments, ranging from ear infections to headaches, nausea and gastrointestinal complaints, that seal products are used specifically to cure.

A person who has a mental disorder or a learning difficulty must also be on the receiving end of a plentiful supply of seal meat, and must eat the meat in both its raw and cooked states, as this is vital for their mental strength. Their condition may be attributed to a lack of seal meat during childhood, or even to the fact that their mother did not eat enough seal meat during her pregnancy. Depression, which results from a lack of balance between body and soul, can also be treated with seal meat.

An indigenous Inuit model of health care sees no clear separation of person and social and physical environment. Wenzel (1981b: 12) has pointed out that Inuit base their own health care on a long-term knowledge of the person and their behaviour. Both patient and carers have mutual experience and understanding of a specific cultural-environmental system. For the Kangersuatsiarmiit disease and illness (both physical and mental) and misfortune can be the result of a violation of an elaborate network of taboos, or the causing of offence to animal spirits. So a diagnosis is made by seeking to discover whether the sick person had inadvertently broken a taboo, for example if a hunter had not propitiated the soul of a hunted animal, such as a seal, by failing to return its kidneys to the sea, or if the patient had offended another person who may have then brought on the sickness by magical means. Illness is not simply an individual affliction, but may endanger the community as a whole.

The Kangersuatsiarmiit say that the more likely cause of sickness and illness for most people is an increasing reliance on various store-bought foods. The young, for example, are said to be especially susceptible to sickness from soda pop and junk food. While store-bought food is not said to be bad in itself, and all households in Kangersuatsiaq supplement their diet with imported foods, it is an unbalanced mixing of Greenlandic food (*kalaalimernit*) with Danish food (*qallunaamernit*) which is believed to constitute a problem for physical and mental health as it contains no medicinal value. The relatives of a sick person thus ensure that Danish foods are eliminated from their diet during the period of sickness and recovery and only fresh *kalaalimernit* is eaten. Medical research on how dietary changes account for health problems in many parts of Greenland, especially the towns, lends support to the indigenous view of the importance of *kalaalimernit* for human well-being. Disorders ranging from heart disease to tooth caries can be attributed in part to an increased reliance on imported foodstuffs high in carbohydrates. In the traditional hunting communities, where people rely more on seal meat, whale meat and various kinds of fish and sea birds, there are lower rates of heart disease. This is probably due to the fact that the traditional Inuit diet is high in polyunsaturated fats.

Wenzel argues that this indigenous continuous model contrasts with a Western, or discontinuous and disassociative model of health care that:

imposes a set of definitions on the patient, his environment, and on the nature of disease that fails to account for the close human ecological association between individual and society . . . the basis of Inuit understanding of health care. (1981b: 13)

Western medical praxis emphasises the diagnosis and treatment of physical symptoms which are regarded in isolation of the complexity of the patient's social and environmental relationships. O'Neil (1989) has discussed the problems arising from conflict between the indigenous and Western models and recommends that medical practitioners respect indigenous cultural meanings of illness. While it could be argued that indigenous and Western models of health care can in fact be complementary, the possibility of reconciling conflicting ideas and practices is made all the more problematic by the cultural distance between doctors and health workers and their patients. Doctors and health workers often decontextualise a patient's condition, even when the patient

has contextualized a health problem by referring to some aspect of his or her life circumstances . . . In most cases, contextual information, even when translated, is ignored, because it does not 'make sense' in the health professional's cultural perspective. (*ibid.*: 335–6)

Before the introduction of Home Rule in Greenland in 1979, the Danish government was responsible for the administration of the Greenland Health Service, which was supervised by the Chief Medical Officer. Part of the Chief Medical Officer's responsibility was to monitor diseases and health conditions of the Greenlandic population, and to oversee programmes of prevention of infectious diseases. The administrative centre in each district was equipped with a small hospital that could provide primary health care. The outlying settlements in each district were visited several times a year by the district doctor. Doctors and most medical staff came from Denmark. The hospital in Nuuk, Greenland's capital, functioned as a referral hospital and patients who could not be treated in Greenland were sent to hospital in Copenhagen. As of 1 January 1992, the Home Rule government has administered the Health Service. All hospital treatment and the prescription of drugs and medicines are free. Although the Home Rule government intends that greater medical specialisation will be available in Nuuk in the future, with the result that fewer people will have to be flown to Copenhagen for treatment, for many who live in small settlements, the achievement of Home Rule has meant little with regard to improvements in non-local health care systems.

People in Kangersuatsiaq who are in need of primary health care must first undergo a five-hour journey by boat to the town of Upernavik, where there is a small hospital. Kangersuatsiaq and other outlying settlements are also visited normally twice a year by the district doctor, who is Danish. As a result, most people's experiences of the doctor are brief and infrequent. The majority of people in Kangersuatsiaq cannot speak Danish and the doctor has no knowledge of Greenlandic, so a Greenlandic-speaking nurse or other interpreter is essential. As a non-Greenlandic-speaking outsider, the doctor has no established role in the daily life of Kangersuatsiaq and because there is a regular turnover of Danish doctors (most come on two-year contracts), people are denied the chance to develop feelings of trust (Nuttall 1992: 105). O'Neil (1989) has also described how, in the Canadian Arctic, patient dissatisfaction with medical services is often attributed to poor communication as health care personnel do not speak local languages.

The lack of available health care for serious illnesses in remoter areas of Greenland often means that a patient still has to be flown to the hospital in Nuuk, or even to Copenhagen. When outside agencies step in to take care of the sick person, and when that person is institutionalised in a hospital, then this becomes a social problem in that both family and community are excluded from an active health care role. It is harder for the patient's family to be kept informed of their situation and progress, and indeed to comment on the kind of treatment they think the patient should be receiving. Telephone communication is often poor and the high cost of travel both within Greenland and to Denmark makes visiting prohibitive, while people also feel constrained by their inability to deal directly with the doctor, a stranger who has no established role in settlement life and who local people believe is like most Danes who only come to Greenland to earn money. When people who are diagnosed as having mental disorder or learning difficulties are taken away from settlements to institutions in other parts of Greenland, or even to Denmark, then there are similar difficulties for the family who remain behind.

States and categories

Jenkins has argued (1993: 17) that 'a broad definition of learning difficulties would stress social and intellectual incompetence: the inability to do things as well as most other people in the appropriate cultural context'. So how do the socially and intellectually incompetent fit in to everyday life in Greenlandic villages? While Inuit do recognise that there are people who are more or less intellectually able than others, they do not draw rigid classificatory boundaries between the able and less able. There are what may be called indigenous diagnostic categories, but the problem is not so much the socially and intellectually incompetent, or how to take care of them or where they fit into the social group, but differences between indigenous and medical models of care. The rest of this essay illustrates how non-indigenous ideas and definitions of intellectual and social incompetence collide with indigenous models of humanity and personhood.

In Greenland, most large towns have a centre for the education of children with disabilities. The children who attend such a centre do so because, from an orthodox medical perspective, 'due to their handicap they were unable to profit from the teaching in an ordinary school' (Marschall and Hjelt 1988). Typically, the children attending such centres have been diagnosed by paediatric consultants as having, among other things, epilepsy, mental retardation and learning disorders. The study of mental retardation and learning disorders in Greenland has focused on the causes, whether clinical or social and economic. As well as being the result of neurological disease, poor social and family backgrounds are also considered to be a major cause of the children's conditions, and paediatricians and health workers claim that handicapped children in Greenland are often neglected or abandoned by their families. Children are then institutionalised because families are seen to be unable, or unwilling, to cope. Marschall and Hjelt have therefore argued that 'there is an urgent need not only for treating the handicapped child but for treating the whole family' (ibid.: 70).

The medical establishment's view of contemporary indigenous care of the handicapped in Greenland is in keeping with a stereotype of how Inuit have traditionally coped with mental and physical disability in the past. While very few narratives and accounts of early travel in the Arctic include any reference or description of insanity or mental illness (Fortuine 1989: 38)[2], the ethnographic literature is rich in examples of Inuit groups abandoning the incompetent, the insane and the physically disabled (e.g. Weyer 1932: 132). The classic instances were at times of lean hunting and environmental uncertainty. The sick and the incompetent restricted movement, so female infanticide was practised, physically deformed babies or children whose mothers had died were drowned, and the elderly would walk off into the dark winter night to relieve stress on the group and its ability to procure enough food.

Yet there is need to be careful when coming to a conclusion about how the Inuit dealt with the old, infirm and disabled. Abandonment of the vulnerable was not necessarily always carried out at a time when the group was faced with the prospect of surviving from scarce resources. For example, the autopsy of a four-year-old mummified child who died in Greenland sometime during the middle of the fifteenth century revealed that it had probably suffered from Down's Syndrome and Calvé-Perthes disease (Hart Hansen *et al.* 1991). The condition of the child would have placed a severe strain on the group as a whole, yet there is no evidence to suggest that the child was abandoned or killed. Rather, this single case from archaeology points to the child being cared for despite its deformity. While archaeology cannot account for why this child survived for so long, anthropologists have suggested that the naming of a child confers upon it the status of a social person and that once named infanticide could not take place (e.g. Balikci 1970: 148). And as the name is believed to contain properties of the deceased, there is a sense in which people do not name a new person, but welcome back a member of family and community (Nuttall 1992: 68–9). The result, whatever the physical or mental condition of the child, is inclusion as a full social person, rather than exclusion and abandonment.

Furthermore, as far as the Inuit considered mental illness or insanity, people who suffered from epilepsy (which Inuit called *qiirsurtuq*, 'sickness in the head') were attributed with spiritual powers (Vallee 1966: 62). While Sonne (1986) attributes the majority of murders in East Greenland prior to the establishment of a Danish trading post in 1894 to mental illness, Fortuine has argued that 'it is likely that most hysterical behaviour observed by the Eskimos themselves was not considered an illness but rather a manifestation of shamanic propensities' (1989: 39).

A person afflicted by mental illness could be cured by a shaman, as the cause was also often attributed to the temporary departure of the soul or to the breaking of a taboo. It was more often the case that a person with mental illness, or with 'sickness in the head', would abandon the community rather than be abandoned by it. In Greenland this is well exemplified by the case of the *qivittoq* (lit. 'one who is disappointed', pl. *qivittut*), a mysterious supernatural wanderer, originally a known person who has left the warmth and security of human society to live alone in the mountains (Nuttall 1992: 112–114).

In Kangersuatsiaq, when people hear about a person who has committed suicide, they will often talk about how suicides are people who want to leave behind kin and friends in the same way as *qivittut* did in the past. A common explanation for a person becoming a *qivittoq* is that they are people who were unlucky in love, they experienced personal pressures, had problems with other people, or had 'sickness in the head'. Local accounts describe how *qivittut* would try and cover up their disppearance by faking a fatal accident. The *qivittoq* has become a metaphor for the rejection of community. *Qivittut* are often sighted by hunters, they pilfer fish from camps, they steal meat and sled dogs, and they return to the settlement during winter to peer through people's windows. For the Kangersuatsiarmiit the *qivittoq* is loneliness personified, the expression of all that it feared about rejection, abandonment and isolation from others. It is notable, however, that those who have 'sickness in the head' have the 'sense' to reject kin and friends. It is they who do the rejecting, rather than being rejected.

In attempting to reach an understanding of contemporary Greenland Inuit ideas of the person, it is important to note that the Kangersuatsiarmiit recognise a difference between states and categories of the person. While it is possible to discover indigenous diagnostic categories for conditions such as madness (*niaqulaarneq*), most terms for mental health and illness describe the state of a person, rather than a category of person. So someone who may in another culture be described as 'mad' would, in Kangersuatsiaq, be *qaatusimasaqanngilaq*, 'not quite in the right state of mind', or someone who may be described as a 'manic depressive' is *tujormivoq*, 'uncomfortable in his/her surroundings'. A person who has a learning difficulty may be described as *sianilluanngilaq*, 'does not have very much sense', or *poqiipoq*, 'is slow at learning/slow at understanding', or even *niaqulaarpoq*, 'half-witted'. Someone who has a breakdown is said to be *silaaruppoq*, 'to have lost his/her reason'.

Many of these states are considered to be temporary and transitory and a person who recovers from a breakdown or depression, or a state of *qaatusimasaqanngilaq*, is said to be *ilisimmarpoq*, 'has come around to consciousness'. The person is then once more 'aware', 'can think' and has the capacity to 'reason' by the correct use of mind (*isuma*), as these abilities have been temporarily absent. *Ilisimmarpoq* also means the ability to connect, to have knowledge and to think about right action. Someone who is *poqiipoq*, 'slow at learning/understanding' or *niaqulaarpoq*, 'half-witted', can also transcend that state and achieve a state of consciousness allowing them to reason and think and to be aware in a way that their previous state prevented them from doing. As Vallee (1966: 61) has put it:

a person is described as in a process of such and such; after the 'sick' condition has passed, the person is not in that state. This way of describing deviant states should be compared with the tendency in English to use substantive categories, such as he *is* a manic depressive, he *is* a criminal, and so on.

This distinction between states and categories is underlined by an emphasis on incorporation rather than rejection, as the following case illustrates.

The tusilartoq

In 1987 Nils, a seven-year-old boy in Kangersuatsiaq, was designated a 'problem' and a special case by both the Greenlandic health and education authorities. Nils was born a *tusilartoq*, 'one who is deaf'. This was not considered a problem by his family or others in Kangersuatsiaq. His parents and his father's brother and sister all learned sign language and Nils, who was named after his mother's grandfather, was regarded as a full member of both his family and community, and was considered *silatuvoq*, 'to have intelligence, understanding and sense'. From the age of four, Nils accompanied his father on hunting and fishing trips. Like other boys in Kangersuatsiaq, Nils would have been expected to begin active participation in subsistence activities when he reached the age of ten, when he would make seal nets and begin to fish. Until then, he would accompany his father on hunting expeditions to watch and learn. During winter, they would walk out on the sea ice each day to check seal nets, and shortly after his seventh birthday he caught a seal in a net he had set under the ice with his father's help. This marked his development as a hunter and the event was celebrated by a first-catch party, where the meat of the seal was shared out among all households in Kangersuatsiaq.

With his seventh birthday, Nils also reached school age. At this point the Danish teacher in the village decided that Nils had severe learning difficulties and would restrict the other children in the school.[3] It was also the opinion of the teacher that Nils could not grow to become a competent person if he remained in the village and therefore announced to his parents that he needed special schooling. The teacher notified the health and education authorities of his concern for the boy and, following the visit of an educational specialist who carried out tests, Nils was labelled officially as having learning difficulties. His parents were informed that Nils would be sent away immediately to a special school in Sisimiut, a large town in central west Greenland. While his parents took the news passively, and initially deferred to the decision taken by the authorities, his father's brother protested and said that he would sit with Nils in the school in Kangersuatsiaq and help him understand his lessons through sign language. The teacher regarded this as unacceptable and Nils left for Sisimiut.

Some two months after Nils had left his home, his parents travelled to Sisimiut to take him out of the boarding school he was now attending.

Nils was suffering from homesickness and his parents had also taken the decision to bring him home because he was *kiserliorneq*, 'living in loneliness'. Although his father had a cousin living in Sisimiut, Nils had very little contact with anyone other than his teachers and fellow schoolchildren. The family was also concerned that Nils's diet in Sisimiut was not giving him the physical and mental strength necessary for his well-being. He was eating only *qallunaamernit* and needed *kalaalimernit*, especially seal meat to ensure a healthy body, soul and mind. But Nils's parents had to reckon with the authorities once more. Nils was soon returned to school in Sisimiut and is now, at the age of fifteen, in Denmark attending a special school for children with learning difficulties, where he continues to live and to be cared for outside his own social and physical environment. Before being categorised as incompetent by those in authority, Nils was, like all boys his age, learning to be a hunter in his own social context where he was allowed to participate as a social person. He now visits his home village once a year during summer.

For the villagers generally, who all agreed that Nils would be better looked after by his own family, this particular case highlighted the tension between formal, institutionalised education and the kind of learning that results in the acquisition of skills and knowledge necessary for survival in an extreme environment. But by taking Nils away from Kangersuatsiaq the authorities had, from the perspective of many Kangersuatsiarmiit, challenged his family's sense of competence and knowledge of how to care for him.

These feelings are consistent with how Nils's family understood their own situation. From the perspective of those in authority, Nils had learning difficulties and was unable to achieve at school. Nils's parents felt unable to challenge this view and experienced a sense of inferiority (*naalagasiorpoq*) when confronted with a dominant and authoritarian form of knowledge. They felt constrained from articulating their worries to the teacher that Nils had been labelled as *poqiipoq* ('slow at learning/understanding') by the authorities because he was unable to achieve a level of educational attainment defined in terms of intellectual competence in school subjects. Nils's parents were also made to feel that because he had been categorised as having learning difficulties they were somehow responsible for restricting his development. Nils's father, in particular, while feeling sure he was teaching Nils the skills he needed in life by taking him out hunting and fishing, none the less felt *ajukkunneq*, 'shy and inferior', when discussing with the teacher the relative merits of being out on the land *vis-à-vis* being in school.

While Nils had been labelled as having learning difficulties, and had been sent to an institution several hundred miles from home (and eventually on to Denmark), his parents worried that this would actually cause him to become less competent as a result of being separated from home and being denied an opportunity to acquire the knowledge to survive on his own terms. Indeed, to his family Nils has become a *piniarte-qanngitsoq*, someone who does not have the means, knowledge and skill to hunt and look after himself. And just as seriously, because Nils was away from the village it was feared that this absence would threaten his knowledge of people and places. Such knowledge is central to the development of a child's social identity. But the teacher and the authorities were not motivated by a concern that Nils would not be a competent hunter or fisherman, nor were they worried that he would be separated from a rich network of social relationships. Rather, the concern was that he would not be able to acquire an education necessary for survival in modern Greenlandic society – a society defined and shaped increasingly by the culture of the market economy, rather than by hunting and fishing. In the process, not only was Nils categorised as incompetent, but his family were also left feeling a sense of inadequacy and incompetence at being deprived of caring for him.

Conclusions

The case of Nils is significant, because it brought to the fore general feelings in Kangersuatsiaq that indigenous understandings are often ignored or not understood by those in positions of authority, such as Danish doctors and teachers. While having an immediate impact in a local context, the subversion of indigenous models of personhood by non-indigenous forms of knowledge is also experienced within a wider political and economic context, where relationships between Danes and Greenlanders are constructed in terms of hierarchies of competent and incompetent persons, in the sense of their ability to participate in modern Greenlandic society. Non-indigenous medical knowledge, or definitions of intellectual incompetence, re-affirm dominant political and cultural interests.

Although Greenland achieved Home Rule from Denmark in 1979, well-educated Danes continue to hold some of the best and the most highly paid jobs. Greenlanders who have no knowledge of Danish or have a rudimentary education have limited access to the labour market and therefore little opportunity to compete for the best jobs. And while Greenlandic is the official language of Greenland, it is the ability to speak Danish which remains an effective indicator of social and intellectual competence. Very few Danes can speak Greenlandic. Greenlanders have a chance of succeeding in education only if they have a reasonable oral and written knowledge of Danish. Likewise, command of the Danish language is one way they are likely to succeed in a social and economic sense in the larger towns, and especially in Nuuk. Interestingly, throughout Greenland frequent mention is made of Danes being unable to learn Greenlandic, either because they do not want to or are unable to because of linguistic incompetence. Danes defend their inability to speak Greenlandic because the language is either too difficult, or because they do not have the opportunity to learn, as Greenlanders speak Danish to them. However, it still remains true that for many Greenlanders (and in the eyes of Danes) an ability to speak Danish is an indication of sophistication and modernity, while those who speak only Greenlandic are ill-equipped to deal with the development and modernisation process underway throughout the country.

What one needs to know in order to survive as a hunter and what it means to live in a socially rich environment are at odds with what one needs to know to participate in a modern society and be meaningfully 'employed' within that society. Greenland is undergoing a process of nation-building and the Home Rule authorities have adopted policies that aim to develop the country in terms of its own social and economic conditions and available natural resources (Nuttall 1994, 1997). To be a modern Greenlander, one must succeed in education and it is the education process which creates categories of competent and incompetent persons. Those who are unable to perform well in school are labelled incompetent by dominant outside interests and agencies. In a local context, however, in a place like Kangersuatsiaq, schooling is seen as a hindrance to full participation in the subsistence economy, as children are denied opportunities to go hunting and fishing when they are confined to the classroom. Nor is proficiency in Danish, or the ability to hear, necessary to successful seal hunting, the propitiation of a seal's soul, or the sharing of its meat among kin and friends. Similarly, those who, for whatever reasons, are unable to hunt for themselves are not marginalised or separated from their immediate social context. They remain, through their kinship ties and their name relationships, full social persons.

Notes

1 For a fuller discussion, see Nuttall (1992).

2 Fortuine (1989: 37) argues that it would have been difficult for outsiders 'to have discerned mental aberration, since many aspects of Native behaviour were already quite beyond their previous experience'.

3 A cynical observer would be surprised by this, as the teacher in question, despite living in Greenland for ten years, could not speak Greenlandic and was teaching in a virtually monolingual community.

9   Learning to become (in)competent: children in Belize speak out

Nancy Lundgren

Every institutionalised educational system (ES) owes the specific characteristics of its structure and functioning to the fact that, by the means proper to the institution, it has to produce and reproduce the institutional conditions whose existence and persistence (self reproduction of the system) are necessary both to the exercise of its essential function of inculcation and to the fulfilment of its function of reproducing a cultural arbitrary which it does not produce (cultural reproduction), the reproduction of which contributes to the reproduction of the relations between the groups or classes (social reproduction).

Pierre Bourdieu (1973: 77)

As far as we know, all cultures determine who is 'in', who is 'out', who is clean, who is unclean, who are the chosen, who are not. Not until the rise of the nation-state, however, and the emergence of capitalism, did social competence take the form of intellectual competence measured by 'scientific' testing, quantifying, measuring and subsequent ranking. Just as Western movies, television, food and ideology have been exported around the globe, so has this 'scientific' sense of competence. Ironically it is reinforced by contemporary sentiments about equality: if everyone is equal and has access to the same things, then the truly gifted, intelligent, competent individuals will rise to the top and the other less competent, dumber and lazier will stay at the bottom (Bowles and Gintis 1976).

Belize, in Central America, is a recently politically decolonised country, which is frequently characterised as a 'poor', 'underdeveloped', 'developing' or 'third world' nation. It is one of the beneficiaries of Western capitalism with its accompanying attitudes about what it is to be (in)competent. As a former colony of Britain, Belize shares what Wallerstein (1980) calls a 'geoculture', with norms and values that serve the same world system. This is a totality where the ruling ideas are the ideas of the ruling class and where small, peripheral countries like Belize, incorporate these ideas and thus are coerced into providing a cheap, unskilled, under-educated and co-operative labour force and market for the dominant core nations (Hunter and Abraham 1987). These peripheral nations have been proletarianised through the forced expropriation of their land and provide a poor surplus labour force and a 'waiting proletariat' (Keren 1987; Magubane 1981; Ake 1981) to serve the needs of capital's never-ending drive to accumulate.

The Western, Christian and capitalist ideas necessary to the production and reproduction of the world capitalist system are transmitted overtly and covertly through the media, the family, the market, the schools and the church (Marable 1983). This cluster of ideas is dominated by bourgeois liberalism and neo-classical economic assumptions. These assumptions are both epistemological and ontological, conveying a sense of what it is to be human, what it means to know things, and how one must act in the world.

These assumptions rest on the essential concept that human beings have a 'self' that is pre-cultural, that this self is free to think for itself, is rational, can make free choices, and will make these choices so as to maximise its opportunities. In this model, the world is, and has always been, limited in its resources and, therefore, creates the inevitability of competition among individuals and groups for these scarce, but desirable resources. Human beings are always desirous of obtaining more (they are naturally greedy) and, therefore, they will devise new technologies, new systems as a natural way to improve their chances to maximise their resources (Heilbroner and Thurow 1981).

According to this world-view, everyone is equal, and everyone has an equal chance to choose, to compete, to create capital, and to join the market. This is as true for nations as it is for individuals. However, the cores and peripheries share a history that, according to Wolf (1994), goes something like this. In the beginning, there was a 'civilised core and the barbarians out there'. The barbarians were either friendly or hostile, while the civilised core made distinctions and people were nuanced. Eventually, according to this history, the 'uncivilised barbarians' and 'monstrous humans' were transformed into the faithful, the unredeemed and the unredeemable (Wolf 1994: 3). Since the 'barbarians out there' provided slave labour for the civilised core, 'race' became an essential element in the game of capital accumulation. There were questions about the innate inferiority of the 'Black' person, which were given support by the obviously inferior position in which they had chosen to keep themselves. Although the notion of 'racial' difference in basic intelligence has been discredited, beginning with Boas (1938) and continuing with Gould (1981) – to name only two – the idea continues to rear its ugly head, as witnessed by the new version of the old story told by Herrnstein and Murray's *The Bell Curve* (1994).

In the contemporary world, incompetence has many names: woman,

Black, Indian, Arab, Chicana, Creole, working-class, poor, and there are others. There are ways to measure the validity of (in)competence in order to reinforce historically and culturally derived commonsense ideas about these categories. (In)competence is a concept that is made real through testing and measuring. This measuring and testing lends support to the reality that certain groups of (incompetent) people are considered appropriate for, and desirous of, certain jobs that the other (competent) people would find tedious, boring and unchallenging. Determining competence and/or incompetence in the modern world political economy contributes to a division of classes, nations and 'races' that serve to maintain the views and behaviours upon which the accumulation of capital rests, and within which it continues to survive (Magubane 1981; Ake 1981; Said 1979; Wallerstein 1980). In its never-ending drive for capital accumulation, capitalism as a social, political and economic system seeks new caches of natural resources, new labour and new markets. Occupational segmentation ensures the constant availability of a cheap, exploited and super-exploited labour force that can be drawn in and pushed out of the labour market at the whim of the needs of capital accumulation (Fernandez-Kelly 1983; Gordon *et al.* 1982).

Ideology and socialisation

My work in Belize illustrates the point. Although I concentrate here on a specific aspect of the educational system, the formal measurement of the children, I have corroborating data on the socialisation process in other arenas: the family, the market, the media and the church. Children in Belize are socialised within the above historical, political, social, economic and ideological context. They live with this interpretation of history, and learn how to see themselves in the world. Because they are socialised with British or American media and a religion transported complete with priests, hymnals, Bible stories and a white Mary and Jesus, and formally educated with books and exams – sometimes even nuns – from somewhere abroad in one of the core countries, it is not difficult to see how, from childhood, Belizeans are introduced to the ideologies and behaviours of the ruling countries and classes. In the case of Belize, this is Britain and, increasingly, the United States. These ruling models do not contain many positive images or roles or places for poor, Black, 'underdeveloped' people like themselves.

There is controversy about the acceptance of 'external' ideas, values and political economies by the people who are forced to participate in world capitalism. Arguments about resistance and human agency dominate present discourses: they insist that human beings do not succumb to negative stereotyping or demeaning work or foreign ideologies just because they are exposed to them; that they have more agency, more freedom to choose, more discernment, than structural, Marxist or World Systems analyses allow (e.g. Bourdieu and Passeron 1977; Cole and Wolf 1974; Comaroff 1985; Marcus and Fischer 1986; Wolf 1994).

While it is important to recognise differences between human beings – in their talents, coping strategies and abilities to understand their own position and resist humiliation and dehumanisation – it takes a very unusual person to critique the basic assumptions upon which their culture rests. The extent to which a culture convinces its members that it is the only one, the best one and the true one, is the extent to which that culture will survive (Skinner 1972). It is adaptive for members of a culture to adopt its rules, values, ways of being and thinking. In fact, the huge success of cultural socialisation and the negative impact it has had on so many people, for so long, should make us shudder. It does not take away from an individual's dignity or humanity to think in structural and/or group terms. Many people's dignity and humanity are taken away by a system that provides them with an ideology and a political economy from which they have no escape, but within which they are considered incompetent workers, incompetent thinkers, incompetent by nature, and within which there are built in, structural limitations that affect their access to critical, life-sustaining resources such as work, healthy food, adequate housing and relevant education.

With this theoretical bias, I look at the specifics of Belize and how (in)competence is conceived, understood, articulated, accepted or rejected by the people who live there and what impact it has on their lives. This touches upon a range of issues about normality, identity and the self. I begin with a brief discussion of socialisation, and of what this means to Belizeans and other peoples as they attempt to create 'normal', competent, socially acceptable human beings.

Socialisation

Socialisation is the process by which initiates become full participating members of a particular culture or way of life. Every group of adult human beings devises ways of accomplishing this task which reflect the ultimate needs and expectations of the group or the culture. As societies have become more complex and stratified, this task becomes similarly more complex. Children are socialised into a specific class, 'race' or ethnic niche within the broader, more inclusive culture (Kohn 1969; Luster and McAdoo 1994; Sennett and Cobb 1973; Marable 1983). Culture is learned, and the social, political and psychological environment plays a part in this learning (LeVine 1980; McAdoo and McAdoo 1985; Zigler *et al.* 1982; Whiting and Whiting 1975).

In the contemporary geoculture of which Belize is a part, certain socially defined categories of people (e.g. people of African descent) have special problems when it comes to integrating their children into the world. In a world that is stratified along lines of power, all children are not socialised equally. Because my work has focused most specifically, though not exclusively, on children of African descent or, as they are called in Belize, Creoles, my discussion focuses more on this group than other groups that, today, are selected out as 'different': Native Americans, Latinos, the industrial poor, migrant workers, etc. My analysis, however, can be generalised to include these 'others' as they and their parents are confronted with many of the same socialisation dilemmas as children of African descent. In a sense, the categories themselves *mean* incompetence. They mean 'not as good', they mean 'less than'. Their children are judged every day by their peers and their 'superiors' and they are judged 'poor', 'underdeveloped', 'backward', of inadequate intelligence (McAdoo and McAdoo 1985; Luster and McAdoo 1994; Kozal 1991). Although all children do not cope with, adapt to, or interpret the culturally inscribed givens of their world in the same ways, the world that they confront creates unusual and specific obstacles, to which the children will be forced to attend. Parents who have been designated as African American, 'Indian', 'Third World', 'underdeveloped', 'Black and ugly', have special problems when it comes to integrating their children into the world or into their world.

Research on how human beings grow and develop and achieve full adult status in social groups is profuse. Out of this plethora of material, it is possible to speculate about particular environments and/or socialisation styles that may be universally advantageous to the growing human organism. There may be some things that all human beings need. A synthesis of the large amount of material on child development (e.g. Zigler and Child 1973; Spindler 1980; Gesell *et al.* 1977; LeVine 1980; Whiting and Whiting 1975) allows me to cautiously suggest the following as possible universal needs of the developing human child.

Human offspring have a prolonged period of dependency and require an extended period of caretaking, including the provision of food, shelter and protection. But evidence indicates that the human infant requires also human verbal and physical contact (Harlow and Harlow 1969). Erickson (1963) is among those who would further suggest that the growing child learns better and thrives better in a predictable environment, where she/he will develop an important adaptive human quality, trust. Arguably also important is an environment that provides the growing person with the possibility of competence (McAdoo and McAdoo 1985), of being effective in the world in which she/he must function. The environment needs to be safe, both physically and psychologically, so that the individual feels comfortable enough to take risks in order to be able to develop his/her full creative intellectual and human potential (Rogers 1961; Maslow 1967; May 1969).

Further, human young need to be taught how to function in their specific culture. They need to learn the rules and values and beliefs of their group. Research suggests that this is best accomplished when it is accompanied by praise and positive, as opposed to negative, training. Punishment is not effective in teaching new behaviours; it may incidentally teach negative ones (Bandura and Walters 1963). Children seem to thrive more successfully and develop more completely when their environment is free from negative appraisals of themselves, where there is an acceptance of their humanity. Human beings are more competent when they are expected to be, and are seen by others as such. There is suggestive evidence that in this kind of environment the individual learns better and has higher self-esteem (Rosenthal and Jacobson 1968; Spencer 1985). It is reasonable to assume that higher esteem for oneself will help one be more successful in one's environment and facilitates higher esteem for one's fellows. Children seem to learn better if their training is consistent and the environment is somewhat orderly and non-violent.

In Belize, the above conditions often do not prevail. Due to varying levels of poverty, food, housing and parental care are not always consistent or dependable. Parents may have to go away in order to find work, leaving children with overburdened grandparents or other relatives. School attendance may be unpredictable due to problems with acquiring uniforms, books and other school-related needs. Parents often do not have time or energy to spend special time with a child due to survival pressures and lack of models for such behaviour. Violence and negative relations often obtain in Belizean households as people try to cope with the extreme pressures of inadequate employment, frustrating relations with people in authority, and the day-to-day scramble to provide even basic necessities for the household.

Probably the most potentially negative aspect of child care in Belize is that corporal punishment is generally the preferred form of child-rearing. Parents beat their children, not because they do not love them, but because they want them to be good and to behave. In their zeal to produce a good, quiet, co-operative child with the appropriate 'manners' and respect for elders, they are using a technique that stifles the potential exuberance and sense of confidence and competence of the child. They may also be inadvertently colluding with capital by producing obedient, docile and unquestioning workers.

Socialisation has to do with individual and group survival. Human beings have a complex set of socialisation needs in order to meet this requirement. Some environments lend themselves more successfully to these socialisation needs. Some soil is bad for certain kinds of flowers:

Certain seeds it will not nurture, certain fruit it will not bear, and when the land kills of its own volition, we acquiesce and say the victim had no right to live. We are wrong, of course, but it doesn't matter. It's too late. (Morrison 1970: 160)

My argument is that the contemporary physical, emotional, environmental, political and economic environment is hostile to the achievement of a properly germinated and fully flowering human individual. While this is true for virtually *all* individuals, it is disproportionately and fatally true for certain populations. The soil is not fertile. But when people fail to blossom, we do not blame the earth, we blame them. We say they did not try. We say they do not know how. We say that they never will.

Belize: the country

Situated inconspicuously beneath Mexico, the tiny nation of Belize is the home of approximately 200,000 people, with a population density of 18.7 persons per square mile (Central Statistics Office 1985). The land area is 8,867 square miles. The climate is subtropical. It is the only English-speaking country on the Central American mainland. Belize is linked to the world economic system through trade, tourism, media, education and other colonial and postcolonial ties. It exhibits features of the typical underdeveloped labour-surplus economy: dependence on foreign exchange, external debt, a somewhat stagnant economy, and inadequate infrastructure. This is the result of nearly 300 years of colonisation, characterised by a mono-economy based upon an extractive industry (forestry) controlled by metropolitan capital, accompanied by absentee landlordism, import dependence, and satellite status within unequal market relations (Ashcraft 1973; Bolland 1986; Central Statistics Office 1985). Belize achieved independence from Britain on 21 September 1981.

The Belizean population is largely made up of Creole-speaking West Indians, with increasing numbers of Spanish-speaking Mestizos from Mexico, Guatemala and other neighbouring Central American countries, and members of other ethnic and linguistic groups: Kekchi, Maya, Garinagu, Mennonite, Chinese. The national language is English and public officials and school personnel use this form of address. Therefore, all of the varying populations speak some Standard English and some form of Creole. Belize is a democracy, governed through a British-style parliamentary system. They have had three peaceful elections since their independence and are now encouraging a free market, competitive economy, based on foreign investment and free trade (Bolland 1986). As with other 'underdeveloped' or 'developing' nations, Belize is often thought to be somewhat backward, in need of outside help and lacking in the basic necessities of 'civilised' life.

Although Belizeans like to think of their country as a melting pot, with no problems with racism, where everyone has equal opportunity, census information suggests a different reality. Quality of life, opportunities for growth, as well as overall life-chances, are heavily determined by whether one is considered 'Indian', 'Garinagu', or 'Mestizo'. While people may understandably take pride in their ethnicity or 'race', the realities of their lives and how they are perceived by a larger culture, are undermined by this same ethnic or 'racial' distinction. They suffer from many of the same stereotypes and prejudices reserved for 'people of colour' in the United States or any of the other core countries.

The children

In Belize competence can be measured. It is measured to a large extent by how well one does in school. From the time the child is three or four, for the rest of his/her life, she/he will be tested and scored and ranked, in similar ways to those discussed by Angrosino, Davies and Reynolds Whyte, elsewhere in this volume. This ranking determines what the child does with her/his life, how he/she will be thought of in the community and how the child will learn to think about her/himself. The scorings and ranking and grading are considered to be objective measures of the child's true self, true potential, true and natural competencies (Davies, in Chapter 5, also reminds us that early testing and labelling help to shape the child's identity). These rankings extend into the family and the community, where they are validated and corroborated. In addition, much of Belize suffers from what Fanon (1967) calls 'internalised oppression', brought with colonisers who assumed their superiority and the 'natural' limited indigenous populations (Nandy 1983; Wolf 1994).

The stigma and racism of the colonial period continue: as a collective identity, in individual minds and hearts. It is reinforced as children worship a white God, read schoolbooks with blond children and green grass, and are bombarded by television, radio and market images of people unlike themselves looking rich and successful and smart, while they look poor and unsuccessful and unable to figure things out as they should (Marable 1983). As Peter Berger says: 'prejudging not only concerns the victim's external fate at the hands of his oppressors, but also his consciousness as it is shaped by their expectations' (Berger 1966: 120). He goes on to develop this theme by suggesting that one of the worst things about prejudice is that it can make people believe they are what the prejudiced image says they are. There is a relationship between what society says and one's identity: 'human dignity is a matter of social permission' (Berger 1966: 121). In Belize we see children articulating the problem of how to maintain dignity in a world where so many messages militate against it.

This prejudicing or assault on the integrity of a people in some ways lends a certain kind of equality to Belizeans who, in general, seem to both judge and forgive all members of the community. Since just about everyone is poor and everyone has to scramble for a living, it is expected that people will do what they can. Most will work 'catch as catch can', fewer will work for the government or have professional jobs. It is more or less accepted that the government workers, teachers, lawyers and doctors are superior and therefore have superior jobs that fit their talents and naturally superior abilities.

The determination of (in)competence, the sense of self, and the development of identity

In Belize, schools were developed hand-in-hand with the establishment of churches (Bolland 1986). When missionaries of all denominations established their churches in Belize, they also established schools. The relationship between church and state has persisted until today; the majority of schools are run jointly. The government is responsible for teachers' salaries and a proportion of the operating expenses, the religious denomination is responsible for all other expenses. The Prime Minister, Manuel Esquivel, told me that his administration considers this relationship desirable, suggesting that the churches should have even more influence on the educational system, so as to reinforce proper ethical and moral standards in the youth of Belize. Each school, or group of schools, has a manager who is, in almost all cases, the representative priest or pastor of the affiliated church. The manager is responsible for fiscal aspects of the school and serves as liaison between the church and the government.

The Chief Education Officer, Mr Andrews, informed me that schools are all the same and therefore, theoretically, provide an identical education to every child in Belize. However, as one of his Education Officers assured me, the education the children receive is not identical. For example, school personnel decide, on the basis of a child's appearance and/or family name, what to expect of them. On the basis of their expectations, the child is placed in a learning group and is liable to remain there throughout his/her school career. Children from 'good' families are favoured by teachers, they perform better and are more likely to go on to secondary school. The others just do not make it. This pattern is consistent with research findings in the United States on 'race' (Silverstein and Krate 1975; Ryan 1981; Marable 1983), class (Bowles and Gintis 1976; Kohn 1969; Sennett and Cobb 1973), and teacher expectations (Rosenthal and Jacobson 1968). It is also consonant with the views of some Belizean educators and with my own observations. In this volume, Angrosino discusses the ways in which labelling contributes to a life-long identity as either able or disabled.

Children are required to attend school until they are fourteen. Mr Andrews explained that, as a result of their testing system, if a child does not take the primary school examination to get into secondary school, she/he has lost the opportunity forever to obtain further education. Without an education – a Western-style education designed for the metropolitan elite – there is little hope for employment in Belize. 'They are the ones,' he explained, 'who we now see hustling, playing cards and smoking weed at the foot of the bridge, the ones we call "bays bwoys".' Prostitution is a possibility for undereducated girls. In this way, he went on, the educational system reproduces a hierarchical, stratified system.

Along with the above sorting process, the financial aspects of education serve further to discriminate. Books must be provided by the child's family. Uniforms are required, as well as the usual equipment such as pencils, tablets, rulers, etc. Mr Andrews estimated that it probably cost a parent approximately $BLZ300 (about $US600) at the beginning of each school year for each child. The more children there are in a family, the more this is a problem; many children attend school without books, pencils, uniforms and/or exercise books.

Mr Brown, another Education Officer, has been doing his own informal research for years and has come to similar conclusions. Although it is a widely shared perception that education should facilitate change in society, in fact he feels that it mostly conforms to the needs of the society. It cannot be revolutionary, he concluded, because it is a system that, once in place, reflects the interests of society. Mr Brown's hope is that in Belize there is some balance between the change-promoting and the reproductive aspects of education. He believes, however, that at this point the system helps to perpetuate inequality: the Education Department found that most students who qualify for scholarships come from homes where the income is over $10,000, the children of civil servants, bankers, politicians. There is a rule that disqualifies these children from scholarships; but it is precisely these children who achieve the highest scores on standardised tests. Income, in other words, is a reliable predictor of children's school success; income and ethnicity because these same children tend to be predominantly Mestizo. A similar theme, that learning difficulties often simply reflect poverty, is acknowledged by Booth and Booth in Chapter 4.

So (in)competence is determined by how well one does in school, and what kind of job or position one has in the work world. The educational system that measures children's (in)competence – social, intellectual, moral – was imported by the British during colonisation. It was devised for the elite of a country most Belizeans will never see, relying on books (and, in many cases, teachers) with ideas, values, information, visual images and language that have meaning for children living in a temperate region in a capitalist core nation. For children living in a subtropical zone, where palm trees replace apple trees, chickens run loose in the sand instead of kittens in the grass, and where there are dusty lanes instead of sidewalks, this education – where a white mother and father and two rosy-cheeked blond children comprise the family – is at best irrelevant, at worst, hostile.

The standard for competence, the information needed to achieve it, and the forms of measurement, are all created by those who have control of capital and therefore control also of the labour process. Although there is a sense in which Belize is its own nation – and this sense is constantly reinforced – the reality is that Belizeans are tied to the core in very real ways. They are tied economically, they are tied politically, and in order to sustain these two ties, they are ideologically tied:

The logic of the ideological apparatuses of the racist/capitalist state leads inextricably to Black accommodation and assimilation into the status quo, a process of cultural genocide that assists the function of ever-expanding capital accumulation. (Marable 1983: 9)

Marable says that this happens as the Black child

attends schools with pedagogies resting on assumptions of her/his inferiority, worships with Renaissance portraits of Christ, a White deity and an irrelevant form of spirituality, and is exposed to aesthetics and popular culture that rests on an Anglo-Saxon ideal, creating self-hatred in the children. (*ibid.*: 10)

I did not have to read Marable, or Wolf, or Wallerstein, to know that Belize is tied in these ways to the capitalist core nations, especially the United States. The children told me. They told me as they described their desires for a Trans-Am, a Tonka truck, to play baseball for the Chicago Cubs, and to go to the United States when they grow up so they can get a job and become rich. The children see their world, their hope, the realisation of their dreams, stretching beyond Belize, as they desire to become a part of the world. And it is no wonder that this should be the case. In every aspect of their lives, the models for what is good, what is competent, and what is best, are models, not of Black poor children who live in wooden houses on stilts, but of white rich children who live in safe, white houses with green grass and sidewalks.

An example

I was fortunate to obtain access to the report cards of all the children who attended Immanuel School during the time of my research.[1] Immanuel is a small school run by the pastor of the independent church that supports it and houses it in rooms underneath the church's sanctuary. Pastor Jones owns the church and school and is the only Belizean who pastors a church that is not owned and operated by foreign missionaries. He is 'Creole' and proud of the fact that he is independent of foreign strings and can offer his people a model of an independent, strong leader. Most Belizeans, he used to say, look up to white foreigners (especially American), which militates against the emergence of local leaders. Pastor Jones wants to provide such a model. He also has a passion for maintaining a school for children in the neighbourhood, who live in some of the poorer households in the city.

Pastor Jones's school functions in one large partitioned room. He is the manager, liaising between the school and the government. His principal has been with him for many years and oversees the everyday running of the school. All but one of his teachers are women, which reflects typical gender stratification in Belizean schools.

The children sit in neat rows on backless benches behind solid wooden desks. Usually they sit two or three at a desk. The rooms are crowded. Thirty to forty children squeeze into a space partitioned off with portable blackboards. Most of the children wear the required uniform. Most of them are neat and clean.

Although all of the schools are ethnically mixed, the majority have a dominant population. This school is mainly 'Creole', as I was told by one of the teachers. Had she not told me, I would have thought that most of the children were either 'Creole', people of mixed European and African background, or 'Garinagu', the descendants of runaway African slaves and 'Indians'. However, I could not differentiate between the two. My teacher guide told me that the way you can tell is that Garinagu are darker and smell and talk differently. These were characteristics that I never recognised. To me, Creole people and Garinagu people, in general, have similar phenotypical characteristics. This same teacher went on to say that Garinagu children do not get along well in her school. Other children tease them. She smiled and said that all children are equal in Belize, but some are more equal than others. She illustrated by putting one hand above the other. She herself does not like the Garinagu, whom she described as too dark. What she was telling me was that they are supposed to treat all children the same and the public message is that everyone is equal, but that in reality lighter is better. Pastor Jones corroborated this view when he once told me that when he was growing up the saying was, 'the lighter the skin, the purer the heart'.

The building is hot, dusty and noisy. Children from infant school to Standard VI (about four years old to about fourteen) are all here. Teachers have to speak loudly to be heard over the general din and the children are constantly entreated to be quiet and obedient. Corporal punishment is frequently used. It is thought that children need a firm hand in order to be taught to have manners and to be respectful. 'Having manners' and 'not being rude' are two behaviours which Belizean children need in order to be considered well cared-for and appropriately raised.

I have heard adults say that if you have manners you can do anything. Therefore parents and teachers work relentlessly on these characteristics. Not unlike public schools in other parts of the world, it seemed to me that learning obedient behaviour was a primary goal, one that overshadowed the goal of acquiring knowledge. Equipment in the school is basic, but the classroom walls are cheerfully decorated with colourful ABC's, kittens, rabbits, balloons, and large numbers in red, yellow and green. In this respect, it could have been any school for young children in the United States or elsewhere. When the children have their art class, they each get only one crayon because otherwise there are not enough to go around. Even though they are hot and dusty there is a constant effort to keep the rooms neat and clean. They assiduously sweep the sandy floors regularly. However, sand and sand flies from the play yard creep in in an annoying and distracting way. Windows, with no screens, look out on to the dry, brown sand. The rooms are oppressively hot.

During free play periods, the children go out into the sandy, hot yard that abuts a busy main street in the front, and family dwellings on both sides. There is no play equipment. Under the unobstructed, piercing sun, the children run around, play tag and occasionally have a jump rope or share a ball. They are aware that they must not soil their uniforms, so their play appears somewhat constrained.

These school conditions are not peculiar to Immanuel. Most of the schools (with the exception of Belize's two private schools) have similar facilities and the children play and learn similarly. Government money goes to teachers' salaries and the mission church provides the buildings, equipment and supplies. The school and worship buildings provided by the missions are usually minimally maintained, too small and cheaply constructed. They stand in quiet, shabby disrepair, a testimony to colonial attitudes. The colonised needed schools and churches, but they didn't need beautiful or comfortable ones.

School performance, ranking, and socio-economic status

Although I obtained access to the report cards of all of the children attending Immanuel, I will discuss the results of close scrutiny of only seventeen. I knew the families of these children. I had been in their homes, talked to their parents, escorted the children to the doctor, played ball with them, had them draw, tell me stories and, in some cases, unobtrusively observed the family for the better part of many days.

Each report card contains a list of the subjects the child is taking with a numerical rating beside each. Subjects include: Maths, Spelling, Social Studies, Science, Scripture and Literature. These scores are totalled, producing an average score. Sometimes the child's rank in the class is included on the card (this usually if the child ranked first, second, or third). At the bottom of the card is a section called Citizenship Qualities, that are ranked: good, poor or fair. These qualities include such things as courtesy to others, co-operation, health habits, and work and study habits (as also in Whyte's study of Uganda, Chapter 7, where in order to be a good student, one must have good conduct as well as high marks).

Most of the children's average scores, unremarkably, ranged in the low 70s. In my sample of seventeen, there were four children whose scores were consistently and noticeably higher, and four whose scores were noticeably lower, forming what appeared to be a normal 'bell curve'. Of the four top-scoring children, three of them were entirely predictable. These three children came from the only families in my sample who could be considered moderately economically comfortable. In one case the child is the only one in the family. In another, the child is one of two in the family, the other of which is many years older. The third child comes from a family of four.

The children with high scores

Jimmy

Jimmy Kline's average was 81; he was the top student in his class when he was six years old and his scores in all subjects were consistently high. The sole and much protected child of relatively older parents, he is one of only two Mestizo children in the sample. A thin, small meticulous child, his very light skin was a source of pride. In class, Jimmy was polite, co-operative, rather physically timid.

The house Jimmy lives in is owned by his maternal grandmother who now resides in the United States. It is a five-room frame house on stilts, on the same street as the school. Only Jimmy, his father and his mother occupy the upstairs portion of the house. It is attractively furnished with matching furniture, pictures on the walls, and window drapes. Jimmy has his own bedroom with his own double bed, a few books, stuffed animals, several small plastic cartoon figure dolls, and several other playthings.

For a child to have her/his own room and own bed with toys and books, was extremely rare among the many average or 'working-class' families in Belize that I visited. Usually the house is crowded, several children may sleep on a bed, often they may sleep on the floor. If there are toys, they are either immediately destroyed or the parents put them away so that the child can't spoil them. There may be one such item for a child over many years. Jimmy received a bicycle for his seventh birthday, an item no other child I knew owned. He was not allowed to ride it, however, because the street was too busy and the father had not yet had time to take the boy to a safe place to practise.

Mrs Kline spends time with Jimmy, talking to him, reading with him, watching television, and occasionally taking him downtown for a slice of pizza during Saturday grocery shopping. She does not allow him to walk alone the two blocks to school, or to use the bathrooms in the school. Jimmy is a child whose parents have the time and resources to be able to invest both in their only son. They have a telephone, television set, refrigerator, indoor plumbing, gas stove and car. The possession of this many household items is extremely rare among the majority of residents of Belize. Most people have a television set, but few have refrigerators; rarely do they have a car and many people, even in Belize City, did not have indoor plumbing or a gas stove.

Linda
Eight-year-old Linda Root, whose average score was a unique 96, has an older brother and sister who are also the top students in their classes. Linda is a plump, rather shy, light-skinned Creole child. She wears clean, pressed uniforms to school where she is quiet, obedient and practically invisible in a classroom full of large numbers of energetic children. She lives with her mother, father and siblings in a neat house owned by the grandparents who live downstairs. Since Mrs Root is their only child, the Root children are their only grandchildren.

Mrs Root was nearly always home when I visited, available to the children and maintaining the household. The house is homey and well-furnished. They, too, have a living-room set, a large kitchen table with chairs, a rug in the living-room, a refrigerator, indoor plumbing, a telephone, television set and gas stove. At the kitchen window hang frilly, clean and attractive curtains. There are always a few hairless dolls lying around and, sometimes, a ball or two. Again, these kinds of amenities are unusual in the average Belizean home I visited.

Although each child in this family does not have his/her own bedroom, there are plenty of beds furnished with pillows and sheets. Again, full sets of bedding are often not possible and the fact that this detail was attended to demonstrates a kind of caring work as well as a little more than usual extra income. The Root children are also watched carefully. They are not allowed to play without supervision and their mother kept careful track of them.

Mr Root has a steady job as a truck driver and, according to Mrs Root, is a good provider. Steady reasonably paid jobs are very difficult to obtain. Such work makes it possible for a family to provide more support to the children. In a recent conversation with a Belizean government official, he indicated that in August 1995 there was 40 per cent unemployment in Belize.

Caroline
Caroline Jamison only had an average of 76, but she was the number one student in her class and her teacher considered her to be a far better student than any of the others. A pretty, medium-brown Creole child with long shiny hair and pretty dresses, Caroline is charming and appealing. At seven years old, she carried herself with confidence and poise, was sensible, co-operative and hardworking. She started school at three years as a result of her own persistence. Little Caroline could handle her class on her own, her teacher proudly revealed.

Caroline's father is a policeman and she is his favourite. Policemen are well-respected in Belize and they make a good, dependable income. Caroline only had one other sibling, a sister who was ten years her senior who had distinguished herself by gaining admittance to the local technical college.

Caroline's mother, Wilma, is a religious woman who prides herself on running an efficient and orderly household. She is protective of her daughters, not allowing Caroline to play on the street, or her older daughter to attend social events unchaperoned by a parent. Caroline has a number of dolls and doll equipment, many of which are not for play. Many of the dolls were still carefully packaged and stood on the mantle for all to admire. The dolls had blonde hair and blue eyes and pretty lace and ribboned dresses of the kind not even Caroline could wear.

The Jamison family is saving for the house they are planning to build on a piece of land they own. In the meantime, the four of them live in a rented frame house on stilts on the large, main unpaved street where the Immanuel School also is located. The two girls have their own shared room. The house was clean, neat and carefully decorated each time I visited. Colourful curtains adorned the windows and they boasted a carpet (the only house I ever visited with one), plastic flowers and pictures on the wall. The style and decoration of the living-room replicated typical forms of decor found in the average North American home. In addition to household amenities such as indoor plumbing, a telephone and refrigerator, this family also had a stereo set and a washing machine. In every other family of my acquaintance, the woman of the house, including in the home where I stayed, washes in a large tin tub with scrub board, usually in the yard.

Both Mr and Mrs Jamison spend more time with this little girl than I found to be usual. They watch television as a family, listen to records and even read an occasional children's book together. Mrs Jamison says that Caroline has always been a bright, verbal, co-operative child who had been responsive to their attention. Her mother also reported to me that the child loves to talk, telling her mother everything that goes on at school that day when she comes home. Mrs Jamison tries to be home for her chatty daughter's recitations.

Misty

What about the other high-scoring child? Seven-year-old Misty Fern was an anomaly. Her average was 90; the top student in her class. Unlike the others, however, she did not have high scores for 'Qualities of Citizenship.' Although her grades were consistently higher than Caroline's, she was not mentioned by the principal or teachers as a shining example of good studentship, as was Caroline. I am not even sure that Misty was considered by her teachers to be particularly bright, despite achieving straight 100s in Maths, Spelling and Social Studies, and 95 in English. Instead, she was considered 'upstart' and ill-mannered, receiving 'fair' or 'poor' on 'co-operation', 'courtesy to others', 'responsibility for the property of others' and 'work and study habits'. Misty belonged to the Morino extended family, which resided around the 'yard' of her grandmother, Sophia. The Latin-sounding surname suggests that Misty was Garinagu, but the family considered themselves to be Creole. A wiry, small, light-brown child, Misty seemed always alert and in motion. Rarely smiling, usually she looked angry, spunky, crabby and all business. Most of the time she wore a dress that did not fit, and rarely wore shoes. Her family frequently called upon her to solve problems or relay information; I often used her as a translator because her English was so much better than other children's.

Misty's cousin, Tammy, was one of the four children whose report card average fell under 50. There were so many children in the extended family that it is impossible to imagine much investment of time or energy in any one of them. Misty's mother did not live there and I never knew who claimed responsibility for her. Financial resources were extremely meagre. At least sixty-five people lived in the yard. The head of the household was clearly Sophia whose daughters and sons lived in small shacks or rooms around the yard. The yard was sand, with an outdoor wood-burning oven, places for washtubs and clotheslines filled with laundry criss-crossing the entire space. The wooden buildings had long ago lost their paint and were built simply, providing shelter but in no way were complete houses. Most looked temporary, some looked as if they would soon collapse, some were barely big enough to hold their residents. I regularly counted around twenty-five children who went home for dinner (the noonday meal) in the Morino yard. Sophia cooked for them all on her open fire outside. She told me that cakes are much better when they are made in the outdoor oven. Various men and women walked in and out, and sometimes joined the children for dinner. Babies ran around bare-bottomed, and cried and chased and fell in the muddy sand. It was noisy and filled with a great deal of general commotion.

Misty Fern is not a child who should have achieved the second-highest school average in my sample. Although her family situation is more the rule than the exception in Belize, it did not provide the kind of emotional or economic support that would predict good academic performance. She may be the exception that proves the rule. But whatever the reason, Misty Fern is an excellent example of how an individual's perceived (or real) station in life can affect what others think about them and, ultimately, their life chances. No one at her school saw her as a clever, exceptionally smart little girl, because all that they could see were her torn clothes, bare feet, snarled hair and irritable countenance. They saw the yard she came from and her last name and assumed that she was incompetent despite clear evidence to the contrary. Thus her clear intellectual competence was ignored because her social incompetence (a situation not of her own making) overwhelmed her personal attributes.

The children with low scores

In the case of the children whose scores were significantly lower than average, all four of them might easily have been predicted.

Tammy

Tammy, as has been noted, is Misty Fern's first cousin and lives in the same yard. The teachers were particularly anxious that I work with Tammy because she was notoriously bad. No one could figure out what was wrong with this six-year-old girl that made her so hostile, pushy and resistant to learning. In class, she frequently fought with the other children and did not co-operate with her teacher. Her average was 44 and her 'Citizenship Qualities' were considered, across the board, terrible. Tammy is a thin, scrappy-looking child, a little darker brown than her cousin, with a shock of usually unkempt short black hair, dresses which usually are too big and heighten her waif's look. Her eyes are dark and intense and she, also, rarely smiled. She handles herself like many of the other children in her family: with anger, loudness, pushiness and, sometimes, long moody sulks. If there was a party, Tammy fought to be first in line and then complained that she did not get enough. When there were games, she wanted to be chosen first, and she had trouble understanding the concept of waiting her turn to be called on before reciting her lessons. She was not afraid to tangle with her teacher, who is a large, formidable-looking woman who has been successfully tangling with five- and six-year-olds since long before Tammy arrived.

The atmosphere in Tammy's household is almost only repressive. Her mother (Misty's aunt) rarely speaks; she beats often. There was little relief from overcrowded, uncomfortable living conditions; the constant worry about obtaining enough cash with which to procure daily survival requirements allowed little relief from her young mother's need to maintain order among her nine children, living with relatives in close quarters.

Tammy's mother, Stephanie, is a young-looking, unusually beautiful, dark brown, twenty-eight-year-old woman. After her last and ninth child, she told me that she planned to have a 'tie off'. She and all of the children live in a room, approximately ten feet by ten feet, just off the main courtyard of her family's set of raggedy, dilapidated buildings. She is one of Sophia's daughters. The father of her last seven children visits regularly, from midnight until early morning, when he leaves to find some work for the day, work which Stephanie described to me as 'catch as catch can'.

When I gave the children the only toys that they received for Christmas, Stephanie said that it would do no good, her bad children would just tear them up. In this household, which is a part of this very large extended family, emotional, psychological, intellectual and material resources are so scarce that they cannot be given much to any child. There are no books, no toys, minimal furniture, a kerosene stove, no oven, no blankets or sheets, no pictures on the walls. Although Sophia seemed to be washing all of the time in her zinc tub in the yard, the children tended to look uncared-for. Their clothes often did not fit, were torn and looked wrinkled and dirty.

The only method for achieving compliance from the children that seemed to be available to the adults of the family was aversive. The older the children became, the more conditioned they became to physical punishment and, thus, the more severe the punishments had to be. Thus, eleven-year-old Rodney was beaten severely many times a day. He was so angry and so much teased about it by his peers that school was becoming a terrible struggle which he increasingly tried to evade. More and more days were spent on the street and he stayed out later and later at night to avoid the inevitable punishment. Tammy was still young, but already school brought her little success and regular frustration. Her behaviour was already so terrible that it was difficult for teachers to warm up to her, despite their familiarity with her difficult situation and claim to be understanding. Already at six, her teachers see her as incompetent and her sense of her own competence is already in question.

Buba, Andre and Shadine
The three other significantly low-scoring children come from the same family. Seven-year-old Andre, whose school average was 36, and his five-year-old brother, Buba, were left with their young aunt while their mother went to the 'States'. During a year's stay in Belize, I noted that no money had been received from their mother and the aunt had barely enough with which to support her own three daughters, aged seven, six, and three. The two boys, Buba and Andre, and the two oldest girls, Shadine and Kareema, all attended Immanuel School. Shadine's school average was 49 and Kareema's 67. These children frequently came to school hungry and without books or proper attire. Their 'Citizenship Qualities' were evaluated as poor, even though they did not present the same sullen, disruptive and disagreeable behaviour as Tammy. These children were affectionate and sometimes cheerful. The little boys are medium-brown with soft, baby faces and sweet smiles. The sisters had grown long and gangly, but with their cousins' same sweet smiles and soft brown skin. They were usually dressed appropriately, clean, and well-groomed.

As resources in this household were negligible, investment in these children is minimal. Their mother and aunt do not beat them with the same regularity as does Tammy's, but the child-rearing style would have to be considered authoritarian. The children are not talked to or reasoned with, they are told what to do and what not to do. They are often left on their own while their caretakers, an assortment of relatives and boyfriends, are busy trying to find ways to provide for their basic care. In the case of Andre and Buba, neither their natural mother nor father were physically present. There were no dolls or bikes or books or toy trucks for these children. They slept wherever they could. The beds frequently had no sheets, there were no pillows or flowers or pictures or washing machines or telephones. These children are some of the very few children I knew who began to show some signs of malnutrition. One of their teachers told me that she had seen them when they could not even keep their heads off their desks.

Discussion: meanings

Buba, Andre and Shadine are examples of what the literature suggests with regard to learning and attention. Work on children and school achievement (Blau 1981; Konner 1977) suggests that the amount of investment parents have in a child correlates positively with school success, among other things. The theory is that the more there is invested, in terms of time, emotion and/or monetary resources, the more the child feels obliged to repay the parents by complying with their wishes. So, for example, if the parent values schooling, and wants the child to be successful in this area, the child who had more invested in him/her will be more inclined to do well in school. In Belize, schooling is valued by all parents and especially so in the case of children in whom the investment is high. Parents see education as a means to later success and well-being, usually with an added expectation that through education the child will attain more status and financial security than they themselves have attained.

It could be anticipated, then, that just on the basis of investment alone, the high-scoring, or most 'competent', children would do well in school. Their households are small, parents' expectations for their children are high, and it is obvious, even to the child, that these parents invest a significant portion of their resources in them. These parents also have more resources to invest than the other parents in my group.

There are other aspects of the socialisation process which also seem to apply here. Verbal style and whether the child-rearing strategy is essentially authoritarian or not, have been found to also contribute to a child's measured school success and, in some cases, IQ score (Blau 1981; Bernstein 1961). The passive compliance parents require of children in an authoritarian-style household is likely also to be extended to formal learning situations and to other authority figures, notably teachers, especially if they also use authoritarian methods. So the child can be forced to attend school but she/he cannot be forced to adopt positive notions about the value and joy of learning. The child has been deprived of an inner sense of responsibility which leaves him/her superficially co-operative, but possibly uncommitted. If this form of coercive control is coupled with a lack of investment in the child, the child is under little obligation to those in a position of authority. The child may, in fact, deliberately subvert parents' or teachers' wishes in an effort to get back at the controlling figure or to escape from the aversive situation altogether.

As was suggested earlier, competence, in the world capitalist formation, is measured to a large extent by the child's school success or failure. Luster and McAdoo (1994), for example, seem to take at face value that academic and behavioural problems are signs of incompetence. Cognitive ability and school adjustment are seen as ways to measure a child's competence as well as a kind of value in itself. The pattern of low investment and high discipline is, according Blau (1981), traditional in some groups of low socio-economic status and/or rural origins who do not place great value on educational achievement. As a gain in resources occurs and/or life expectations change, these parents begin to change their behaviour towards their offspring. There may, however, be a lag period when child-rearing methods have not yet adapted to the changing needs of the child. This process can be observed in Belize.

Another clearly observable aspect of the issue of the socialisation process and children's measured school success, has to do with verbal styles. Bernstein (1961) has identified differences in verbal styles which he believes are correlated with differences in the *exhibited* intellectual abilities of children (Blau 1961: 107–8). 'Restricted' verbal codes, Bernstein suggests, are stereotypical, use short sentences, and are:

distinguished by the rigidity of the syntax and the limited . . . use of structural possibilities for sentence production. Thus, these speech elements are *highly* predictable for any one speaker. It is a form of relatively condensed speech in which certain meanings are restricted and their elaboration is reduced. (Bernstein 1961: 291)

On the other hand, in an 'elaborated' code, a wider and more complex range of meanings can be expressed:

the structure and syntax are relatively difficult to predict for any one individual and . . . the formal possibilities of sentence organisation are used to clarify meaning and make it explicit. (*ibid.*)

The use of the more restricted style tends to restrict the child and does not encourage internalisation of the parent's values. Others (Kozal 1991; Ward 1986) have commented in different ways on aspects of this phenomenon.

It was my observation, reinforced by comments made by some Belizean educators, that a restricted verbal code is the one most frequently used by parents as well as by teachers, especially in the primary grades. This is the preferred form of communicating with the children, as children are seen as needing to be controlled and managed. They are encouraged to obey, to be quiet and not to speak up. Otherwise they are considered to be 'rude' and without manners.

In the cases of Caroline, Linda and Jimmy, the pattern of high authority and restricted verbal codes is still prevalent, but not to the degree that it obtained in the other households. Probably the key in these instances is the investment factor. In all three instances, these households have more resources of every kind to invest, and fewer offspring upon which to spend them, than the others in my sample. Although these parents still require obedience from their children, use authoritarian methods, and stress the usual manners and obedience, they balance it with, for example, walking the child to school, spending time combing their hair, talking and listening. These parents also make sure the children know they are investing the time and the mental and physical energy. All three of these children obviously want to please their parents and their elders. They are unusually 'good' and 'polite'. These children had already internalised their elders' values to do with being co-operative, and doing what was expected of them as well as possible, so external control was rarely necessary any more.

Ramifications of school evaluations

This sample is small and, therefore, the results merely suggestive. However, this brief analysis of one aspect of the formal evaluation process supports the hypotheses of others (e.g. Bowles and Gintis 1976; Freire 1983; Marable 1983) that, whereas the process purports to be evaluating children's intellectual accomplishments, and thus their competence as human beings, it is really measuring the child's socio-economic status and 'race'. I saw what should be even intuitively obvious: that parents who have more resources have more to invest in their children. If they have fewer children, they also can invest more in each child. Parents whose material resources are minimal need to expend so much of their emotional and temporal resources on securing material resources, that they have little time or emotion to invest in the child. They are, for the same reasons, more inclined to be more authoritarian in their child-rearing style because they do not have the time or patience for children who question their authority or cause them too much trouble. These children consistently score poorly in the formal educational evaluative system. It is insidious, because the scores seem so objective and teachers, parents and the children accept them as a true measure of who the child is. The evaluations are accepted as an impartial measurement of the child's capabilities as well as their achievements.

Theoretical implications

This argument that children are socially constructed – the constructivist view (Levine 1992) – has created a lively dialogue. Lamenting the loss of the self, many scholars seem to feel somehow cheated by the idea that there may not be a central, core self, which unfolds and bears witness to one's innate, pre-cultural being, guided on the journey by one's soul and the desire to eventually attain the God-like status which is the right of all human beings. How can one be respected, be taken seriously, if one is but a culturally created creature (Alford 1991)? What then is the meaning? Without an inherent, essential self, one would not have agency, would not be free.

While some are mourning the death of the self, some are resurrecting it in the form of resistance or human agency (Clifford 1983, 1988; Comaroff 1985; Crapanzano 1986). Competence, then, would have to do with an inner being and how well that inner essence evolved into an autonomous, secure, fully developed, integrated personality (Maslow 1967). I perused the literature on psychopathology and looked at the DSM-III (the current, third edition of the US *Diagnostic and Statistical Manual, Mental Disorders*) to get an idea of which characteristics make a person competent and which make him/her incompetent, or even 'crazy' by American standards. In general, a person is incompetent if they have improper affect, are anxious, depressed or too elated, or are out of touch with 'reality.' Some, like Szasz (1969) and Laing (1965), argue that the world we have created is crazy, so therefore those who do not conform to it are the ones who are the most 'sane' or adjusted. However, their views have been pretty much ignored. To continue with the more mainstream or accepted and sanctioned views, the 'healthy' person expresses individuality, explores options, has an awareness and integration of the self, engages in social interaction, is aware of his/her own dynamics and needs, is dynamic, not static, and full of energy, explores and grows, tries to understand others, and engages in social dialogue. Even the most psychotic behaviour can be understood within the above framework.

One does not have to think too hard before recognising that much of what we consider pathology has to do with contemporary Western cultural and Christian values. What makes a person competent is being one who fits into their society, and in the West we value particular forms of morality, aggression or lack thereof, sexual maturity (heterosexuality), self-esteem, self-knowledge and sociability. To be competent is to be 'normal'. For this, one must develop a sense of one's identity (Erickson 1963) and a sense of self which is moral and good. To be abnormal is not to develop individuation, identity, self. One must be individuated, but social, good in school and work, and have a moral sense. 'Abnormal' is to have self blurred, as in schizophrenia, which is too many selves (Levine 1992).

So the Modern, coming out of the Enlightenment, created a self which gave a sense of meaning, purpose and direction to the human population embarking upon the dehumanising technological capitalist social formation. It was a new subsistence strategy and it needed a new concept of what it meant to be human. It was a Judaeo-Christian sense of humanness, which made it divine to be individualistic, somewhat aggressive, acquisitive, prudent, opportunistic, competitive, hard-working, scientific, thrifty, moral, xenophobic, ethnocentric, sexually mature (heterosexual for procreation), monogamous, obedient. Most Americans and Europeans are familiar with the promise that God gives out talents and it is up to the individual to develop them. If one does well financially, socially, personally (according to the guidelines), one is successful. If one does not, one is incompetent, either intellectually, socially, financially or psychologically. It is easy to see how, in this scenario, racism and sexism are so virulent. People of colour and women are different from white men. They may have their talents, but they are not the same ones as Christian white men and they may, in fact, be so different as not to be recognised as part of a real person. These people may be incompetent simply because they are threateningly different.

Thus the poor simply suffer from 'bad character'. Women suffer from too much emotion and not enough 'rationality'. People of colour are not as highly 'developed'; they are 'uncivilised', and their moral development is 'impaired', as is that of women (Gilligan 1977; Kohn 1969). Things have always worked out well because the best are on the top, they are the most 'actualised' (Maslow 1967), they are the moral leaders. If you are 'down', if you cannot pull yourself up, you are defective, you haven't worked hard enough, you have a criminal mind, you cannot delay gratification (Moynihan 1965; Lewis 1959): you are not morally fit and you need someone to take care of you, to teach you, to guide you. Interestingly, Devlieger's argument in Chapter 3, that the 'mentally retarded' are also Americans, supports my view of the power of culture to convince its members of what is normal, moral and usual.

Competence has just about the same meaning in Belize as it does in the United States. However, almost no one achieves what could be considered clear competence and the 'incompetent' are not noticed as much. There is only one 'special' school in the country, and that is for deaf children. All the others go to the regular schools. Children are seen as having a human essence which includes a personality, sensibility, an articulated self. The child should be kept from staying home from school, being rude or upstart, should learn to have manners and do what the teacher says. If the child succeeds she/he is achieving, she/he is competent. If the child does poorly, doesn't study, is loud or belligerent, she/he is considered to be lazy or stupid or uncooperative. She/he will probably be beaten more often and maybe harder so that she/he will do what she/he should in order to be considered competent. I once accompanied the truant officer to a school where he was to punish a small child for some misdemeanour he had committed. As we got to the school, the principal greeted us and they began discussing the boy. The truant officer recounted some grisly story about the boy's grandfather and finished with 'the limb does not fall far from the tree'. The boy had obviously come from bad genes, so what could you expect of him?

Toni Morrison once wrote about a family who lived in an old store front: 'because they were poor and Black, and they stayed there because they believed they were ugly. No one could have convinced them that they were not relentlessly and aggressively ugly.' There was nothing in their world to convince them otherwise. For Belizeans there is not much to convince them otherwise. I was often told, by children and adults, that it is hard to feel competent in a world where you are small, poor and Black. There was solicitude for many, however, and that was in the church. For the women, the saviour is God; for the men it is a new government. God and a better government, or maybe both, offer hope, solace, patience and the possibility of redemption.

Conclusion

What it means to be a competent human is clearly a theoretical issue. Most of the personality theorists – Freud, Jung, Adler, Maslow, Fromm, Rogers, Rank, Gesell, Kelly, McClelland – with the exception of Skinner, assume an essential self, an identity, a personality, something independent of, perhaps even predating, culture. Anthropologists have debated this question since Boas, who taught that culture shapes its members, and that each culture has its own plan, design, traditions, ceremonies. However, whether the plans are cognitive structures (Lévi-Strauss) or spider webs (Geertz), or come from the earth (Harris), the coherence of their parts (Evans-Pritchard), from somewhere inside (Fischer), or from somewhere outside (Wolf), remains controversial.

Each time I am in Belize, it seems obvious to me that what it is to be human for Belizeans is a combination of their history as a part of a larger world process, their history as a people displaced from their homelands, creating new human beings, and the realities of their contemporary political economy. They live with this history and sometimes believe that they are the faithful, sometimes the unredeemed, and, often, that they are the unredeemable. To be poor is bad, I was told; to be rich is good. Belize is a 'poor little country' and, therefore, not as good as the rich ones. Also, the core rich countries are graced with mostly white people and Belize is filled with Black and Brown and mixed shades of people. They do not look like the straw-haired, pale dolls they buy, or that they find in magazines and movies.

The Belizeans I met, for the most part, accepted their fate as their burden, and felt that they need to work harder, pray more and be better. Although everyone copes with the realities of their situation in different and unique ways, the message given to them in the British schoolbooks and American magazines, from the missionaries and from the foreign 'helpers', is that they are not competent to rise out of poverty, they are not competent in school, and that they need the help of more competent foreign (usually white) technology, knowledge and access to resources.

Competence is not something they have control over because the standard, the measuring stick, is not theirs. If they were to measure, they might determine competence by how well you could clear your *milpa* with only one machete, or by how far you could walk to get your water so that you could wash all your clothes, cook and bathe several children and get them off to school every day. Or competence might be measured by how well you could tend your small herd of cows, or how you could heal and comfort your neighbours.

However, these are not their measures and they would not want them now if they could have them. Now their ability is measured against that of everyone with whom they are connected through trade, ideology, labour and resources. They have long provided the labour; many of the resources have been taken from them and given to the powerful core nations. They do not have control over their land, their labour, the product of their labour, their subsistence, their religion, their language, their schools, or their sense of their own worth. When a people are in such an overpoweringly unequal relationship with those upon whom they depend, when they cannot control their own livelihood and feed their own babies, their sense of capability, of strength, is seriously undermined.

They can choose to reject the world's assessment of them by virtue of their 'otherness' and seeming incompetence. They can decide that they are competent anyway despite all of the information to the contrary. And many do. However, it is the job of a culture to make its members want to do what the culture requires. There are many ways this can be done and usually it works. Most members of most cultures believe that theirs is best and right and closest to God, and they therefore have a committed relationship to their culture. Thus, most of the people of Belize, even with its beautiful array of ethnically marked sizes and shapes and shades, are committed participants in the world political economic system, with all of its expectations, values and world-view. They believe, also, as a part of their cultural information, that one day things will change, one day they will be better, one day they will be as competent and strong and successful as their overdeveloped counterparts appear to be.

As Fanon (1967), Nandy (1983), Memmi (1965) and others have so poignantly suggested, people who have been colonised, or otherwise defiled, have a tendency to internalise their oppression and to believe in their own incompetence. Powerful core nations depend upon this internalisation of an ideology of inferiority, as one way to control segments of the world population which might otherwise rebel, and to ease the competition for power. In Belize, as in other colonised worlds, boys and girls, men and women can easily derive from their environment a sense of their own inadequacies, and therefore collude with those who would evaluate them by calling themselves 'poor', 'Black and ugly', 'backward' and, sometimes, basically and essentially incompetent. If people have accepted a view of themselves as less able, lazy, too dumb to compete, incompetent, they may lose the incentive to try. And this lack of confidence, this resignation, can cause them to exclude themselves from job options, educational options, business options and other aspects of life that might produce a better life and, thus, a sense of accomplishment, of competence.

Note

1 All names have been changed to protect the privacy of informants.

10   Towards a social model of (in)competence

Richard Jenkins

The contributors to this collection have discussed the social construction of (in)competence in a range of local cultural contexts and from different points of view. Although their arguments and ethnographies are very varied, they nonetheless suggest some general conclusions.

The most obvious, in agreement with the few other available comparative discussions of (in)competence, is that there is no consistency *between* cultures – if it is possible to talk like this without reifying the notion of culture – with respect to the definition and understanding of (in)competence or the treatment of people who are categorised as incompetent. This is perhaps most clearly apparent in Patrick Devlieger's comparison of central Africa and the United States in Chapter 3, and in the differences between Greece and Wales – which are no less striking because of their subtlety – documented by Sylvia van Maastricht in Chapter 6. These two which make explicit comparisons aside, however, if the other papers are read side-by-side, cultural variability and the relativity of (in)competence are among the collection's central themes. All models are local models.

Perhaps even more interesting is the equally inescapable conclusion that we should not expect consistency, coherence, or consensus *within* cultures. Michael Angrosino argues in Chapter 2, for example, that in the United States the notion of 'mental retardation' is an 'umbrella' category, lumping together fundamentally un-alike individuals, reflecting bureaucratic priorities more than anything else. It is also a label that is contested and negotiated by those individuals in many different everyday ways. Similarly, Devlieger argues that 'mental retardation' in America has very different meanings for different individuals. This is also the forceful conclusion to be drawn from Booth and Booth's discussion of resilience in Chapter 4. Charlotte Davies, discussing the situation in Wales in Chapter 5, goes even further. For her the category of 'learning difficulties' is so heterogeneous with respect to the individuals who are included within it that it is incoherent. She goes on to observe, however, that, even though it does not cohere, as a categorisation that is typically applied to minors by adults it has considerable power to shape individual lives.

A different perspective on consistency is offered by Nancy Lundgren's discussion of Belize in Chapter 9. She emphasises the stratification, by class and ethnicity, of attributions of (in)competence. Similar themes have long been central to the sociology of education in Europe and North America (e.g. Bourdieu and Passeron 1977; Bowles and Gintis 1976; Halsey *et al.* 1980; Jencks *et al.* 1973; Karabel and Halsey 1977), indicating that the institutionalised labelling processes which judge (in)competence and classify individuals may be broadly similar in many different local contexts. Lundgren's paper also suggests that there is continuity – of process and thematic principle – between the classificatory and stratificatory work done in the processes of 'normal' socialisation and education, and the grosser classifications of (in)competence that underpin the social construction of 'mental retardation' or 'learning difficulties' and the allocation of individuals to those categories. This is also indicated by Mark Nuttall's discussion of Greenland in Chapter 8.

If this general argument is correct, there is continuity and overlap between – and should ideally be a shared purpose among – the narrow academic specialisation of 'disability studies' and the broader sociological 'mainstreams' occupied by studies of stratification and education (cf. Jenkins 1991). Competence and incompetence are inseparable, conceptually and in lived experience. Hence the notion of (in)competence, to denote a unified domain of social identification in which competence and incompetence are socially constructed.

A further perspective on the 'internal' cultural inconsistency or incoherence of classifications of (in)competence comes from Susan Whyte's discussion in Chapter 7. In eastern Uganda there is a wide range of classificatory or diagnostic models, drawing upon a range of aetiological notions. Her exegesis of those models and notions, of the threads which are woven into local understandings of (in)competence, is a compelling argument for the value of ethnographic research. So, too, is Nuttall's material from north-western Greenland in Chapter 8. This suggests not only that locals have a wide variety of classificatory categories available with which to understand any particular case – there do not seem to be gross categories of intellectual disability or anything similar – but that they also express no rigid distinction between the 'able' and the 'less able'. In both of these cultural contexts, individual difference and context seem to be the key factors.

The point here is that classificatory coherence and consistency are in the eye of the beholder. A European or North American eye has been trained to see, at least in part, through the filter of the decontextualised and totalising gross categories that have been assembled over the last century or so into models of 'normality' (and its opposites). The local eye may have had a very different schooling.

Gross categories of (in)competence are not just classificatory categories (if there is any such thing as *just* classification, that is). Historically, they have been developed as part and parcel of the institutional practices of categorisation that are bound up in bureaucratic government, and have consequences in the lives of people with respect to the allocation of resources and penalties; they may be *imagined* but they are anything but *imaginary* (Jenkins 1996). The place of testing and categorisation in the formal institutions of the state, and its consequential significance, cannot be over-emphasised (Hanson 1993). The role of formal testing in the social construction and legitimation of hierarchies of (in)competence among the schoolchildren of Belize is documented in detail by Lundgren in Chapter 9. Formality of a different kind is a central theme in van Maastricht's account of Wales and Greece. Less formality seems, in this case, to create more cracks in the system through which people can slip into more-or-less 'ordinary' lives, and there are more available spaces for them to slip into. To return to education, I suspect that Whyte's observation about Uganda, that schools produce intellectual incompetence in a way that ordinary life does not, has an almost universal resonance. Nuttall's discussion of the 'modernisation' of Greenland, with its accompanying 'educationalisation', is also relevant here. What all of these authors have to say in this respect may have unsettling implications for our verdict on the systematic provision of care in the social democratic welfare systems of the affluent North and West.

The distinction between 'mental retardation' or 'learning difficulties' and 'mental health problems' or 'psychiatric illness', that is so familiar in Europe and North America, is another example of gross categorisation. It is not always locally applicable or sensible. This is abundantly clear from Nuttall's Greenlandic ethnography, from Whyte's chapter on Uganda, from Devlieger's brief discussion of the Shona, and from van Maastricht's Greek material. No less interesting, however, is the suggestion that categorical clarity is not always apparent even in the United States, where the distinction is one of the axiomatic bases for constructing dramatically different institutionalised care regimes for individuals. Angrosino suggests that young 'retarded' people who are experiencing emotional difficulties – and it seems to be the case that people with intellectual disabilities are disproportionately likely to experience the kind of life events that often give rise to such difficulties (Hattersley *et al.* 1987: 158) – will be channelled into the 'mental health' system rather than 'special education'. In the process individual complexities are ironed out to fit into the classificatory organisation of care.

The history of the care and treatment of the incompetent in Western societies makes it clear that distinguishing between 'idiots' and the 'mad' was, in the long term, a move in the right direction, towards more humane and more effectively therapeutic institutional provision. That does not necessarily mean, however, that the distinction, as conventionally drawn, continues to make analytical sense today, or that it makes sense in all contexts and for all persons. Issues such as these are reflected in the difficulties that some of the contributors have in establishing stable, workable terminologies and categories for the material that they are analysing. Angrosino, for example, favours the use of the broadest possible category of *mental disability* – rather than 'mental retardation' – in order to allow for the widest possible range of incompetence. Approaching the same problem from a different place, Whyte advocates the use of *mental* rather than *intellectual*, as a reminder that we are talking about matters to do with the mind in all of its complexity and – following G. H. Mead, perhaps – all of its social embeddedness. To further underscore the confusion here, in the introductory chapter I proposed, for different reasons, the use of 'intellectual disability' rather than 'mental retardation' or 'learning difficulties'.

Tim Booth and Wendy Booth, discussing parents with 'learning difficulties' and their children in England, make a point that is intimately related to questions of social embeddedness. They argue that individual competence is not simply a matter of *skills*, however – and however widely – the notion of 'skill' may be construed. There are several dimensions to their argument. In the first place – and this is something that can be drawn out of other chapters, most strikingly perhaps Lundgren's discussion of Belize – it is difficult to disentangle endogenous incompetence from the impact of exogenous disadvantage of one kind or another. This point cannot be made too often or too emphatically. Second, they argue that (in)competence is an *attributed status*, allocated to individuals by others in terms of recognition, support, and so on. We are back to labelling and classification. Competence and incompetence are as much emergent properties of the social networks in which individuals participate, products of the actions of significant others in those networks, as they are anything else. Hence their suggestive and original notion of 'distributed competence'.

None of which should be understood as suggesting that individual difference is insignificant. Quite the reverse. In looking at what they call, following Rutter, *resilience* or *resiliency*, Booth and Booth explicitly focus on the 'positive pole' of individual difference. As demonstrated by their careful unpacking of its strands in the context of individual case histories – more testimony to the virtues of qualitative research, in this case with a focus on narratives – this too is generated socially. Resilience is a matter of what others do as well as the individual's behaviour, of collective resources and support as much as individual talents and capacities. Resilience and (in)competence are in this model properties of social situations and networks, rather than individuals.

Another perspective on (in)competence as an emergent property of social relations and interaction can be found in the chapters by Nuttall and Lundgren. Lundgren, looking at the social construction of (in)competence for children in ex-colonial Belize, is clear that what she is documenting is the imposition of a set of essentially *external*, metropolitan categories of (in)competence, that are rooted in the international division of labour of 'development' and 'underdevelopment', of white and black, of rich and poor, of big and small. Within Belize, these distinctions are transformed into a local ethnic hierarchy of worth and (in)competence, which is in turn legitimated by the extensive use of externally derived procedures of formal testing. Here we have a glimpse of the international political economy of (in)competence.

Nuttall's discussion of indigenous and non-indigenous knowledges about (in)competence in Greenland allows a similar point to be made. However, his material also suggests a further interesting observation in this respect. Incompetence is not just a matter of and for those who are explicitly or formally categorised as incompetent. Those who have local responsibilities and duties, to care for their kin who cannot care adequately for themselves, experience a loss of *their* own sense of competence – both as kin and as adults in the local context – when those for whom they are locally responsible are taken elsewhere, to be 'cared for properly' by a non-indigenous regime. This is the creation of a *double incompetence*. To turn around the Booths' expression, it is 'distributed *in*competence'.

All of the chapters have underlined the importance of *context*. Social context is, in some respects, everything. This is in part what is meant by suggesting that all models are local models. But a number of more specific comments about context can be drawn out of particular chapters. Lundgren and Nuttall both indicate the need to recognise the widest possible context. In Lundgren's study of Belize, for example, the ultimate context within which the classification of individual children must be understood is nothing less than the global political economy. Devlieger's account of (in)competence in America is also relevant in this respect. Incessant mobility, the transformation of space and distance into opportunity and biography that inheres in 'the American dream', is the backdrop to the lives of those who are called incompetent no less than those who are called competent. It is among the defining constituent themes of (in)competence in America. Another contributor who very clearly spells out the role of context is van Maastricht, in her comparison of Greece and Wales. It is broad social context – the more formal organisation of social life in general in Wales, slightly different conceptions of adulthood, and the greater availability of modest economic opportunities in Greece, none of which are specific to 'people with learning difficulties' – that makes the difference between the two places.

If context is so important, and (in)competence so much a matter of the variable relativities of context, setting and locality, are there any senses in which it might be possible to think about (in)competence in terms which are universal to all humans? Are there *any* human competences which are *not* locally defined and culturally variable? The generic capacity to use and to understand language is probably the first answer to this question which comes to mind, and perhaps the least controversial (which doesn't mean that there is no debate to be had about this, however). Other directions in which answers might be sought are suggested by some contributors. Angrosino, for example, argues that the only truly cross-cultural competence is the individual capacity to construct personally satisfying identities. Davies, in her discussion of adulthood and 'people with learning difficulties', can be read as implying that a degree of reflexivity, in particular, is a generic basis for competent adulthood. Whyte's paper, too, has something to offer this particular discussion. (In)competence here is a matter of participation in the local lifeworld. The lifeworld is a social creation, and competence is the capacity to expand it from an individual point of view: competence expands the lifeworld, incompetence diminishes it. An equally plausible, and complementary, reading of Whyte's ethnography and argument is that greater, more extended participation in the social world encourages or produces greater and extended competence. In the social world about which she is writing, exclusion from the ins-and-outs of everyday life makes a potent contribution to heightened incompetence.

These all seem to come down to something similar, as indeed does the notion of socially 'distributed competence', put forward by Booth and Booth. It is, in fact, the direction in which *all* of the papers point: (in)competence, from this point of view, is as much an emergent property of social networks and interactional context as it is an endogenous quality of individuals. Perhaps the most basic competence is the capacity for the *sociality*, rooted in the reciprocations of mutually intelligible, complex communication, that characterises human beings and human social life (Carrithers 1992). As G. H. Mead suggested long ago, *mind* exists in the social spaces, in the mutuality of interaction, between embodied individuals (cf. Jenkins 1996: 29–53). It is in interactional processes of social construction that mind, selfhood and society emerge. Competence is, in this respect as in so many others, fundamentally the same kind of phenomenon as incompetence.

(In)competence is also closely related – or at least comparable – to many other kinds of social states of being. When Tim and Wendy Booth talk about *resilience*, for example, they are clearly talking about something which is difficult to distinguish clearly from competence. Similarly, we know from our own experience that there is a whole vocabulary for talking how this or that person behaves and acts with respect to both process and outcomes – confidence, decisiveness, precision, effectiveness, efficiency, stylishness, tact, aggression, cheek, flair, imagination, and so on – which, in appropriate context, refer to something that might be glossed as an aspect of competence. There is a concomitant vocabulary which refers to aspects of incompetence. Yet the meaning of none of these words is utterly reducible to (in)competence; there appear to be other things going on as well.

We have many locally and culturally variable ways to talk about the complexities of how well or how badly people – me, you and others – do things. But we also have many local classificatory hierarchies of which things are important and which are not. For example, where I live and where I was brought up, whether or not I am deemed to have 'a good ear for music', 'a good sense of rhythm', or 'artistic talent' – all of which are undoubtedly communicative and cognitive competences – is neither here nor there. These are widely recognised as social graces and virtues, and may, unusually, provide the basis for making a living, but their absence is not stigmatising. Not being able to sing is not the same as not being able to speak. Having a poor ear for music is not the same as having a specific language disorder. Not being able to dance well is not the same as not being able to walk well. And being colour blind – as I am – is not the same thing as being partially sighted. These examples may strike the reader as trivial – and if they do that is a telling enough exemplification of my argument – but they make the point. The practical aptitudes that are identified as (in)competences in any given local or cultural setting are always, at least to some extent, an arbitrary selection from the spectrum of aptitudes and potentialities that make up the human behavioural portfolio. The degree to which they are marked or emphasised is also – once again, to some extent – arbitrary.

At its most fundamental we need to liberate our thinking about (in)competence – competence and incompetence – from the constraints of a mechanistic individualism which understands competence or incompetence as residing solely 'in the wiring' of embodied persons. This is the taken-for-granted point of departure of much medicine and psychology and much Western common sense. Mine is not, however, an argument for turning our backs on the accumulated science of the psychologists or dismissing the wisdoms of everyday life. If nothing else, this is true because (in)competence resides *in part* in the physiology of embodied persons. However, we must establish a properly *social* framework for understanding and engaging with those traditions of scientific and everyday knowledge, and with the phenomena which they address. This collection of papers is offered as a contribution towards that understanding and that engagement.

Bibliography

Accardo, P. and Whitman, B. 1990. 'Children of mentally retarded parents', *American Journal of Diseases of Children*, vol. 144, pp. 69–70.

Ainlay, S. C., Becker, G. and Coleman, L. M., (eds.) 1986. *The Dilemma of Difference: A Multidisciplinary View of Stigma*, New York: Plenum Press.

Ake, C. 1981. *A Political Economy of Africa*, Harlow: Longman.

Alford, C. F. 1991. *The Self in Social Theory: A Psychoanalytic Account of its Construction in Plato, Hobbes, Locke, Rawls and Rousseau*, New Haven: Yale University Press.

Andron, L. and Tymchuk, A. 1987. 'Parents who are mentally retarded', in A. Craft (ed.), *Mental Handicap and Sexuality: Issues and Perspectives*, Tunbridge Wells: D. J. Costello.

Angrosino, M. V. 1981a. *Quality Assurance for Community Care of Retarded Adults in Tennessee*, Nashville: Vanderbilt Institute for Public Policy Studies.

1981b. *A Survey of the Impact of a Proposed Medicaid Cap on State Spending for the Mentally Retarded*, Washington, D.C.: National Association of State Mental Retardation Program Directors.

1989. *Documents of Interaction: Autobiography, Biography, and Life History in Social Science Perspective*, Gainesville: University of Florida Press.

1992a. 'Benjy's tale: Faulkner and the sociolinguistics of mental retardation', *RE Arts and Letters*, vol. 18, pp. 5–22.

1992b. 'Metaphors of stigma: how deinstitutionalized mentally retarded adults see themselves', *Journal of Contemporary Ethnography*, vol. 21, pp. 171–99.

1994. 'On the bus with Vonnie Lee: explorations in life history and metaphor', *Journal of Contemporary Ethnography*, vol. 23, pp. 14–28.

Angrosino, M. V. and Zagnoli, L. J. 1992. 'Gender constructs and social identity: implications for community-based care of retarded adults', in T. Whitehead and B. Reid (eds.), *Gender Constructs and Social Issues*, Urbana: University of Illinois Press.

Anthony, E. 1974. 'A risk-vulnerability model for children of psychotic parents' in E. Anthony and C. Koupernik (eds.), *The Child in His Family: Vol. 3. Children at Psychiatric Risk*, New York: John Wiley and Son.

1987a. 'Children at high risk for psychosis growing up successfully', in E. Anthony and B. Cohler (eds.), *The Invulnerable Child*, New York: Guilford Press.

1987b. 'Risk, vulnerability and resilience: an overview', in E. Anthony and B. Cohler (eds.), *The Invulnerable Child*, New York: Guilford Press

Antonak, R. F., Fieldler, C. R. and Mulick, J. A. 1989. 'Misconceptions relating to mental retardation', *Mental Retardation*, vol. 27, pp. 91–7.

Appelbaum, P. S. 1994. *Almost a Revolution: Mental Health Law and the Limits of Change*, New York: Oxford University Press.

Ashcraft, N. 1973. *Colonialism and Underdevelopment: Processes of Political/Economic Change in British Honduras*, New York: Teachers' College Press.

Atkinson, D. 1988. 'Research interviews with people with mental handicaps', *Mental Handicap Research*, vol. 1, pp. 75–90.

Atkinson, D. and Williams, F. (eds.) 1990. *'Know Me As I Am': An Anthology of Prose, Poetry and Art by People with Learning Difficulties*, London: Hodder and Stoughton.

Atkinson, D., Jackson, M. and Walmsley, J. (eds.) 1997. *Forgotten Lives: Exploring the History of Learning Disability*, Plymouth: BILD Publications.

Atkinson, N. 1989. *The Broken Promise and Other Traditional Fables from Zimbabwe*, Harare: Academic Books.

Balikci, A. 1970 *The Netsilik Eskimo*, New York: The Natural History Press.

Bandura, A. and Walters, R. H. 1963. *Social Learning and Personality Development*, New York: Holt, Rinehart and Winston.

Barnes, C. 1996. 'Theories of disability and the origins of the oppression of disabled people in western society', in L. Barton (ed.), *Disability and Society: Emerging Issues and Insights*, London: Longman.

Batavia, A. I., DeLong, G. and McKnew, L. B. 1991. 'Toward a national personal assistance program', *Journal of Health Policy and Law*, vol. 16, no. 3, pp. 523–46.

Baudrillard, Jean. 1989. *America*, trans. C. Turner, New York: Verso (original: *Amérique*, Paris, 1986).

Begun, A. 1993. 'Human behaviour and the social environment: the vulnerability, risk, and resilience model', *Journal of Social Work Education*, vol. 29 (1), pp. 26–35.

Bellah, R., Madsen, R., Sullivan, W. M., Swidler, A. and Tipton, S. M. 1985. *Habits of the Heart: Individualism and Commitment in American Life*, Berkeley: University of California Press.

Berger, P. L. 1966. *Invitation to Sociology: A Humanistic Perspective*, Harmondsworth: Pelican.

Berger, P. L. and Luckman, T. 1967. *The Social Construction of Reality*, London: Allen Lane.

Bernstein, B. A. 1961. 'Social class and linguistic development: a theory of social learning', in A. H. Halsey, J. Floud and C. A. Anderson (eds.), *Education, Economy and Society*, Glencoe: Free Press.

Berrios, G. 1995. 'Mental retardation: clinical section – part II', in G. Berrios and R. Porter (eds.), *A History of Clinical Psychiatry: The Origin and History of Psychiatric Disorders*, London: Athlone Press.

Billington, S. 1984. *A Social History of the Fool*, Brighton: Harvester.

Bird-David, N. 1990. 'The giving environment: another perspective on the economic system of hunter-gatherers', *Current Anthropology*, vol. 31 (2), pp. 189–96.

Blau, Z. S. 1981. *Black Children/White Children: Competence, Socialization, and Social Structure*, New York: Free Press.

Boas, F. 1888. *The Central Eskimo*, Sixth Annual Report of the Bureau of American Ethnology, Washington, D.C.: Smithsonian Institution.

1938. *The Mind of the Primitive*, New York: Macmillan.

Bogdan, R. and Taylor, S. J. 1976. 'The judged, not the judge: an insider's view of mental retardation', *American Psychologist*, vol. 31, pp. 47–52.

1982. *Inside Out: The Social Meaning of Mental Retardation*, Toronto: University of Toronto Press.

1989. 'Relationships with severely disabled people: the social construction of humanness', *Social Problems*, vol. 36, pp. 135–48.

1994. *The Social Meaning of Mental Retardation: Two Life Stories*, New York: Teachers' College Press.

Bolland, O. N. 1986. *Belize: A New Nation in Central America*, Boulder: Westview Press.

Bolles, A. L. 1985. 'Economic crisis and female-headed households in urban Jamaica', in J. Nash and H. Safa (eds.), *Women and Change in Latin America*, New York: Bergin and Garvey.

Booth, T. 1996. 'Sounds of still voices: issues in the use of narrative methods with people who have learning difficulties', in L. Barton (ed.), *Disability and Society: Emerging Issues and Insights*, London: Longman.

Booth, T. and Booth, W. 1993. 'The use of depth interviewing with vulnerable subjects: lessons from a research study of parents with learning difficulties', *Social Science and Medicine*, vol. 39 (3), pp. 415–24.

1994. *Parenting Under Pressure: Mothers and Fathers with Learning Difficulties*, Buckingham: Open University Press.

1996. 'Sounds of silence: narrative research with inarticulate subjects', *Disability and Society*, vol. 11 (1), pp. 55–69.

Borre, K. 1994. 'The healing power of the seal: the meaning of Inuit health practice and belief', *Arctic Anthropology*, vol. 31 (1), pp. 1–15.

Bourdieu, P. 1973. 'Cultural reproduction and social reproduction', in R. Brown (ed.), *Knowledge, Education and Cultural Change*, London: Tavistock.

Bourdieu, P. and Passeron, J.-C., 1977. *Reproduction in Education, Society and Culture*, London: Sage.

Bowles, S. and Gintis, H. 1976. *Schooling in Capitalist America: Educational Reform and the Contradictions of Economic Life*, New York: Basic Books.

Boykin, A. W. and Toms, F. D. 1985. 'Black child socialization: a conceptual framework', in H. P. McAdoo and J. L. McAdoo (eds.), *Black Children: Social, Educational, and Parental Environments*, Beverly Hills: Sage.

Briggs, J. 1986. 'Expecting the unexpected: Canadian Inuit training for an experimental lifestyle', paper presented at the Fourth International Conference on Hunting and Gathering Societies, London.

Brooks, R. 1994. 'Children at risk: fostering resilience and hope', *American Journal of Orthopsychiatry*, vol. 64 (4), pp. 545–53.

Brothwell, D. R. 1960. 'A possible case of mongolism in a Saxon population', *Annals of Human Genetics*, vol. 24, pp. 141–50.

Brown, H. and Smith, H. 1989. 'Whose "ordinary life" is it anyway?', *Disability, Handicap and Society*, vol. 4, pp. 105–19.

Bruininks, R. H., Meyers, C. E., Sigford, B. B. and Lakin, K. C. (eds.) 1981. *Deinstitutionalization and Community Adjustment of Mentally Retarded People*, Washington, D.C.: American Association on Mental Deficiency.

Bruner, J. 1987. 'Life as narrative', *Social Research*, vol. 54 (1), pp. 11–32.

Buchmann, M. 1989. *The Script of Life in Modern Society: Entry into Adulthood in a Changing World*, Chicago: University of Chicago Press.

Buck, F. and Hohmann, G. 1983. 'Parental disability and children's adjustment', in E. Pan, T. Backer and C. Vash (eds.), *Annual Review of Rehabilitation*, vol. 3, New York: Springer.

Budd, K. and Greenspan, S. 1984. 'Mentally retarded mothers', in E. Blechman (ed.), *Behaviour Modification with Women*, New York: Guilford Press.

Burleigh, M. 1991. 'Racism as social policy: the Nazi "euthanasia" programme, 1939–1945', *Ethnic and Racial Studies*, vol. 14, pp. 453–73.

1994. *Death and Deliverance: 'Euthanasia' in Germany 1900–1945*, Cambridge: Cambridge University Press.

Burleigh, M. and Wippermann, W. 1991. *The Racial State: Germany 1933–1945*, Cambridge: Cambridge University Press.

Byrne, E. A., Cunningham, C. C. and Sloper, P. 1988. *Families and their Children with Down's Syndrome: One Feature in Common*, London: Routledge.

Campbell, J. K. 1983. 'Traditional values and continuities in Greek society', in R. Clogg (ed.), *Greece in the 1980s*, London: Macmillan.

Carrithers, M. 1992. *Why Humans Have Cultures: Explaining Anthropology and Social Diversity*, Oxford: Oxford University Press.

Carrithers, M., Collins, S. and Lukes, S. (eds.) 1986. *The Category of the Person: Anthropology, Philosophy, History*, Cambridge: Cambridge University Press.

Carson, R. C. 1969. *Interaction Concepts of Personality*, Chicago: Aldine.

Central Statistics Office. 1985. *Abstract of Statistics*, Belmopan: Government Printing Office.

Chapman, A. J. and Jones, D. M. (eds.) 1980. *Models of Man*, Leciester: British Psychological Society.

Chappell, A. L. 1992. 'Towards a sociological critique of the normalisation principle', *Disability, Handicap and Society*, vol. 7, pp. 35–51.

Clark, K. 1965. *Dark Ghetto: Dilemma of Social Psychology*, New York: Harper and Row.

Clark, K. and Clark, M. 1939. 'The development of consciousness of self and the emergence of racial identity in negro preschool children', *Journal of Social Psychology*, vol. 10, pp. 591–5.

1958. 'Racial identification and preference in negro children', in E. Maccoby (ed.), *Readings in Social Psychology*, New York: Newcomb and Hartly.

Clifford, J. 1983. 'On ethnographic authority', *Representations*, vol. 2, pp. 118–46.

1988. *The Predicament of Culture: Twentieth-Century Ethnography, Literature, and Art*, Cambridge, Mass.: Harvard University Press.

Cockburn, D. (ed.) 1991. *Human Beings*, Cambridge: Cambridge University Press.

Cohen, S. 1985. *Visions of Social Control: Crime, Punishment and Classification*, Cambridge: Polity.

Cohler, B. 1987. 'Adversity, resilience, and the study of lives', in E. Anthony and B. Cohler (eds.), *The Invulnerable Child*, New York: Guilford Press.

Cole, J. W. and Wolf, E. R. 1974. *The Hidden Frontier: Ecology and Ethnicity in an Alpine Valley*, New York: Academic Press.

Comaroff, J. 1985. *Body of Power, Spirit of Resistance: The Culture and History of a South African People*, Chicago: University of Chicago Press.

Crapanzano, V. 1986. *Waiting: The Whites of South Africa*, New York: Vintage.

Cronk, C. E. 1993. 'Down Syndrome', in K. F. Kyple (ed.), *The Cambridge World History of Human Disease*, Cambridge: Cambridge University Press.

D'Andrade, R. 1987. 'A folk model of the mind', in D. Holland and N. Quinn (eds.), *Cultural Models in Language and Thought*, Cambridge: Cambridge University Press.

Davies, C. A. and Jenkins, R. 1997. ' "She has different fits to me": how people with learning difficulties see themselves', *Disability and Society*, vol. 12 (1), pp. 95–109.

unpublished. *Time for a Change: People with Learning Difficulties Negotiating the Transition to Adulthood*, Swansea: Department of Sociology and Anthropology.

de Beauvoir, S. 1953. *America Day by Day*, trans. Patrick Dudley, New York: Grove Press (original: *L'Amérique au jour le jour*, Paris, 1948).

Devisch, R. 1990. 'The Mbwoolu cosmogony and healing cult among the Northern Yaka of Zaire', in A. Jacobsen-Widding and W. van Beek (eds.), *The Creative Communion: African Folk Models of Fertility and Regeneration*, Stockholm: Almqvist and Wiksell.

Devlieger, P. 1991. *Integration of People with Disabilities in Zimbabwean Communities*, Geneva: International Labour Organisation.

1995a. *On the Threshold of Adult Life: Life Course and Dis-course of Mental Retardation in American Culture*, Ph.D. dissertation, Department of Anthropology, University of Illinois at Urbana-Champaign.

1995b. 'Why disabled? The cultural understanding of physical disability in an African society', in B. Ingstad and S. Reynolds Whyte (eds.), *Disability and Culture*, Berkeley: University of California Press.

Devlieger, P. and Hunter de Bessa, G. 1994. ' "Processing" or "channelling" into adult life: the impact of the culture of mental retardation', paper presented at the 93rd Annual Meeting, American Anthropological Association, Atlanta, Georgia.

Dowdney, L. and Skuse, D. 1993. 'Parenting provided by adults with mental retardation', *Journal of Child Psychology and Psychiatry*, vol. 34 (1), pp. 25–47.

Doyle, B. 1995. *Disability, Discrimination and Equal Opportunities: A Comparative Study of the Employment Rights of Disabled Persons*, London: Mansell.

Dybwad, G. 1970. 'Treatment of the mentally retarded: a cross-national view', in H. C. Hayward (ed.), *Socio-Cultural Aspects of Mental Retardation*, New York: Appleton-Century-Crofts.

Edgerton, R. B. 1966. 'Conceptions of psychosis in four East African societies', *American Anthropologist*, vol. 68, pp. 408–25.

1967. *The Cloak of Competence: Stigma in the Lives of the Mentally Retarded*, Berkeley: University of California Press.

1970. 'Mental retardation in non-Western societies: towards a cross-cultural perspective on incompetence', in H. C. Hayward (ed.), *Socio-Cultural Aspects of Mental Retardation*, New York: Appleton-Century-Crofts.

1979. *Mental Retardation*. Cambridge, Mass.: Harvard University Press.

1984. 'Introduction', in R. B. Edgerton (ed.), *Lives in Process: Mildly Retarded Adults in a Large City*. Monographs of the American Association on Mental Deficiency, no. 6, Washington, D.C.: American Association on Mental Deficiency.

1993 [1967]. *The Cloak of Competence*, revised ed., Berkeley: University of California Press.

1994. 'Mental retardation and disability', paper presented at the 93rd Annual Meeting, American Anthropological Association, Atlanta, Georgia.

Edgerton, R. B. and Gaston, M. A. 1991. *'I've seen it all!': Lives of Older People with Mental Retardation in the Community*, Baltimore: Paul H. Brookes.

Egeland, B., Carlson, E. and Sroufe, L. 1993. 'Resilience as process', *Development and Psychopathology*, vol. 5 (4), pp. 517–28.

Erickson, E. H. 1963. *Childhood and Society*, New York: W.W. Norton.

Estroff, S. E. 1981. *Making it Crazy: An Ethnography of Psychiatric Clients in an American Community*, Berkeley: University of California Press.

Fanon, F. 1967. *Black Skin, White Masks*, New York: Grove Press.

Faraday, A. and Plummer, K. 1979. 'Doing life histories', *Sociological Review*, vol. 27, pp. 773–98.

Feldman, M. 1986. 'Research on parenting by mentally retarded persons', *Psychiatric Clinics of North America*, vol. 9 (4), pp. 777–96.

Ferguson, D. L. and Ferguson, P. M. 1993. 'The promise of adulthood', in M. E. Snell (ed.), *Instruction for Students with Severe Disabilities*, New York: Merrill.

Ferguson, P. M., Ferguson, D. L. and Taylor, S. J. (eds.) 1992. *Interpreting Disability: A Qualitative Reader*. New York: Teachers' College Press.

Fernandez-Kelly, M. P. 1983. *For We Are Sold, I and My People*, Albany: State University of New York Press.

Fienup-Riordan, A. 1983. *The Nelson Island Eskimo*, Anchorage: Alaska Pacific University Press.

Flynn, M. C. 1986. 'Adults who are mentally handicapped as consumers: issues and guidelines for interviewing', *Journal of Mental Deficiency Research*, vol. 30, pp. 369–77.

1989. *Independent Living for Adults with Mental Handicap: 'A Place of My Own'*, London: Cassell.

Fortuine, R. 1989. *Chills and Fever*, Anchorage: University of Alaska Press.

Fotheringham, J. 1980. *Mentally Retarded Persons as Parents* (unpublished manuscript), Kingston, Ontario: Department of Psychiatry, Queen's University.

1981. *Mild Mental Retardation, Poverty and Parenthood*. (unpublished manuscript), Kingston, Ontario: Queen's University.

Frank, G. 1986. 'On embodiment: a case study of congenital limb deficiency in American culture', *Culture, Medicine and Psychiatry*, vol. 10, pp. 189–219.

Fraser, S. (ed.) 1995. *The Bell Curve Wars: Race, Intelligence, and the Future of America*, London: HarperCollins.

Freire, P. 1983. *Education for Critical Consciousness*, New York: Continuum.

Friedman, P. R. 1976. *The Rights of Mentally Retarded Persons*. New York: American Civil Liberties Union and Avon Books.

Gaines, A. D. 1994. 'Local ability: time, space and the ability of relativity', paper presented at the 93rd Annual Meeting of American Anthropological Association, Atlanta, Georgia.

Garmezy, N. 1974. 'The study of competence in children at risk for severe psychopathology', in E. Anthony and C. Koupernik (eds.), *The Child in His Family: Vol. 3. Children at Psychiatric Risk*, New York: Wiley.

1985. 'Stress resistant children: the search for protective factors', in J.

Stevenson (ed.), *Recent Research in Developmental Psychopathology*, Oxford: Pergamon.

1991. 'Resiliency and vulnerability to adverse developmental outcomes associated with poverty', *American Behavioural Scientist*, vol. 34 (4), pp. 416–30

Geertz, C. 1983. *Local Knowledge: Further Essays in Interpretive Anthropology*, New York: Basic Books.

Gelman, S. 1980. 'A system of services', in C. Cherington and G. Dybwad (eds.) *New Neighbors: The Retarded Citizen in Quest of a Home*, Washington, D.C.: US Department of Health and Human Services.

Gerber, D. 1990. 'Listening to disabled people: the problem of voice and authority in Robert B. Edgerton's *The Cloak of Competence*', *Disability Handicap, and Society*, vol. 5, pp. 3–22.

Gesell, A., Ilg, F. L., Ames, L. B. and Bullis, G. E. 1977. *The Child From Five to Ten*, New York: Harper and Row.

Gilligan, C. 1977. 'In a different voice: women's conceptions of the self and of morality', *Harvard Educational Review*, vol. 47, pp. 481–51.

Goodey, C. F. 1995. 'Mental retardation: social section – section I', in G. Berrios and R. Porter (eds.), *A History of Clinical Psychiatry: The Origin and History of Psychiatric Disorders*, London: Athlone Press.

Gordon, D. M., Edwards, R. and Reich, M. 1982. *Segmented Work, Divided Workers: The Historical Transformation of Labor in the United States*, Cambridge: Cambridge University Press.

Gorer, G. 1948. *The Americans: A Study in National Character*, London: The Cresset Press.

Gould, S. J. 1981. *The Mismeasure of Man*, New York: Norton.

Greenhouse, C. J. 1992. 'Signs of quality: individualism and hierarchy in American culture', *American Ethnologist*, vol. 19, pp. 233–54.

Grossman, H. J. (ed.) 1973. *Manual on Terminology and Classification in Mental Retardation*, Washington, D.C.: American Association on Mental Deficiency.

Gubrium, J. F. 1986. 'The social preservation of mind: the Alzheimer's disease experience', *Symbolic Interaction*, vol. 9, pp. 37–51.

Gudorf, C. E. 1995. 'Assigning meaning to mental retardation', *NAPMR Quarterly*, vol. 26, no.1, pp. 16–21.

Guemple, L. 1979. *Inuit Adoption*, Ottawa: National Museum of Man.

Hacking, I. 1990. *The Taming of Chance*, Cambridge: Cambridge University Press.

Hahn, H. 1987. 'Civil rights for disabled Americans: the foundation of a political agenda', in A. Gartner and T. Joe (eds.), *Images of the Disabled, Disabling Images*, New York: Praeger.

Halpern, J., Sackett, K. L., Binner, P. R. and Mohr, C. B. (eds.) 1980. *The Myths of Deinstitutionalization: Policies for the Mentally Disabled*, Boulder: Westview Press.

Halsey, A. H., Heath, A. F. and Ridge, J. M. 1980. *Origins and Destinations: Family, Class and Education in Modern Britain*, Oxford: Clarendon Press.

Hanson, F. A. 1993. *Testing Testing: Social Consequences of the Examined Life*, Berkeley: University of California Press.

Harding, P. and Jenkins, R. 1989. *The Myth of the Hidden Economy: Towards a New Understanding of Informal Economic Activity*, Milton Keynes: Open University Press.

Harlow, H. F. and Harlow, M. K. 1969. 'Learning to love', *American Scientist*, vol. 54, pp. 244–72.

Harrington, C. and Whiting, J. W. M. 1972. 'Socialization process and personality', in F. L. K. Hsu (ed.) *Psychological Anthropology*, Cambridge, Mass.: Schenkman.

Hart Hansen, J. P., Meldgaard, J. and Nordqvist, J. (eds.) 1991. *The Greenland Mummies*, Washington, D.C.: Smithsonian Institution Press.

Hattersley, J., Hosking, G. P., Morrow, D. and Myers, M. 1987. *People with Mental Handicap: Perspectives on Intellectual Disability*, London: Faber.

Heilbroner, R. L. 1980. *The Worldly Philosophers*, New York: Simon and Schuster.

Heilbroner, R. L. and Thurow, L. C. 1981. *Macroeconomics*, Englewood Cliffs: Prentice-Hall.

Herrnstein, R. and Murray, C. 1994. *The Bell Curve*, New York: Free Press.

Herskovits, E. 1995. 'Struggling over subjectivity: debates about the "self" and Alzheimer's disease', *Medical Anthropology Quarterly*, vol. 9 (2), pp. 146–64.

Herzfeld, M. 1980. 'Honour and shame: some problems in the comparative analysis of moral systems', *Man*, vol. 15, pp. 339–51.

Hetzel, B. S. 1989. *The Story of Iodine Deficiency: An International Challenge in Nutrition*, Oxford: Oxford University Press.

Hirst, P. and Woolley, P. 1982. *Social Relations and Human Attributes*, London: Tavistock.

Hockey, J. L. and James, A. 1993. *Growing Up and Growing Old: Ageing and Dependency in the Life Course*, Newbury Park: Sage.

Holy, L. and Stuchlik, M. 1983. *Actions, Norms and Representations: Foundations of Anthropological Inquiry*, Cambridge: Cambridge University Press.

Hsu, F. L. K. 1975. 'American core values and national character', in J. R. Spradley and M. A. Rynkiewich (eds.), *The Nacirema: Readings on American Culture*, Boston: Little, Brown and Company.

Hughes, E. C. 1945. 'Dilemmas and contradictions of status', *American Journal of Sociology*, vol. 50, pp. 353–9.

Hunter, H. M. and Abraham, S.Y. (eds.) 1987. *Race, Class and the World System: The Sociology of Oliver Cox*, New York: Monthly Review Press.

Ingstad, B. 1995a. 'Mpho ya Modimo – a gift from God: perspectives on "attitudes" toward disabled persons', in B. Ingstad and S. R. Whyte (eds.), *Disability and Culture*, Berkeley: University of California Press.

1995b. 'Public discourses on rehabilitation: from Norway to Botswana', in B. Ingstad and S. R. Whyte (eds.) *Disability and Culture*, Berkeley: University of California Press.

Ingstad, B. and Whyte, S. R. (eds.) 1995. *Disability and Culture*, Berkeley: University of California Press.

Jackson, M. and Karp, I. (eds.) 1990. 'Personhood and agency: the experience of self and other in African cultures', *Uppsala Studies in Cultural Anthropology* 14, Uppsala: Acta Universitatis Upsaliensis.

Janssen, C. G. C. 1982. *Ouders van geestelijk gehendicapte kinderen*, Lisse: Swets and Zeitlinger.

Jencks, C. *et al.* 1973. *Inequality: A Reassessment of the Effect of Family and Schooling in America*, London: Allen Lane.

Jenkins, R. 1977. 'Witches and fairies: supernatural aggression and deviance among the Irish peasantry', *Ulster Folklife*, vol. 23, pp. 33–56.

1990. 'Dimensions of adulthood in Britain: long-term unemployment and mental handicap', in P. Spencer (ed.), *Anthropology and the Riddle of the Sphinx: Paradoxes of Change in the Life Course*, London: Routledge.

1991. 'Disability and social stratification', *British Journal of Sociology*, vol. 42, pp. 557–80.

1993. 'Incompetence and learning difficulties: anthropological perspectives', *Anthropology Today*, vol. 9 (3), pp. 16–20.

1996. *Social Identity*, London: Routledge.

1998. 'From criminology to anthropology? Identity, morality, and normality in the social construction of deviance', in S. Holdaway and P. Rock (eds.), *Thinking About Criminology*, London: UCL Press.

Jensen, A. 1969. 'How much can we boost I.Q. and scholastic achievement?', *Harvard Educational Review*, vol. 39, pp. 1–123.

Karabel, J. and Halsey, A. H. (eds.) 1977, *Power and Ideology in Education*, New York: Oxford University Press.

Keren, D. J. 1987. 'The waiting proletariat: a new industrial labour force in rural Maquilas', in D. Haaken and H. Lessinger (eds.), *Perspectives in US Marxist Anthropology*, Boulder: Westview.

Kidd, C. B. 1970. 'The nature of mental retardation in different settings: some problems in cross-cultural study', in H. C. Hayward (ed.), *Socio-Cultural Aspects of Mental Retardation*, New York: Appleton-Century Crofts.

Kitwood, T. and Bredin, K. 1992. 'Towards a theory of dementia care: personhood and well-being', *Ageing and Society*, vol. 1, pp. 269–87.

Koch, L. 1996. *Racehygiejne i Danmark 1920–56*, Copenhagen: Gyldendal.

Koegel, P. 1986. 'You are what you drink: evidence of socialized incompetence in the life of a mildly retarded adult', in L. L. Langness and H. G. Levine (eds.), *Culture and Retardation: Life Histories of Mildly Retarded Persons in an American City*, Dordrecht: D. Reidel.

Kohn, M. L. 1969. *Class and Conformity: A Study of Values*, Homewood, Ill.: Dorsey Press.

Kondo, D. K. 1990. *Crafting Selves: Power, Gender, and Discourses of Identity in a Japanese Workplace*, Chicago: University of Chicago Press.

Konner, M. 1977. 'Infancy among the Kalahari Desert San', in P. Herbert, S. R. Tulkin and A. Rosenfeld (eds.), *Variations in the Human Experience*, New York: Academic Press.

Kozal, J. 1991. *Savage Inequalities: Children in America's Schools*, New York: Harper Perennial.

Krefting, L. and Groce, N. 1992. 'Anthropology in disability research and rehabilitation', *Practicing Anthropology*, vol. 14, no. 1, pp. 3–5.

La Fontaine, J. S. 1985. 'Person and individual: some anthropological reflections', in M. Carrithers, S. Collins and S. Lukes (eds.), *The Category of the Person: Anthropology, Philosophy, History*, Cambridge: Cambridge University Press.

Laing, R. D. 1965. *The Divided Self*, Harmondsworth: Pelican.

Langness, L. L. and Levine, H. G. (eds.) 1986. *Culture and Retardation: Life Histories of Mildly Retarded Persons in an American City*, Dordrecht: D. Reidel.

Lasch, C. 1978. *The Culture of Narcissism: American Life in an Age of Diminishing Expectations*, New York: W. W. Norton.

Leighton, A. H., Lambo, T. A., Hughes, C. C., Leighton, D. C., Murphy, J. M. and Macklin, D. B. 1963. *Psychiatric Disorders among the Yoruba: A Report of the Cornell-Aro Mental Health Project in the Western Region, Nigeria.*, Ithaca: Cornell University Press.

Leland, H. 1973. 'Adaptive behaviour and mentally retarded behaviour', in G. Tarjan, R. K. Eyman and C. E. Meyers (eds.), *Sociobehavioural Studies in Mental Retardation*, Los Angeles: American Association on Mental Deficiency.

Levine, G. (ed.) 1992. *Constructions of the Self*, New Brunswick: Rutgers University Press.

Levine, H. G. and Langness, L. L. 1986. 'Conclusions: themes in an anthropology of mild mental retardation', in L. L. Langness and H. G. Levine (eds.), *Culture and Retardation: Life Histories of Mildly Retarded Persons in an American City*. Dordrecht: D. Reidel.

LeVine, R. A. 1980. 'Anthropology and child development', in C. M. Super and S. Harkness (eds.), *Anthropological Perspectives on Child Development, New Directions for Child Development*, vol. 8, pp. 71–86.

Lewis, O. 1959. *Five Families: Mexican Case Studies in the Culture of Poverty*, New York: New American Library.

Lienhardt, G. 1985. 'Self: public, private. Some African representations,' in M. Carrithers, S. Collins and S. Lukes (eds.), *The Category of the Person: Anthropology, Philosophy, History*, Cambridge: Cambridge University Press.

Löfgren, O. 1989. 'Anthropologizing America', *American Ethnologist*, vol. 16, pp. 366–74.

Lunt, N. and Thornton, P. 1994. 'Disability and employment: toward an understanding of discourse and policy', *Disability and Society*, vol. 9, pp. 223–38.

Luster, T. and McAdoo, H. P. 1994. 'Factors related to the achievement and adjustment of young African American children', *Child Development*, vol. 65, pp. 1080–94.

McAdoo, H. P. and McAdoo, J. L. (eds.) 1985. *Black Children: Social, Educational and Parental Environments*, Beverly Hills: Sage.

McGaw, S., and Sturmey, P. 1993. 'Identifying the needs of parents with learning disabilities: a review', *Child Abuse Review*, vol. 2, pp. 101–17.

McIntyre, K., White, D. and Yoast, R. 1990. *Resilience among High Risk Youth*, Wisconsin Clearinghouse: University of Wisconsin Madison.

Magubane, B. 1981. *The Political Economy of Race and Class in South Africa*, New York: Monthly Review Press.

Manion, M. and Bersani, L. 1987. 'Mental retardation as a Western, sociological construct: a cross-cultural analysis', *Disability, Handicap and Society*, vol. 2, pp. 231–45.

Marable, M. 1983. *How Capitalism Underdeveloped Black America*, Boston: South End Press.

Marcus, G. and Fischer, M. 1986. *Anthropology as Cultural Critique*, Chicago: University of Chicago Press.

Marschall, B. and Hjelt, K. 1988. 'Children attending the local centre for education of handicapped children in Maniitsoq/Sukkertoppen, Greenland: medical data and living conditions', *Arctic Medical Research*, vol. 47 (2), pp. 67–70.

Marshall, M. 1994. 'Social isolation, cultural competence, and disability in the Carolines', *The Micronesian Counselor*, Occasional Paper No. 13.

1996. 'Problematizing impairment: cultural competence in the Carolines', *Ethnology*, vol. 35 (4), pp. 249–263.

Maslow, A. H. 1967. 'A theory of metamotivation: the biological rooting of the value – life', *Journal of Human Psychology*, vol. 7, pp. 93–127.

May, D. and Hughes, D. 1988. 'From handicapped to normal: problems and prospects in the transition from school to adult life', in D. May and G. Horobin (eds.), *Living with Mental Handicap: Transitions in the Lives of People with Mental Handicaps*, New York: St Martin's Press.

May, R. 1969. *Love and Will*, New York: Norton.

Memmi, A. 1965. *The Colonizer and the Colonized*, Boston: Beacon Press.

Mercer, J. 1973. *Labeling the Mentally Retarded: Clinical and Social System Perspectives on Mental Retardation*, Berkeley: University of California Press.

Michiko, I. 1988. 'Ishimure Michiko's "The Boy Yamanaka Kuhei" ', trans. C. Stevens, in E. P. Tsurumi (ed.), *The Other Japan: Post War Realities*, Armonk, NY: M. E. Sharpe/Bulletin of Concerned Asian Scholars.

Miles, M. 1992. 'Concepts of mental retardation in Pakistan: towards cross-cultural and historical perspectives', *Disability, Handicap and Society*, vol. 7, pp. 235–55.

Miller, E. 1995. 'Mental retardation: clinical section – Part 1', in G. Berrios and R. Porter (eds.), *A History of Clinical Psychiatry: The Origin and History of Psychiatric Disorders*, London: Athone Press.

Miller, R. D. 1982. 'The least restrictive alternative: hidden meanings and agendas', *Community Mental Health Journal*, vol. 18, no. 1, pp. 46–55.

Moffat, M. 1992. 'Ethnographic writing about American culture', *Annual Review of Anthropology*, vol. 21, pp. 205–29.

Morris, B. 1994. *Anthropology of the Self: The Individual in Cultural Perspective*, London: Pluto Press.

Morrison, T. 1970. *The Bluest Eye*, New York: Holt, Rinehart and Winston.

Moynihan, D. P. 1965. *The Negro Family: The Case for National Action*, Washington D.C.: US Department of Labor.

Mrazek, P. and Mrazek, D. 1987. 'Resilience in child maltreatment victims: a conceptual exploration', *Child Abuse and Neglect*, vol. 11, pp. 357–66.

Müller-Hill, B. 1988. *Murderous Science: Elimination by Scientific Selection of Jews, Gypsies and Others. Germany 1933–45*, Oxford: Oxford University Press.

Murphy, E. M. and McNeill, T. E. 1993. 'Human remains excavated at Doonbought Fort, Co. Antrim, 1969', *Ulster Journal of Archaeology*, vol. 56, pp. 120–38.

Murphy, R. F. 1987. *The Body Silent*, London: Phoenix House.

Murphy, R. F., Scheer, J., Murphy, Y. and Mack, R. 1988. 'Physical disability and social liminality: a study in the rituals of adversity', *Social Science and Medicine*, vol. 26, pp. 235–42.

Murphy, S. T. 1992. *On Being L.D.: Perspectives and Strategies of Young Adults*, New York: Teachers' College Press.

Nandy, A. 1983. *The Intimate Enemy: Loss and Recovery of Self Under Colonialism*, Bombay: Oxford University Press.

Nelson, R. 1969. *Hunters of the Northern Ice*, Chicago: Chicago University Press.

New York State Commission on Quality of Care for the Mentally Disabled. 1993. *Serving Parents who are Mentally Retarded: A Review of Eight Parenting Programs in New York State*, New York: New York State Commission on Quality of Care for the Mentally Disabled.

Nicolaisen, I. 1995. 'Persons and nonpersons: disability and personhood among the Punan Bah of Central Borneo', in B. Ingstad and S. R. White (eds.), *Disability and Culture*, Berkeley: University of California Press.

Nuttall, M. 1992. *Arctic Homeland: Kinship, Community and Development in Northwest Greenland*, Toronto: University of Toronto Press.

1994. 'Greenland: emergence of an Inuit homeland', in Minority Rights Group (ed.), *Polar Peoples: Self-determination and Development*, London: Minority Rights Group Publications.

1997. 'Nation-building and local identity in Greenland: resources and the environment in a changing North', in S. A. Mousalimas (ed.), *Arctic Ecology and Identity*, Budapest and Los Angeles: Hungarian Academy of Sciences/ISTOR.

Okano, K. 1993. *School to Work Transition in Japan: An Ethnographic Study*, Clevedon: Multilingual Matters.

Okech, J. B. 1992. 'Mental retardation', *UNISE Bulletin*, vol. 1. Kampala: Ministry of Education.

Oliver, J. 1977. 'Some studies of families in which children suffer maltreatment', in A. Franklin (ed.), *The Challenge of Child Abuse*, New York: Grune and Stratton.

Oliver, M. 1990. *The Politics of Disablement*, London: Macmillan.

O'Neil, J. 1989. 'The cultural and political context of patient dissatisfaction in cross-cultural clinical encounters: a Canadian case study', *Medical Anthropology Quarterly*, vol. 3 (4), pp. 325–44.

O'Neil, J. and Kaufert, P. A. 1990. 'The politics of obstetric care: the Inuit experience', in W. Penn Handwerker (ed.), *Births and Power: Social Change and the Politics of Reproduction*, Boulder: Westview Press.

Orley, J. 1970. *Culture and Mental Illness: A Study from Uganda*, Nairobi: East African Publishing House.

Pahl, R. E. 1988. 'Introduction: work in context', 'Editor's introduction to part one', and 'Epilogue: on work', in R. E. Pahl (ed.), *On Work: Historical, Comparative and Theoretical Perspectives*, Oxford: Basil Blackwell.

Parker, S. 1962. 'Eskimo psychopathology in the context of Eskimo personality and culture', *American Anthropologist*, vol. 64, pp. 79–96.

Parker, S. 1983. *Leisure and Work*, London: George Allen and Unwin.

Perin, C. 1988. *Belonging in America: Reading Between the Lines*, Madison: University of Wisconsin Press.

Pollner, M. and McDonald-Wikler, L. 1985. 'The social construction of unreality: a case study of a family's attribution of competence to a severely retarded child', *Family Process*, vol. 24, pp. 241–54.

Poulsen, M. 1993. 'Strategies for building resilience in infants and young children at risk', *Infants and Young Children*, vol. 6 (2), pp. 29–40.

Rogers, C. 1961. *On Becoming a Person*, Boston: Houghton Mifflin.

Ronco, W. and Peattie, L. 1988. 'Making work: a perspective from social science', in R. E. Pahl (ed.), *On Work: Historical, Comparative and Theoretical Perspectives*, Oxford: Basil Blackwell.

Roosens, E. 1979. *Mental Patients in Town Life: Geel – Europe's First Therapeutic Community*, Beverly Hills, CA: Sage.

Rosaldo, M. Z. 1984. 'Toward an anthropology of self and feeling', in R. A. Shweder and R. A. LeVine (eds.), *Culture Theory: Essays on Mind, Self and Emotion*, Cambridge: Cambridge University Press.

Rosen M., Clark, G. D. and Kivitz, M. S. (eds.) 1976. *The History of Mental Retardation: Collected Papers*, 2 vols., Baltimore: University Park Press.

Rosenthal, R. and Jacobson, L. 1968. *Pygmalion in the Classroom*, New York: Holt, Rinehart and Winston.

Rutter, M. 1974. 'Dimensions of parenthood: some myths and some suggestions', in Department of Health and Social Security, *The Family in Society: Dimensions of Parenthood*, London: HMSO.

1979. 'Protective factors in children's responses to stress and disadvantage', in M. Kent and J. Rolf (eds.), *Primary Prevention of Psychopathology: Vol. III. Social Competence in Children*, Hanover, NH: University Press of New England.

1985. 'Resilience in the face of adversity: protective factors and resistance to psychiatric disorder', *British Journal of Psychiatry*, vol. 147, pp. 598–611.

1987. 'Psychosocial resilience and protective mechanisms', *American Journal of Orthopsychiatry*, vol. 57 (3), pp. 316–31.

Ryan, J. and Thomas, F. 1987. *The Politics of Mental Handicap*, revised edn., London: Free Association Books.

Ryan, W. 1981. *Equality*, New York: Vintage Books.

Said, E. 1979. *Orientalism*, New York: Vintage.

Sayers, S. 1988, 'The need to work: a perspective from philosophy', in R. E. Pahl (ed.), *On Work: Historical, Comparative and Theoretical Perspectives*, Oxford: Basil Blackwell.

Scheerenberger, R. C. 1983. *A History of Mental Retardation*, Baltimore: Brooks.

Schilling, R. F., Schinke, S. P., Blythe, B. J. and Barth, R. P. 1982. 'Child maltreatment and mentally retarded parents: is there a relationship?' *Mental Retardation*, vol. 20 (5), pp. 201–9.

Schoon Eberly, S. 1991. 'Fairies and the folklore of disability: changelings, hybrids and the solitary fairy', in P. Narvaéz (ed.), *The Good People: New Fairylore Essays*, New York: Garland.

Sen, A. 1992. *Mental Handicap among Rural Indian Children*, New Delhi: Sage.

Sennett, R. and Cobb, J. 1973. *The Hidden Injuries of Class*, New York: Vintage Books.

Sentumbwe, N. 1995. 'Sighted lovers and blind husbands: experiences of blind women in Uganda', in B. Ingstad and S. R. Whyte (eds.), *Disability and Culture*, Berkeley: University of California Press.

Serpell, R. 1993. *The Significance of Schooling: Life-journeys in an African Society*, Cambridge: Cambridge University Press.

Shweder, R. A. and Bourne, E. J. 1984. 'Does the concept of the person vary cross-culturally?', in R. A. Shweder and R. A. LeVine (eds.), *Culture*

Theory: Essays on Mind, Self and Emotion. Cambridge: Cambridge University Press.

Silverstein, B. and Krate, R. 1975. *Children of the Dark Ghetto: A Developmental Psychology*, New York: Praeger Publishers.

Singer, P. 1979. *Practical Ethics*, Cambridge: Cambridge University Press.

Skinner, B. F. 1972. *Beyond Freedom and Dignity*, New York: Vintage.

Smith, W. E. and Smith, A. M. 1975. *Minamata*, London: Chatto and Windus.

Sonne, B. 1986. 'Sindssyge og blodhævn i Østgrønland', *Grønland*, vol. 34 (8–9), pp. 321–7.

Spencer, M. B. 1985. 'Racial variations in achievement prediction: the school as conduit for macrostructural cultural tension', in H. P. McAdoo and J. L. McAdoo (eds.), *Black Children: Social, Educational and Parental Environments*, Beverly Hills: Sage.

Spindler, G. D. (ed.) 1980. *The Making of Psychological Anthropology*, Chicago: University of Chicago Press.

Spindler, G. D. and Spindler, L. 1983. 'Anthropologists view American culture', *Annual Review of Anthropology*, vol. 12, pp. 49–78.

Squibb, P. 1981. 'A theoretical structuralist approach to special education', in L. Barton and S. Tomlinson (eds.), *Special Education: Policy, Practices and Social Issues*, London: Harper and Row.

Stiker, H.-J. 1982. *Corps Infirmes et Sociétés*, Paris: Aubier.

Stone, D. A. 1985. *The Disabled State*, London: Macmillan.

Szasz, T. 1969. 'The myth of mental illness', in O. Milton and R. G. Wahler (eds.), *Behaviour Disorders: Perspectives and Trends*, New York: J. B. Lippincott.

Talle, A. 1995. 'A child is a child: disability and equality among the Kenya Maasai', in B. Ingstad and S. R. White (eds.), *Disability and Culture*, Berkeley: University of California Press.

Taylor, C. 1986. 'The person', in M. Carrithers, S. Collins and S. Lukes (eds.), *The Category of the Person: Anthropology, Philosophy, History*, Cambridge: Cambridge University Press.

Thom, D. 1995. 'Mental retardation: social section – Section II', in G. Berrios and R. Porter (eds.), *A History of Clinical Psychiatry: The Origin and History of Psychiatric Disorders*, London: Athlone Press.

Thompson, P. 1981. 'Life histories and the analysis of social change', in D. Bertaux (ed.), *Biography and Society*, London: Sage Publications.

Tomlinson, S. 1981. *Educational Subnormality: A Study in Decision-making*, London: Routledge and Kegan Paul.

1982. *A Sociology of Special Education*, London: Routledge and Kegan Paul.

Trent, J. W. 1994. *Inventing the Feeble Mind: A History of Mental Retardation in the United States*, Berkeley: University of California Press.

Turkington, C. 1992. 'New definition of retardation includes the need for support', *APA-Monitor*, no. 24, pp. 26–7.

Tymchuk, A. 1990. *Parents with Mental Retardation: A National Strategy*, SHARE/UCLA Parenting Project, Department of Psychiatry, School of Medicine, UCLA.

1992. 'Predicting adequacy of parenting by people with mental retardation', *Child Abuse and Neglect*, vol. 16, pp. 165–78.

Tymchuk, A. and Andron, L. 1990. 'Mothers with mental retardation who do or do not abuse or neglect their children', *Child Abuse and Neglect*, vol. 14, pp. 313–23.

Tymchuk, A. and Feldman, M. 1991. 'Parents with mental retardation and their children: review of research relevant to professional practice', *Canadian Psychology*, vol. 32 (3), pp. 486–96.

Unger, O. and Howes, C. 1986. 'Mother–child interactions and symbolic play between toddlers and their adolescent or mentally retarded mothers', *The Occupational Therapy Journal of Research*, vol. 8 (4), pp. 37–249.

Vallee, F. G. 1966. 'Eskimo theories of mental illness in the Hudson Bay region', *Anthropologica*, vol. 8 (1), pp. 53–83.

van Gennep, A. 1960 [1909]. *The Rites of Passage*, Chicago: University of Chicago Press.

van Gennep, A. 1980. *Het recht van de zwakste*, Boom: Meppel.

Vanier, J. 1979. *Community and Growth*, Toronto: Griffin House.

Varenne, H. 1977. *Americans Together: Structured Diversity in a Midwestern Town*, New York: Teachers' College Press.

Vaughan, M. 1983. 'Idioms of madness: Zomba Lunatic Asylum, Nyasaland, in the colonial period', *Journal of Southern African Studies*, vol. 9 (2), pp. 218–38.

Wadel, C. 1973. *Now, Whose Fault is That? The Struggle for Self-Esteem in the Face of Chronic Unemployment*, St. John's: I.S.E.R., Memorial University of Newfoundland.

Wallace, A. 1961. 'Mental illness, biology and culture', in F. Hsu (ed.), *Psychological Anthropology: Approaches to Culture and Personality*, Homewood: Dorsey Press.

Wallerstein, I. 1980. *The Modern World-System II: Mercantilism and the Consolidation of the European World Economy*, New York: Academic Press.

Wallman, S. 1979. 'Introduction', in S. Wallman (ed.), *Social Anthropology of Work*, London: Academic Press.

Ward, M. C. 1986. *Them Children: A Study in Language Learning*, Prospect Heights: Waveland Press.

Webster-Stratton, C. 1990. 'Stress: a potential disruptor of parents' perceptions and family interactions', *Journal of Clinical Child Psychology*, vol. 19 (4), pp. 302–12.

Welsh Office 1983. *The All-Wales Strategy for the Development of Services for Mentally Handicapped People*, Cardiff: Welsh Office.

Wenzel, G. W. 1981a. *Inuit Ecology and Adaptation: The Organisation of Subsistence*, Ottawa: National Museum of Man.

1981b. 'Inuit health and the health care system: change and status quo', *Etudes Inuit Studies*, vol. 5 (1), pp. 7–15.

Werner, E. 1986. 'Resilient offspring of alcoholics: a longitudinal study from birth to 18', *Journal of Studies on Alcohol*, vol. 47 (1), pp. 34–40.

1989. 'High-risk children in young adulthood: a longitudinal study from birth to 32 years', *American Journal of Orthopsychiatry*, vol. 59 (1), pp. 72–81.

Weyer, E. 1932. *The Eskimos: Their Environment and Folkways*, New York: Yale University Press.

Whiting, B. B. and Whiting, J. W. 1975. *Children of Six Cultures: A Psycho-Cultural Analysis*, Cambridge, Mass.: Harvard University Press.

Whyte, S. R. 1990. 'Uncertain persons in Nyole divination', *Journal of Religion in Africa*, vol. 20, no. 1, pp. 41–62.

1991. 'Family experiences with mental health problems in Tanzania: a survey of treatment histories and social stiuations', in F. Schulsinger and A. Jablensky (eds.), *The National Mental Health Programme in the United Republic of Tanzania, Acta Psychiatrica Scandinavica Supplementum*, no. 364, vol. 83.

1995. 'Constructing epilepsy: images and contexts in East Africa', in B. Ingstad and S. R. Whyte (eds.), *Disability and Culture*, Berkeley: University of California Press.

1997. *Questioning Misfortune: The Pragmatics of Uncertainty in Eastern Uganda*, Cambridge: Cambridge University Press.

Whyte, S. R. and Ingstad, B. 1995. 'Disability and culture: an overview', in B. Ingstad and S. R. Whyte (eds.), *Disability and Culture*, Berkeley: University of California Press.

Whyte, S. R. and Whyte, M. A. 1998. 'The values of development: conceiving growth and progress in Bunyole', in H. B. Hansen and M. Twaddle (eds.), *Developing Uganda*, London: James Currey.

Wolf, E. R. 1994. 'Perilous ideas: race, culture, people', *Current Anthropology*, vol. 35, pp. 1–12.

Wolfensberger, W. 1972. *The Principle of Normalisation in Human Services*, Toronto: National Institute on Mental Retardation.

Wood, J. F. 1970. 'Psychiatry: half a century of growth', in S. A. Hall and B. W. Langlands (eds.), *Uganda Atlas of Disease Distribution*, Nairobi: East African Publishing House.

Young, O. 1993. *Arctic Politics: Conflict and Cooperation in the Circumpolar North*, Hanover: University Press of New England.

Zetlin, A. G. and Turner, J. L. 1984. 'Self-perspectives on being handicapped: stigma and adjustment', in R. B. Edgerton (ed.), *Lives in Process: Mildly Retarded Adults in a Large City*, Washington, D.C.: American Association on Mental Deficiency.

Zetlin, A., Weisner, T. and Gallimore, R. 1985. 'Diversity, shared functioning, and the role of benefactors: a study of parenting by retarded persons', in S. Thurman (ed.), *Children of Handicapped Parents: Research and Clinical Perspectives*, New York: Academic Press.

Zevenbergen, H. 1986. *Zwakzinnigen in verschillende culturen*, Lisse: Swets and Zeitlinger.

Zigler, E. F. and Child, I. L. 1973. *Theories of Socialization*, Reading, Mass.: Addison-Wesley.

Zigler, E. F., Lamb, M. and Child, I. 1982. *Socialization and Personality Development*, 2nd edn., New York: Oxford University Press.

Zigler, E. F. and Hodapp, R. M. 1986. *Understanding Mental Retardation*, Cambridge: Cambridge University Press.

Zimmerman, J. and Dickerson, V. 1994. 'Using a narrative metaphor: implications for theory and clinical practice', *Family Process*, vol. 33 (3), pp. 233–45.

Index